The Preliminary Teaching Test

by

Hazel Reed BHSAI (Reg'd)

Please Note

As from January 2001 the syllabus for the Preliminary Teaching Test has been revised slightly. There is now a written section within this Exam covering such subjects as how to complete an Accident Report Form, receiving liveries or producing exercise plans etc.

Please contact the British Horse Society for a new syllabus.

The Preliminary Teaching Test.

First published in Great Britain by Nova Publications, 1999.
Reprinted 2000
Nova Publications,
Olive House, 22, Frys Lane, Yateley, Hants. GU46 7TJ, Great Britain
(+44) 0 1252 874981

ISBN 0 9525859 4 4
British Library Cataloguing in Publication Data.
A Catalogue record for this book is available from the British Library.

Typeset in Yateley by Dreke.
Printed and bound by Intype, Input Typesetting Ltd., Wimbledon, London, Great Britain.

Illustrations and computer graphics by Hazel Reed.

Photographs by Sophie Reed

Contents

Section Two - The Preliminary Teaching Test

Foreword

Being successful in the Preliminary Teaching Test takes sound, practical knowledge and experienced gained by many hours of practice. This book will give its readers the theory and guidance that are so necessary to become good teachers and to help them pass the Preliminary Teaching Test.

The most important word when teaching is 'HOW' to do something and this is where this book will prove to be most valuable to both teachers and students, as it has been written in an easy to understand text.

I feel this book should be a constant companion to all aspiring teachers and I am sure it will prove to be as popular and as beneficial as the Stage 1, 2 and 3 books in the same series.

I recommend this book highly to all those involved in teaching both riding and stable management.

Valerie Lee B.H.S.I.

Valerie Lee, BHSI

Chief Examiner.

Acknowledgements

My sincerest and warmest thanks go to all those who have helped and supported me in writing these books. All those who saw me through the dark hours when it did not seem possible that each book would be finished.

Thanks to the proof-readers, the typesetter, the photographers, the aiders and abettors, the props persons, the printers and everyone who took part in this venture.

Robert Pickles FBHS, Derek Reed BSc., Robert Dibben BHSII BHSSM, Jody Redhead, BHSAI, Karen O'Sullivan, Val Lee BHSI, Dr. Amy Jones, Margaret Heritage BSc., Fiona and Stephen Jones, Christine Walsh, Fiona Inglis-Hunter BHSI, Bronia Hill BHSII, Dr. Jamie Whitehorn, Ian Spalding, Diane Salt BHSAI, Rob Kennedy, Jerry France, Ann Stoate, Caroline Lycett BHSII BHSSM, Jean Gill HND (HS) BHSII, BHSSM, Sarah Goodall.

Thanks particularly to Sophie, Martyn and Helena who with infinite patience have put up with 'Writer's Grump'. Thank you for your support, help and fortitude under difficult circumstances; we will take that long promised holiday, I promise!

Special thanks to Paul and Claire Turner at Varndell Dressage Farm, Odiham for their patience and support.

Thanks also to Nereide and John Goodman, Phillipa Muir, James Burtwell, Gemma Softley, Darren Hynes and all the staff at Wellington Riding.

To all the models for their endurance, energy and control, Caroline Church, Paul Turner, Helena Reed, Gemma Softley, Sophie Reed, Darren Hynes, Eeyore, Rufus, Bruno, Apple Pie and Felix.

Thanks also to all those instructors who through the years have managed somehow to teach me to sit on a horse.

Cover photograph by David Hart taken at Wellington Riding Establishment, Hampshire, England.

Photographs by Sophie Reed taken at Varndell Dressage Farm and Wellington Riding Establishment.

Introduction

This guide to the Preliminary Teaching Test (PTT) is part of a series taking the student to Preliminary Instructor level. The series includes the Stage I, the Stage II (incorporating the Riding & Road Safety Test) and the Stage III, Riding & Stable Management books.

As with the other books, this guide is designed *specifically* for one particular Examination. All the relevant subjects are covered thoroughly so students know exactly what and how much they need to learn.

Consequently the school figures and movements described and explained in this book are all those that will be requested at Stage II up to Stage III level. Though extremely important and useful for working the horse, movements such as shoulder in and haunches in, collected or extended paces, are not explained because they are not required for this standard of teaching.

Written in a practical and concise manner, the information is easy to read and understand. Students can learn in a logical, step by step way, developing and increasing their ability and confidence.

The book is divided into two sections. The first, entitled 'Teaching', describes the techniques of teaching, the qualities of a teacher, how to teach pupils in different types of lessons, adults and children. It also explains how to teach school figures, movements, jumping, flatwork and how to define equestrian terms.

The second section covers the Preliminary Teaching Test giving general information, Test Information and Format, how to apply for the Test and where to train. The Theory session, Group Lesson, Lecturette, Lunge Lesson and the Lead Rein are all explained including the preparation and planning required to enter the Test with confidence.

Purpose of the PTT Guide

Teaching is an art. It may be easy to 'instruct' by giving a variety of commands, but to **teach** pupils and help them to improve their standards takes practice, skill, technique and knowledge. The successful teacher needs to know the subject and have the ability to communicate this to others. He or she needs to be adaptable to teach pupils at varying standards who may have different ways of learning.

The teacher has to be a professor, a diplomat, a communicator and a psychologist. He or she must have the desire to teach, doing so with enthusiasm, patience and creativity.

Sometimes the difficulties seem insurmountable and teaching can be an exhausting job. The rewards, however, are tremendous, from the beginner rider who suddenly beams with joy having mastered a simple technique to the pupil who goes on to achieve at the top of their profession.

The importance of teaching should never be underestimated. The knowledge we gain from our teachers, we pass on to others; and so it goes on through the generations.

In this book we hope to enthuse others with our own enthusiasm for this profession. We are aware that the knowledge we print in these pages must be accurate and thorough yet, at the same time, flexible for there are always different ways of achieving an aim, especially with horses.

Though designed for students of the Preliminary Teaching Test, the emphasis being on the theoretical and practical knowledge necessary to pass this Test, the information contained is also useful to all instructors, those teaching at riding establishments and those who freelance.

As well as being informative, we do hope this book will be enjoyed. Teaching needs to be enjoyable both for the teacher and the pupil.

Section One

Teaching

CHAPTER 1
The Psychology of Teaching

The skill of teaching is gained through instruction, practice, observation and experience. The art of teaching is achieved through learning the skill and combining this with the ability of communication to empower the pupils.

Requirements of a Teacher

A teacher is a person who helps others to learn. Though an instructor is generally a teacher, there is a difference between instructing only and teaching. Instructing is commanding the pupils to do something; teaching is explaining the essential points, demonstrating and helping the pupils to increase their knowledge and improve.

The instructor (teacher) needs three basic requirements:

- *Knowledge of the subject matter*
- *Communication*
- *Observation*

The instructor will need **a thorough knowledge of the subject matter** and the ability to **communicate this knowledge to others**. **Observation** of both horse and rider is essential, the perception and skill to analyse problems, and the ability to give corrections to improve the rider.

Knowledge

A sound foundation of knowledge is vital especially of the basic principles.

- The rider's position and seat.
- The rider's influence on the horse through the natural aids.
- The horse's ability, his paces, his 'way of going'.
- Safety for both horse and rider.

Good instructors will build on this basic knowledge through experience and continue to learn throughout their careers.

Communication

The skill of communication, that is transmitting information and ideas to others, depends on language, voice quality and listening. This technique can be developed through study and experience.

* **Communication is based on the use of language**. Explanations and corrections need to be in the language that the pupils understand. Pupils will need to be taught the equestrian terms so that they will learn as they improve.
* The information should be **logical and concise**. Pupils will be confused with complicated, tedious or unnecessary conversation.
* The instructor needs to **develop different styles** to which the **pupils can relate and understand**. This is especially important with **children**.
* The instructor needs to be **imaginative and adaptable**, constructing alternative ways of conveying the message. Sometimes imaginary phrases or metaphors will increase understanding.
* The instructor **needs to be heard**. This is achieved through **voice projection and control**.
* The instructor needs to **convey confidence and inspire the rider**.
* The instructor also needs to **listen**. **Communication is a two-way system**. The instructor should assess if the pupils have understood and are able to comply. This can be determined by observing the pupils and asking for questions.
* The instructor should also be able to **communicate with other instructors**, have the ability to exchange ideas or ask for help with lessons or lectures.

Observation

Observation is essential to distinguish and correct faults. To improve the pupil it is important to be able to focus on the problem rather than the symptom.

For example, an incorrect leg position may be caused by an incorrect position of the seat. The good instructor should improve the rider constantly and avoid becoming 'blind to', or only noticing, certain faults.

There is an equestrian cliché that **'the best teacher is the horse'**. The horse informs the instructor (and rider) by body language, facial expression and 'way of going' exactly how he feels and therefore how the rider is riding.

The Qualities of a Teacher

Whilst knowledge, communication and observation, are the basic requirements of teaching, the instructor needs other qualities to interrelate with the pupils, develop their skills and improve their abilities.

Positive Qualities

* **Awareness of safety** - the instructor should maintain the safety of pupils and horses. Whilst pupils often need encouragement, the instructor should avoid pushing them beyond their capabilities.

* **Enthusiasm and confidence** - the foundation for these is a thorough knowledge of the subject. Enthusiasm is the belief in a principle and the desire to impart this to others. Confidence is gained from knowledge and experience.

* **Patience and understanding** - *patience and understanding are the ultimate virtues of the teacher.* At times the instructor needs to firmly encourage the pupils in a positive way; this should be combined with a real understanding for their limits.

* **Humour** - pupils need to enjoy learning and, though teaching is a serious subject, humour helps the pupils relax. It is part of the teacher and pupil rapport.

* **Rapport and respect** - the teacher/pupil relationship. There is a fine balance between rapport and respect, creating rapport with the pupils so that they react to the teaching whilst at the same time earning respect to maintain discipline. These are gained by a thorough knowledge of the subject matter, control over situations and a genuine desire to help the pupils advance.

* **Understanding human and equine psychology** - an instructor needs to observe and understand the body language of rider and horse, facial expression or change of mood. Human psychology is important when dealing with working pupils, other teaching staff, clients, employers; this is 'man-management' within the establishment.

* **Consistency** - the teaching should be consistent and progressive.

* **Adaptability** - whilst keeping the basic principles of equitation consistent, the instructor also needs to adapt to suit each pupil's requirements, each horse's ability. There are times when different ways are required to achieve a goal; both rider and horse are individuals. Often lessons will need to be adapted and altered to suit a rider or horse's capabilities.

* **Tact and diplomacy** - the instructor needs to learn the quality of positive criticism. Most of an instructor's time is spent in correcting faults and problems. It is good psychology to start with a positive statement, praising good points and then correcting the faults. Tact and diplomacy are required to increase the rider's confidence.

Negative Characteristics

- **Sarcasm** - it is wiser to avoid sarcasm especially those sarcastic remarks that bring the person down.
- **Impatience, aggressiveness, intolerance, bad temper** - these traits kill the desire to learn, the rapport between pupil and instructor.
- **Egotism** - instructors full of their own self-importance often cannot understand the pupils' problems and difficulties.
- **Lack of confidence and enthusiasm** - come from a lack of experience and knowledge.
- **Inconsistency** - if pupils are taught different methods they may become confused and lose their confidence.
- **Negative criticism** - a lesson full of 'don'ts' rather than 'do's'. This creates negativity in the pupils. Continual negative criticism is demoralising.

After each lesson the pupils should feel that they have improved, learnt something new and increased in ability. Most importantly, they should enjoy the time and learning.

Methods of Teaching

Each individual instructor has his or her own personality and will create a different method of teaching, a different approach and atmosphere to each lesson. Instructors will have varied aims and ideals based on their knowledge, experience, age, focus and the methods by which they themselves were taught.

Lessons will vary, too, as a consequence of the type of pupils; children need teaching in a different way to adults, working pupils focusing on exams need another form of instruction from beginners learning to ride on a weekly basis.

Each type of lesson will require a different focus, group lessons, private lessons, flatwork or jumping, lunge lessons and lectures on stable management.

As well as bringing their own individuality to each lesson, instructors influence pupils by their example.

The instructor who dresses smartly will encourage a smart class.

An instructor who is always punctual will encourage this quality in the pupils.

An instructor who is disciplined will create a disciplined group, for instance insisting that the horses are all lined up neatly and safely for mounting; ensuring that the tack is always checked.

Voice

Good voice projection is vital; the pupils need to hear. Posture is an important factor for vocal control. The instructor needs to stand straight, but relaxed, head up and chest expanded. The voice needs to come from the lungs rather than the throat.

Not everyone has a naturally loud voice, but voice projection can be increased by developing a good body posture and through deep breathing exercises to expand the lung capacity.

The instructor will also need to speak more slowly than normal. The speed of sound carries the words to the pupils, who are usually on the move, and rapid speech will reach the pupils as a jumble of inaudible words. The words need to be spoken clearly and slowly as in public speaking.

Voice projection gives an indication of how confident the instructor is, or how nervous and tense. A quiet, subdued voice or one that is squeaky because of a tense larynx will show a lack of confidence which is easily passed on to the pupils. This develops a lack of trust and rapport between instructor and pupil.

The tone of voice is as important as voice projection. This needs to be soothing, confident and enthusiastic without being overzealous, friendly without being familiar. The instructor should sound varied, interesting and encouraging.

A monotonous voice, boring and dull, indicates a lack of interest in the lesson and pupils. A voice too varied in pitch can be irritating and sound patronising. Strong accents can cause problems; soft accents though can often be soothing and interesting.

An instructor who is too loud or who constantly shouts will irritate the pupils. The pupils (and the horses) will eventually 'switch off' and ignore the instructor. If a firmer control is required or a greater degree of encouragement, this can be implied through the tone of the voice and the use of language.

Language

Language is the medium by which we communicate our ideas, our experiences, our knowledge and our objectives. Language can be limited through misinterpretation and a lack of understanding.

As well as learning how to teach, instructors also need to understand the use of language. This is the most powerful tool in the successful teacher's armoury.

The instructor needs to be adaptable with words to create various images that will appeal to different types of people. For instance children need simple explanations, often with the use of imaginative descriptions to help them understand. Beginners will not have learnt equestrian terminology and will need these explaining in 'layman' terms first. Different words create different images and the instructor needs a stock of meanings, explanations and imagery to encourage pupils to accept the ideas.

For more advanced adults the vocabulary will need to be suited to their standard. Some concepts are difficult to grasp and should be explained clearly, for instance, 'collection', 'impulsion' and 'softness'. If a pupil is not achieving a goal it may be through a lack of understanding.

Successful instructors ration their words, using sufficient to explain their ideas. Whilst it is pleasant to have a short chat at the beginning and end of the lesson, the instructor who endlessly gossips, particularly if the topics are not relevant, will lose the pupil's interest and respect. Equally an instructor who says nothing, gives no help towards improvement, will not build up a rapport.

Body Language

Body language can be as important as the spoken word. The way an instructor stands and the mannerisms used convey confidence, control, authority, enthusiasm and interest in the group.

The head should be held up, with the instructor making eye contact with the pupils. Holding the head down makes the instructor look inattentive and, by constricting the larynx and directing the voice downwards, inaudible.

The hands can be held behind the back or by the sides and at times used to support spoken language when giving an explanation. An instructor who keeps his hands in his pockets may look slovenly and disinterested. Folded arms will restrict the chest cavity and may decrease the voice; it also makes an instructor look unapproachable.

Instructor's Appearance

The instructor's appearance needs to be neat and tidy. This gives the impression of efficiency and an interest in the group.

It also encourages the class to be neat and tidy, suggesting high standards and a professional approach. The clothes will need to be practical in case a horse needs to be ridden.

It is important for instructors to understand how they influence their pupils, through teaching, personality and manner.

Teaching Tips

One method of improving your own teaching is to watch other instructors; observe their body language, listen to the terms and phrases they use, notice how they control the group. Assess instructors, your own instructor and those who taught you in the past. Objectively make a list of their good points and bad points, their teaching styles, the methods that you felt improved you and those aspects of the teaching that you felt prevented improvement.

Some good points may be that he or she is enthusiastic, positive, disciplined, gives confidence, constructive criticism, praise, adds variety to lessons, maintains continuity between lessons. The instructor may have a good personality, is humorous, audible, is adaptable being able to teach classes of different standards.

Some bad points may be; not critical enough or over-critical, sarcastic, shouts, becomes impatient, too aggressive, does not give enough teaching, lacks control of lessons, voice not loud enough, no humour.

Naturally not every pupil will agree on the good and bad points, but this will encourage you to become more observant and discriminating about instructors and their teaching methods.

It will assist you in deciding how you may like to teach and those aspects of instructing that you may wish to avoid. Building on the experience of others and developing your own individual style will help you to progress and expand your teaching ability.

To develop and practise your voice projection speak to someone standing at a distance of about 20 metres, then increase the distance to 40 metres. Experiment by speaking quickly, then more slowly, and by altering voice tone. Breathing exercises may help, particularly if you have a soft, quiet voice.

Often indoor schools are not good auditoriums; the voice seems to be 'sucked' away into nothing. Outdoor schools are occasionally noisy particularly if near to a main road. Practice will be necessary in different types of school. One helpful aid is to be recorded either on video or cassette whilst teaching. This will show if your voice is sufficiently loud and clear.

CHAPTER 2
Lessons

To cater for riders with different aims and at various stages in their training, riding centres offer a choice of lessons. Riders may need the intensive training of a private lesson, at other times it is of more benefit to join a group; some riders may wish to improve their jumping abilities whilst others wish to focus on dressage. Each type of lesson is designed to help riders' progress and fulfil their objectives.

Another important point in a rider's training schedule is the environment in which the lessons take place. As well as offering variety, the training areas require maintenance for the rider's safety and improvement.

Aims of Lessons

The aim of every lesson is to increase the pupil's knowledge about a subject and to improve their skill. An increase in knowledge develops confidence when riding, caring for and handling horses. Deciding on the best type of lesson for each pupil will depend on certain considerations.

1. **The pupil's ability**

   The pupil's level of training will influence the standard of lesson for riding or stable management. A rider's fitness and ability will determine the length of lesson, the structure and the type, that is, a lunge or private lesson, or a group.

2. **The pupil's own wishes and aims**

   Lessons may be designed specifically for those working towards some aim, a competition or examination. The rider may wish to concentrate on one discipline such as dressage.

3. **Availability of lessons**

   It may not be possible to give the type of lesson required. For instance, the cross-country lesson is not feasible if the course is waterlogged or frozen. The instructor may have to design an alternative lesson to help the pupil towards his goals.

Types of Lessons

The types of lesson are:

- ❖ Private or semi-private
- ❖ Group
- ❖ Lunge
- ❖ Lead rein
- ❖ Instructional hack
- ❖ Stable management

Each has its own advantages and disadvantages for the pupils, instructors and horses.

The Private Lesson

This consists of one instructor to one pupil, either for riding or stable management.

Advantages

- ✳ The pupil receives the **complete attention of the instructor**.
- ✳ **Problems are dealt with more quickly** in a concentrated private lesson.
- ✳ **Progress is accelerated** through the concentrated aspect of this lesson, **beginners and advanced students** gain particular benefit.
- ✳ The pupil can **build up a rapport** with the instructor.
- ✳ Often the client is given **a horse of a higher standard**.

Disadvantages

- Private lessons can be **demanding**. The **rider may not be sufficiently physically or mentally fit**. An alternative is a **semi-private lesson** (two riders per instructor); the teaching is not as concentrated but the riders still receive an amount of individual attention.
- There are **no other horses or riders to observe, learn from or use as a demonstration**.
- **Unsociable** - may not have the opportunity of meeting other riders.
- **Safety**; may not have the opportunity to relate to other riders in the school, keeping safe distances, or learning the school rules.

The Group Lesson

Specific group lessons are designed for children and adults: beginner, novice, intermediate and advanced. Each lesson may be structured around one particular theme, for instance flatwork, show jumping or cross-country.

Advantages

* **Time saving**, often whilst the teacher is correcting one pupil's problem, the others in the group correct themselves.
* **Pupils can learn by watching others**.
* **Competition** between pupils encourages some to try harder.
* The group lesson is **less demanding** for the unfit or novice rider.
* **Social event**; pupils have the chance to meet others of their standard.
* The riders learn **awareness** of others in the school, learning the school rules.
* Riding in a group can help to **improve the horse's manners**.
* Riders can be used for **demonstration purposes**.

Disadvantages

- May be **hazardous** if one or more riders forget or disobey the school rules.
- **Difficult for the instructor and frustrating for the riders** if the group is of **varying standards**.
- Horses, being herd animals, can **nap or cut corners** to return to the others.
- The **pecking order with horses can cause dangerous behaviour** in a school.
- The instructor may **concentrate on one person to the detriment of others**, though a good instructor will avoid this situation.

The Lunge Lesson

This is a private lesson usually lasting 30 minutes; the pupil is taught whilst being lunged on a horse.

Advantages

* Efficient method of **improving the rider's position** helping to develop a more secure, independent seat.
* The rider can **concentrate on improving their position** without having to think about controlling the horse.
* Helps the rider to **understand and develop feel** of the horse's movement in the paces and through transitions.

* Builds up a **rapport with the teacher**.
* The rider has the **individual attention** of the instructor.
* The rider receives **concentrated teaching** and improves more quickly.
* Particularly **beneficial for beginners** offering security and, for **more advanced riders,** concentrated teaching towards improvement.
* Builds up **confidence** through a secure, safe method of riding.

Disadvantages

- Lungeing can put **physical stress and strain on the horse** if the lesson is continued for too long or the horse is used for lunge lessons too often.
- Can be **detrimental if the horse is disobedient on the lunge**. The horse needs to be well behaved and capable of being lunged.
- If the pace is too fast or unbalanced the **centrifugal force** created by working on a circle can be detrimental to both the rider and the horse. The rider may learn to sit incorrectly to compensate; the horse may lean in or pull away from the circle.

The Lead Rein Lesson

There are different types of lead rein lesson. In the private lead rein lesson the instructor leads and teaches the rider. In the lead rein group the instructor teaches the class whilst assistants do the leading.

Advantages

* Best method **of teaching small children from the beginning**, as they do not have the strength or knowledge to control ponies or to apply the leg aids effectively, (especially if the child's legs do not reach below the saddle flap!).
* Offers **individual teaching**.
* Allows **rapport with the instructor**.
* **Develops confidence**.

Disadvantages

- It is sometimes **difficult to see problems** when leading and instructing a rider.
- Can be **physically exhausting for leader or leaders** especially at trot.
- **Not easy to teach canter** and can be **dangerous if the pace becomes too fast for the leader**.
- If on the **lead rein over a long period of lessons the rider can become bored**.

The Instructional Hack

In this type of lesson the instructor, mounted, escorts the class on a hack, giving advice at the same time. In the lead rein hack the horses and ponies are led from the ground by staff or helpers.

Advantages

* **Variety,** especially for beginners who may often not experience hacking.
* **Expands the rider's knowledge** about the horse, his psychology and the reactions of horses or ponies away from the school.
* **Beneficial for the horses and ponies**; varies their routine.
* **Interesting** and **stimulating** for riders and horses.
* Gives the chance for riders to **practise the lessons learnt in the school**.

Disadvantages

- **May be dangerous** unless the horses and ponies are quiet, sensible and the riders are sufficiently competent. **Ponies should wear grass reins**. If a pony puts his head down to eat the grass a small child may easily slip off.
- The **instructor cannot always see everyone in the ride**. The group should be accompanied by an escort to assist the instructor.

The Stable Management Lesson

This is a lecture on aspects of stable management and horse care. The lectures need to be a combination of theory and practice. Students need to relate the theory to practical experience so that this can be used in the day to day running of the yard. The lectures should include observation, demonstrations and practice of the safe methods of working with, caring for and handling horses and ponies.

Advantages

* **Creates an interest in other areas of horse management**. Some clients do not have the opportunity to experience horse care or stable management.
* **Increases knowledge and ability**. Working pupils and clients benefit from proper instruction on how to care for and work around horses.

Disadvantages

- May become **repetitive and boring** unless organised and records kept of previous lectures to ensure a progressive programme.

Taken individually all types of lessons should provide and fulfil the pupil's requirements, needs, aims and objectives.

Teaching Environment

One important aspect is the environment in which the lessons take place, the indoor or outdoor school, the jumping arena and lecture room. These need to provide a safe area, one in which the instructor can teach efficiently.

The School or Menage

Most establishments have an outdoor menage or an indoor school; some have both. The size and quality of schools can vary but all need to provide a safe and suitable environment.

The school area needs to be sufficiently large to cope with the size and number of classes. An international sized arena, at least 20m by 60m can accommodate two classes at the same time providing these are not large groups.

An arena measuring 20m by 40m can also accommodate two lessons, but these would need to be either two private lessons where the riders do not need to use the whole school or two lunge lessons.

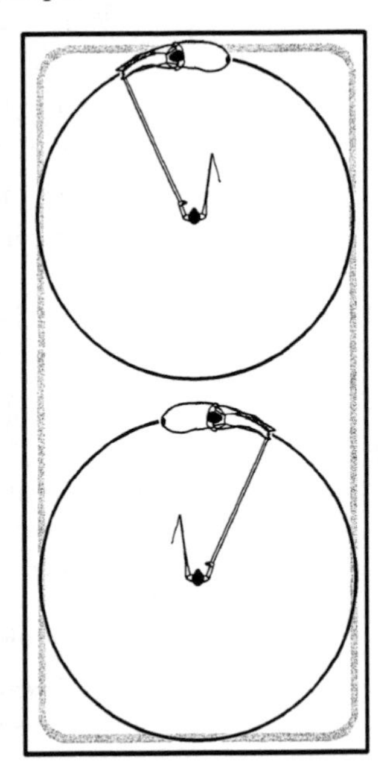

For safety the school can be divided into two areas by poles, either laid on the ground or placed on blocks.

Alternatively if lunging horses without a division, the horses may be lunged on different reins so that they are travelling in the same direction, one on the left rein, one on the right

Trying to accommodate and organise two large groups in a smaller sized school can put the riders at risk.

With all schools the essential aspects are the surface, drainage, enclosure (fencing or wall) and the fixtures and fittings.

Surface

Ideally the ground needs to be flat; riding on a sloping surface like the side of a hill is dangerous. The surface should be sufficiently soft and deep to prevent concussion on the horse's feet and legs, and free of stones or other sharp objects that may bruise or puncture the horse's sole and frog. The surface material needs to be of a consistency that is neither too fine, as with fine sand, nor too solid as with heavy sand or clay soil.

Fine sand can cause respiratory problems, as well as sore eyes, nostrils and friction burns where it lodges between the saddle, girth and skin. Heavy sand and soil becomes packed into the feet and can cause thrush.

Good efficient surfaces can be expensive but are worth the cost for the quality of work and the health of the horse and rider.

Drainage

To protect the surface of the outdoor school, keeping it free of puddles, pools or even ponds, efficient drainage is essential. Though it is sometimes an advantage for horses to be ridden or lunged through pools to accustom them to water, constantly riding for weeks or months through a waterlogged surface is not safe, efficient or a pleasure.

The horse's feet and legs will eventually suffer from thrush, mud fever and, if the surface is heavy, from strain injuries. The horses are more liable to slide, slip or even fall over. Some schools become so saturated that they cannot be used during periods of wet weather.

With indoor schools the surface needs to be kept moist to prevent the material becoming dry and too fine. When dry the track is more likely to become rutted exposing and damaging the underneath surface as well as causing injury to the horses.

Enclosure

In Riding Schools where beginners, novices and children are taught, the school or menage ideally needs to be enclosed on all sides. Indoor schools will normally have walls, which are covered by kicking boards to protect the walls from damage and the horses from injury. For outdoor schools a solid fence high enough to discourage the horses from jumping is suitable.

Any type of fencing that will cause injury should be avoided, such as wire, barbed wire or rough walls.

Fixtures and Fittings

If the school is used for jumping, wings, poles, jumpkins and blocks need to be stored efficiently when not in use to prevent injury to horses and riders. Storage space for jumping equipment outside the school, with easy access, is the most efficient method.

For commercial yards good lighting is essential for economical use of the schools after dark and on murky days during the winter. For livery yards this is of benefit for the liveries owners and an asset for the yard.

Mirrors are extremely useful, as they help the riders check their position and riding ability; they also help with lighting by reflection.

Schools and menages are normally equipped with markers. These are used for dressage, for school figures and movements. In schools where children are taught these markers are often painted to help them remember the letters of the school.

Maintenance

A good quality school is an asset to the yard, and benefits the horses, the riders and the instructors. The school needs to be properly maintained to keep its value.

- The surface needs to be kept as free of droppings as possible to maintain the consistency of the material.
- Frequent and regular harrowing or rolling of the surface helps to eliminate any deep areas such as the outer track.
- At intervals new surface material will need to be added. No matter how careful the maintenance, some surface will naturally be lost, in the horse's hooves, being blown in the wind or leached out by rain. At some establishments the horse's hooves are picked out before leaving the school. Alternatively the horses may be walked in a circle just outside the door or gate; any excess surface may be swept back into the school.
- The surface needs to be kept moist, particularly during hot periods; otherwise some material will be lost in the wind.
- Drainage ditches need to be kept clear and commercial drainage may need renewing at periods.
- The sides of the school, the fence, kicking boards should be repaired when damaged. The doors or gates should be easy to open and close.
- Any wind or storm damage to roof, guttering, walls, door, fences or gates should be repaired quickly.
- Any damage to mirrors or lighting should also be repaired.
- Electric cables should be insulated and all electricity supply and lighting regularly checked and maintained.

Other training areas such as a show jumping arena or a cross-country course are just as important. Jumping equipment should be kept dry, especially wings, poles, cups and pegs made of wood or metal, to prevent rotting and rusting. Cross-country jumps will need repairing or rebuilding regularly.

Maintenance of the ground is essential particularly on a cross-country course to prevent deep and slippery take off and landing areas, to keep ditches clear and to maintain the track around the course. Many establishments stop their cross-country lessons during the winter to preserve the ground.

The Lecture Room

This room needs to be in a quiet area away from the distractions of the yard and should provide adequate facilities for educating the pupils.

The equipment may include:

- chairs and tables, on which to write
- a blackboard, white board or an overhead projector
- a television and video
- props such as feed samples, types of bits, shoes, Farrier's tools, medical kit
- photocopier, if possible, to copy notes
- books on stable management and equitation, diagrams of horse anatomy

All equipment needs to be properly maintained and kept up to date, for instance, new feed samples or new medical items introduced onto the market.

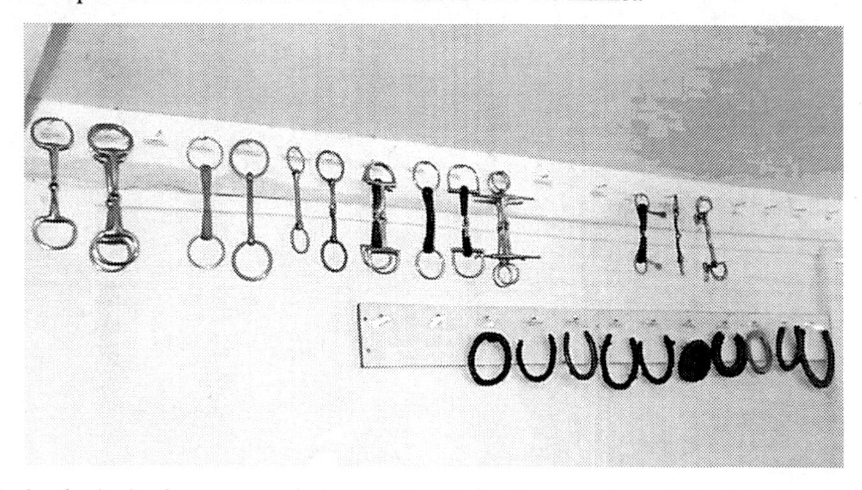

Technological advances are being made all the time, new products introduced and more efficient equipment invented. The pupils need to be made aware of current equipment as well as learning traditional methods.

Teaching Tips

You will need to know about the different types of lessons, their relative advantages and disadvantages. This will help you to advise pupils which type of lesson will be of most benefit. For instance, if a beginner who has never sat on a horse before asks what type of lesson he needs you can suggest lunge lessons first before he joins a group.

The quality and maintenance of the school, menage, jumping arena and cross-country course are of vital importance to any yard, whether a commercial establishment or a private livery yard. Safety is the first aspect of any area in which horses are ridden, schooled, lunged, loose schooled or jumped.

To gain knowledge about quality of training areas, visit and assess different yards, their teaching facilities, the schools, their sizes, situations and the different surfaces used for flatwork and jumping arenas.

CHAPTER 3
Lesson Structure

All types of lessons need to have a structure, a framework, so that the teaching is organised in a logical, practical and effective way. Preparation is an important part of the lesson; the subjects need to be arranged into the framework efficiently, so that the pupils learn by working through the stages in a progressive pattern.

Lesson Preparation

For inexperienced instructors each lesson may need to be prepared in detail possibly including practice in giving explanations and definitions of the relevant subjects to be covered. Experienced instructors expand their repertoire of lessons so that preparation becomes minimal.

As part of the preparation for each lesson information concerning the pupil or pupils will be required. How many there are in the lesson, their names, ages, possible weight, standards, abilities, fears and aims.

For the instructor who is new to the yard this information can be obtained by asking the yard receptionist or previous instructor. Information will also be required about the previous lessons, what subjects were covered. Preparation includes deciding on the situation of the lesson, indoors, outdoors, cross-country and, for stable management, the lecture room or outside on the yard.

Whilst preparing the lesson, keep safety in mind, organising the class efficiently, teaching safety measures and precautions so that this becomes ingrained within the minds of the pupils. The lesson can then be prepared and structured accordingly to suit these requirements.

Lesson Structure

The structure of the lesson is its plan or framework and consists of

- the introduction (with warm-up phase)
- the lesson content
- the conclusion (with cooling down phase)

The Introduction

During the introduction ask for the pupils' names, their standards, aims and any problems they may be experiencing. It may also be relevant to ask about the horses, their abilities and temperaments.

Check all the horses' tack for fitting and condition. If an accident occurs through ill-fitting or worn tack the rider can hold the yard responsible. Check that the riders are wearing the correct clothing.

After the girths and stirrups are checked and altered, assist the riders to mount safely and correctly. The girths and stirrups can be checked again after mounting.

The Warm-up or 'Loosening'

This phase is required to supple muscles, tendons and ligaments for work; it can also be used to create relaxation in the riders and horses. By starting with a familiar routine (normally work on a longer rein at walk and trot) the riders and horses are put at ease and will be more receptive to the teaching.

The 'warm-up' session should consist of simple loosening exercises, to create relaxation and suppleness, not difficult manoeuvres that would only tense and stiffen the riders and consequently the horses.

During this phase the instructor can assess the abilities of the pupils and the horses.

Lesson Content

The content of the lesson is its aim and contains the main theme. This theme, based on new topics or revision of previous knowledge, influences the types of exercises, school figures or movements to be included.

It will also determine any 'props' that are required, such as poles, jumps or equipment for a stable management lesson. The lesson theme can also influence which horses to use for which riders and how the riders are to be organised, as a ride or in open order as individuals.

Teaching Format for New Topics

When introducing new topics there is a recognised format that may be followed to ensure that the teaching is clear, thorough and understandable.

- Introduction
- Explanation
- Demonstration
- Practice
- Repetition
- Conclusion

This order allows time for the pupils to absorb the information given.

❖ *Introduction*

Introduce the topic so that the pupils are mentally prepared; for instance *'Today I am going to teach you the school movement leg yield'*. To suddenly launch into something new causes confusion.

❖ *Explanation*

Describe the subject explaining the definition (leg yield is a lateral or sideways movement with the horse moving on two tracks), the benefits or functions, the aids and the aims.

❖ *Demonstration*

Demonstration is a powerful method of teaching; often pupils will understand more by watching rather than by being commanded. Ask a rider to demonstrate the procedure.

❖ *Practice*

The pupils are now given time to practise. This should be at a slow pace first, in walk, to give time for pupils to assimilate new information and to practise the co-ordination of the aids.

❖ *Repetition*

After practising the pupils repeat the exercise to increase their understanding and improve their ability. Assess the pupils at this time to check if anyone has failed to understand. Often pupils will say that they have learnt a point just to please or because they are fearful of not understanding. Anyone who is struggling can be given further guidance.

The rider (and the horse) should always be praised when something has been achieved or at least when the rider has made the effort. Praise should not be given needlessly when the work is poor.

Do not ask the pupils to repeat any exercise or school figure for too long. The lesson should progress onto other types of work to maintain the pupil's interest and the horse's freshness.

❖ *Conclusion*

In conclusion answer any questions the pupils may ask about the subject, give further information if required, assess and praise the pupils on their work.

Explanation is 'hearing', demonstration is 'sight', practice and repetition are 'feel'.

The pupils should be given periods of rest, particularly when introducing new techniques, to prevent rider fatigue. It will also be necessary during hot weather to prevent dehydration.

Bringing the rider or group into the centre of the school to give a short lecture or a demonstration on the relevant subject is an efficient method of giving a rest. Periods of discussion should be kept fairly brief; the horse and rider may become bored and restless. During cold weather the horses and riders need to be moving to keep warm.

Conclusion

The conclusion of the whole lesson will include a 'cooling down' period when the horses are allowed to relax on a long rein. Both pupils and horses will need to wind down gradually especially if hot.

The pupils are given the chance to ask any questions or discuss relevant points. Naturally at some time there will be the question that cannot be answered immediately. No instructor knows everything all the time.

Explain that the information will be obtained and the question answered at the next lesson. Avoid giving an incorrect or irrelevant answer just for the sake of answering (pupils become aware of this very quickly).

Each pupil should be given an assessment and advice on how to progress and improve in the future. If relevant the pupils can be given 'homework' so that they can study, revise or practise the techniques already taught.

It is a nice touch if the pupils also thank the instructor and give praise for a good lesson. Instructors need just as much encouragement.

Stable Management Lectures

The same qualities are required when giving stable management lectures. A neat and tidy appearance, good voice projection, use of language, knowledge of the subjects.

The lecture will be structured with an introduction, content and conclusion and involve prior preparation based on the standards and aims of the group.

The introduction may include revision of previous topics or a new subject. If notes are required during the lecture, inform the pupils at the beginning. It is less disturbing if they go to find pen and paper first than in the middle of the lecture.

The content section will start with the basic information first, emphasising the main points and then expanding on these with more facts.

- ❖ Keep the subject flowing in a logical progression so that the pupils follow and understand. Changing from one subject to another causes confusion and loss of attention.
- ❖ Give the main part of the lecture without questions first. Then, if required, have a short question and answer session. If the pupils are constantly interrupting with queries the flow of the lecture will be broken.
- ❖ Speak clearly and a little more slowly than normal (not too slow), so that each sentence is audible. Change the voice tone; avoid a monotonous drone (a cure for insomnia).

- Personal experiences can be included providing they are relevant to the topic being discussed. Avoid continuously telling personal stories that have no relevance to the lecture, or wander from point to point with no continuity. This will only confuse the class.

- Keep the language clear, concise and understandable, explaining any technical terms and expressions that may not be familiar. Avoid slang, strange or unusual expressions.

- Include any safety aspects of the subject being covered, and emphasise safety features and precautions relevant to the topic.

- Include practical demonstrations and practice where possible. Stable management is mostly about practical knowledge and ability; the theory needs to be supported by actually doing the tasks.

- Give homework so that the pupils continue to learn in the periods between the classes.

- Watch for the quiet pupil who may be apprehensive about asking or answering questions. Encourage everyone to be active in the lecture; this may even help this pupil later in life, by building their confidence and ability.

For the conclusion the main points can be summarised; pupils should be encouraged to ask questions or have repeated any points that they did not understand. The topic may be opened for general discussion, when pupils can give personal views, showing that they have understood the lecture.

Props

During the lecture, using props adds interest. These may be handed around for pupils to observe. There should be diagrams and books on the horse's anatomy, different breeds and various types of tack. A television and video are good investments as there are many good stable management videos available on the market.

The lecture though should never solely be made up of watching a video, as pupils can lose interest. Lectures should be based around a short video or part of a video with the majority of the time being spent in taking notes, asking questions and having discussions.

Prepare the props prior to the lecture. Though many can be kept permanently in the lecture room, some will need to be collected before so that the flow is not interrupted searching for the required items.

All lessons need a structure if they are to run smoothly and efficiently. The same applies to hacks out in the country or on the Public Highway.

Hacking

Hacking is one of the most dangerous aspects of riding; the horses can be excited or nervous, the riders are away from the security of the school. There are more hazards, traffic, other riders, pedestrians and their dogs, livestock, farm machinery.

Lead rein hacks, instructional hacks and even normal hacks need planning and structuring if the riders are to be safe and enjoy their time.

Practically every rider at some time goes on a hack, for many riders hacking is their purpose for attending a riding school. Some schools cater almost exclusively for hacking.

Hacking offers variety in the work schedule, for those horses who are mainly used in the school. It allows time for riders and horses to relax, offers enjoyment and pleasure. Horses enjoy it, particularly those who do not hack out often.

Hacking increases the rider's experience of the horse's psychology, his reactions to a different environment, how he behaves when faced with unfamiliar surroundings. The horse will be more keen, active, forward going; the rider learns to feel this change in the horse's energy and forwardness. It is amazing how some seemingly sluggish school horses change character completely when given the chance to hack.

It is a good part of training a young horse or competition horse. The horse becomes accustomed to different areas, different sights, sounds, smells; this helps when going out to compete.

Types and Lengths of Hack

After several lessons children can be taken on a 'walk out' either on a lead rein hack or with several competent escorts in control. This will normally last from 15 to 30 minutes.

Most hacks last for one hour; this allows sufficient time for the rider to enjoy the hack; longer periods could tire an unfit or novice rider. Also one hour fits in with the school routine, as most lessons are an hour long. Longer rides, up to two hours, are regularly available for fitter, more experienced riders.

Most schools do offer even longer hacks particularly at special times of the year. For special events, such as Christmas or during the summer months, a hack may be arranged for three or four hours, but this will include a rest at the local pub or a picnic in between.

Horses

Choosing suitable horses and ponies is vital. Both the leader and escort need sensible, steady, reliable horses who are happy to be in the lead or be ridden home alone if necessary. If riding on the roads, the horses should be traffic proof.

It is impossible to look after a group of riders if the lead horse is temperamental, nervous or unreliable. It is a risk to the whole group including the leader.

The horses and ponies need to be suitable for each type of rider, their ability, weight, height and standard. All the horses should have been hacked out previously and be known to be safe or at least sufficiently safe for that particular rider. Sending out a beginner on a new horse just arrived at the yard could be risky.

Each horse should suit the rider, possibly the horse should be slightly below the rider's standard. This is safer than sending a rider out on a horse he cannot handle.

Tack and Equipment

The horse's tack should always be inspected before leaving the yard. Any worn or unsafe tack should be replaced.

GP saddles should be used with a correctly fitted girth.

The bridle is normally a snaffle but a stronger bit can be used if necessary, providing the rider is capable.

Martingales may be required, particularly if the horse tosses his head. A breastplate or a neckstrap will be essential for beginners, children and novices; a breastplate will also keep the saddle secure. Grass reins are definitely required for ponies.

The horses should all be correctly shod. A worn or loose shoe can cause problems, particularly if the shoe is cast whilst on the hack and the horse goes lame. Worn shoes can be slippery on road surfaces.

The leader and escort should take at least one lead rope each. These can be wound up and fastened to the 'D' rings on the saddles.

Other useful items to take are a hoof pick preferably a folding one, a clean handkerchief or triangular bandage and some string or twine, in case a horse needs to be tied up to a fence. A portable phone can be taken providing it is carried safely, so that it does not drop out. If a portable phone is not practical, some money or a phone card is useful for a phone call. The leader and escort should carry a short whip.

If hacking into an area that requires a permit, the permit discs may need to be carried or fastened to the bridle.

Bright clothing, fluorescent during bright days and reflective during dull days or in the evening, helps riders to be visible, hat covers, tabards, horse's brushing boots anything that will be seen. A grey horse is more easily visible and can be placed at the front or back of the ride, particularly if riding on the road.

The horses should ideally be wearing brushing boots, possibly over-reach boots and knee boots. Though most horses are safe, it is always possible, particularly on slippery road surfaces, for a horse to fall down onto his knees.

Road Safety

Revision

Stage II - Riding & Road Safety, rules, regulations, groups, clothing, Highway Code.

Riding on the Public Highways is hazardous. However most hacking means roadwork at some point, so knowledge of the road and the Highway Code will be required to keep rider and horse safe.

Follow the rules of the Highway Code; obey signs and signals. Be aware of other traffic, cars, bicycles, motor bikes and heavy vehicles. Always look, signal and position the horse at junctions and roundabouts. Keep checking, keep looking, be aware of the surroundings.

Take extra care around parked vehicles, particularly if having to pass them.

Look out for unexpected noises and movement in gardens, behind hedges, fences or walls.

If the horse begins to shy at an object by the side of road, turn the horse's head away so that he flexes his head towards the traffic. Use the right leg aid to prevent him from swinging his hindquarters out in front of a vehicle.

Avoid, if possible, riding near road works, heavy traffic, farm machinery or anything that may cause problems, where the horse may shy or refuse to continue. If a horse does stop and completely refuses to go on do not continue trying to force him. You may have to dismount and walk past the hazard or turn back and find an alternative route. The road is not the place to train or teach the horse obedience.

Keep the pace active but not fast; avoid trotting around corners or roundabouts and where the road surface can be slippery.

Do not ride on pavements, footpaths and grass verges if possible. Verges may contain rubbish, ditches, drains and potholes.

Ride in single file on narrow roads, country lanes, in heavier traffic.

Always thank considerate drivers, it encourages them to be considerate around horses in the future.

Group Hacks

When taking a hack out always let someone at the stables know the approximate route and estimated return time. If an incident does occur and the hack is late returning, the yard knows which route to follow to find the ride.

If the riders in the group have not ridden on this hack previously, make a note of the their names and of their abilities, whether they hack frequently or not. Find out about the horses, their names, abilities and their characteristics when hacking.

Check each rider's clothing to ensure that this is safe. Anything that could become caught up in branches or fall off en route should be put away safely or removed. Loose jackets should be fastened. If a rider wears glasses check that these are secure.

Before leaving the Yard, check that each rider is suitably mounted. If one rider is on a horse that may be dangerous or too difficult for that rider to handle, either ask for a change of horse or swap riders.

Check that the horses are all sound and well shod. Though horses do occasionally go lame on a hack, good organisation before the ride departs will minimise this risk.

When the ride is ready, instruct them to form a ride in the required order. If necessary, for new riders or those who are not familiar with this hack, explain about the rules, keep in single file, no over-taking, keep a safe distance behind the horse in front, keep up with the horse in front, never allow the ride to split.

The Hack

Keep the ride safe; avoid doing anything that may be risky or dangerous.

Keep the standard of the hack to that of the least experienced rider. Ideally the group should be compatible, at similar standards, but this does not always happen. When groups consist of riders of varying standards avoid dividing the group and sending riders off for a canter whilst the others wait. The horses left behind will become agitated and may misbehave or even bolt.

A group should consist of four to six riders; this is sufficient for one leader and escort to control. Sometimes for more experienced riders, groups may number up to eight.

The escort will normally be at the rear of the ride except if needed, for example crossing a road, when the escort may need to stand in the road to control the traffic whilst the group crosses in safety.

The first five minutes of the hack should be in walk to allow the riders and horses time to warm up. The girths and stirrups can be checked again.

Always prepare the ride before changing pace or direction. The riders need time to prepare and to be in balance.

For a downward transition preparation time is essential to prevent the ride bumping into each other when the front riders stop. Raise a hand to signal that the downward transition is about to be made and then shout for the ride to walk or trot.

The places for trot and canter should be carefully chosen. Single enclosed lanes are excellent; they keep the riders in line and prevent overtaking. The surface should be fairly soft, smooth and free of stones.

Keep looking behind to check the ride. Even with experienced riders incidents can happen, the ride may need to stop fairly quickly to deal with the situation.

Riders should take a slightly forward position for canter, keeping the weight pushed down into the heel. This is good practice for the jumping seat.

Avoid cantering on the way home from a hack, many horses will quicken towards home and may bolt.

Riding in open spaces, such as fields and common land, can be unsafe, especially at a fast pace with a number of riders who are less experienced. Ride around the edge of fields, keep in single file and keep the pace slow unless the riders are experienced and capable of controlling the horses.

If the riders are to jump, they must all be capable of jumping and all want to do so. Check that the fences or obstacles are safe, particularly the take off and landing areas. Keep the riders at a safe distance from one another without splitting the ride, the horses can become excited if they see others jumping.

For the last ten minutes of the hack, the whole ride should walk and allow the horses to cool down. If safe the riders can give the horses a long rein. Avoid this on a road.

Hazards

In forests or woods, low branches can often cause injury. Warn the ride if riding through low branches; the pace should be a slow walk and the riders should fold onto the horse's neck to avoid being hit. Avoid trotting and cantering under low branches. Even slender trees can cause injury, especially if splinters lodge in the rider's or the horse's eye.

When walking through narrow spaces, the rider needs to be aware and control the horse to prevent being knocked, injured or trapped. Avoid riding at a trot or canter through areas of dense woodland where trees grow close together.

Some horses will not step through puddles, ditches or drains. Warn the rider that the horse may side step or jump.

Single Riders

It is safer to hack with someone else, but this is not always possible. Inform someone at the yard of the planned route and the estimated return time.

Have some identification in a pocket; the horse should also have identification on him including the name and address of the stables. If he is found wandering on his own, the yard can be contacted. A card inside a plastic luggage label fastened to the saddle or bridle is a good idea.

The Country Code

The purpose of the Country Code is to protect the countryside, the people who live there, those who visit and use the country.

Horses can be quite destructive, their hooves churn up the ground, they may graze on protected areas, they may break tree branches.

- Keep to the designated bridleways.
- Do not drop litter.
- Avoid starting fires.
- Leave gates as you found them.
- Do not destroy plant life in designated areas.
- Avoid damaging or destroying trees or bushes.
- When riding in fields keep to the designated paths.
- Ride around the boundary, the edge of the field, do not destroy crops.
- Do not disturb livestock; walk past other animals.
- Walk slowly past pedestrians.
- Pass other riders at a safe distance in walk.
- To overtake other riders ask permission first and then walk past slowly.

If horses and riders are to continue to use the country areas the country code should be respected and followed.

Teaching Tips

When observing lessons given by experienced instructors, notice how they structure their lessons, adapting when necessary to their pupils' abilities. Notice how they introduce and teach new subjects giving time for practice and repetition.

Observe how instructors explain the subject for the content of the lesson; watch how they organise the riders around the school, controlling them so that the riders use the space effectively. Listen to the instructors explanations of the methods, aids, aims for each new subject taught.

Practise as often as you can either hacking out with friends, leading or escorting hacks. It is an experience and there is nothing that will increase your knowledge as much as experience!

CHAPTER 4
Beginner Lessons

Beginner lessons are one of the most important aspects of teaching. This is the first impression that the adult or child may have of horses and these initial lessons can either encourage or deter them.

Teaching the correct methods from the start is important if beginner riders are to progress. Economically, lessons for beginners are good revenue in many commercial yards.

The Beginner

The important elements of the first lessons are **safety and enjoyment**. The pupil may feel apprehensive but will develop confidence if the instructor maintains safety in the lessons.

For the complete beginner, or even those returning to riding after some years, this could be a new doorway opening up in their lives. They may, after some lessons, decide it is not for them and give up, but equally they may take up riding seriously and continue to grow in skill, perhaps progressing to the top.

Stable Management lectures are often a benefit to beginners for the more they learn about the 'mysteries of horsemanship' the more interested and competent they become.

The Instructor

The instructor needs to create confidence, a good atmosphere, be enthusiastic and have a friendly manner. Patience and understanding are all necessary qualities for teaching beginners. The pupil may not have the ability to progress as quickly as the instructor would like but impatience, aggressiveness or apathy will all discourage the beginner.

The teaching should be consistent otherwise the pupil can become confused. Explanations need to be given step by step in simple terms, thorough without being complicated. The instructor needs to decide between essential information for safety and education, and information that, at this stage, would overload the pupil unnecessarily.

The instructor has to imagine himself as the pupil, looking through their eyes, never assuming knowledge. What seems an automatic action for the instructor will be totally new and unfamiliar to the pupil.

For the first lessons, at least, the beginner should be taught by the same instructor. This develops a continuity and rapport. The pupil will develop confidence in one instructor and, through familiarity, begin to relax.

Clothing

Beginners will not normally possess the correct riding clothes and they may wish to wait before purchasing items such as hat and boots as these are expensive.

The riding school should give advice on suitable clothing at the time the booking is made. The instructor will need to check again when the beginner arrives for the lesson.

Some schools hire out equipment; some offer a lease arrangement so that items can be purchased over a period of time.

The hat should be inspected for fit and condition, especially if this has been borrowed or rented from the office. The boots should be strong, heeled and have a smooth sole.

Trousers should be loose fitting without a seam down the inside of the leg. Gloves will be needed to protect the fingers and hand. Jackets, if worn, should be fastened. A stick or whip should not be necessary at this stage.

The Horse

Choosing the right type of horse for the beginner is important. The horse (or pony) should be the right size for the rider in height and width. Putting a small rider on a wide horse can strain the rider's hips. If the horse is too narrow this may feel uncomfortable.

The horse should be reliable, sensible, with balanced, rhythmical paces and obedient when being lunged. He needs to have a fairly strong back and build.

Gentle 'Mr. Plod' is suitable for the first few lessons but as the rider progresses a slightly more forward-going horse may be needed. As the rider begins to learn how to use the aids these will be more effective on a more responsive horse.

The saddle should be a GP saddle, the correct size for the rider and horse. The use of a saddlecloth, gel pad or numnah will, to some extent, protect the horse's back. The bridle should be a snaffle with single reins. *There should be a neckstrap.*

The First Lesson

For an adult beginner the first lesson will normally be on the lunge. Normal lungeing equipment will be used with the exception of side reins.

If the rider is apprehensive or very unbalanced, it is possible to give the first couple of lessons on the lead rein. For smaller children whose balance is not sufficient for lungeing (under 10 or 12 depending on their size), the first lessons will be on the lead rein.

The length of the lesson at this stage may be kept to 30 minutes until the rider has developed some physical fitness (riding fitness) and improved the balance. It is better for the rider to have two lessons per week rather than a single hour, which can be physically and mentally demanding.

At all times basic safety procedures and the reasons for these should be explained, such as never walking too close to a horse's hindquarters. The horse, being a prey animal, will strike out at what he considers is a predator.

The beginner needs to know that horses and ponies are living creatures with a mind and will of their own. They each have their own temperaments, reacting in individual ways and having different moods.

Approaching the Horse

Explain and demonstrate how to approach the horse. Then lead the horse from the stable whilst explaining to the pupil how to do this safely. Continue talking to the beginner to put him at ease and to keep him in sight. Sometimes the beginner, walking more slowly, can find himself placed directly behind the horse.

Entering the School

Explain the rule about entering the school, knocking on the door and asking permission to enter. Opening the door abruptly could startle the horses, walking in without warning could cause a collision.

The horse is led into the middle of the school and turned correctly. Explain that horses should be kept at a safe distance from one another to prevent fights, kicking, biting and injury.

Mounting

Demonstrate tightening the girth (offside as well as the nearside) how to take the stirrups down the leathers gently and how to measure the stirrups against an arm for length. A mounting block should be used for the beginner, who will probably not be sufficiently fit or agile to mount from the ground or by a leg up.

Demonstrate and explain mounting.

- Hold the reins and some mane in the left hand.
- Place the right arm over the saddle to the far side, not holding onto the cantle.
- Place the left foot into the stirrup (the beginner may become confused and place the right foot in) keeping the toe down to avoid prodding the horse's side.
- Spring lightly into the saddle landing gently to avoid bumping the horse's back. (This is important to teach from the start, as beginners may not know how their weight can hurt or damage the horse's spine.)

Demonstrate adjusting the stirrups whilst keeping the foot in the iron, checking the girth whilst mounted and how to hold the reins correctly. Explain and demonstrate the horse's movements at walk and trot, describing briefly the footfalls. Then show the correct method of dismounting. Assist the beginner to mount explaining the procedure again.

Riding

Once the beginner has settled into the saddle and adjusted the stirrups to a comfortable length, which may be slightly shorter at this stage, explain simply the following points:

- The rider's basic position on the horse.
- How to hold the reins feeling a light contact on the horse's mouth.
- How to ask the horse to go forward into walk by using the leg aids in a series of nudges and allowing with the hand.
- How to stop the horse by sitting up straight, leg in contact and by applying a slight resistant squeeze or pressure on both reins equally.

For the first few minutes lead the horse on a couple of circuits until the rider becomes accustomed to the movement. The rider may hold the front of the saddle.

When the rider feels more confident, the horse can be sent out onto the lunge circle.

The teaching begins with simple exercises and instructions.

- Transitions between halt and walk.
- Encourage the rider to use the voice aid, which will also help the rider to breathe and relax.

Change the rein periodically so that the rider and horse do not become 'one-sided'. Explain about the method and reasons for changing the rein.

The Rider's Position

Teach the rider to sit centrally in the saddle. It is essential that the rider learns to distribute the weight correctly from the start, developing the correct musculature and physical fitness. Positional corrections can be made throughout the lesson.

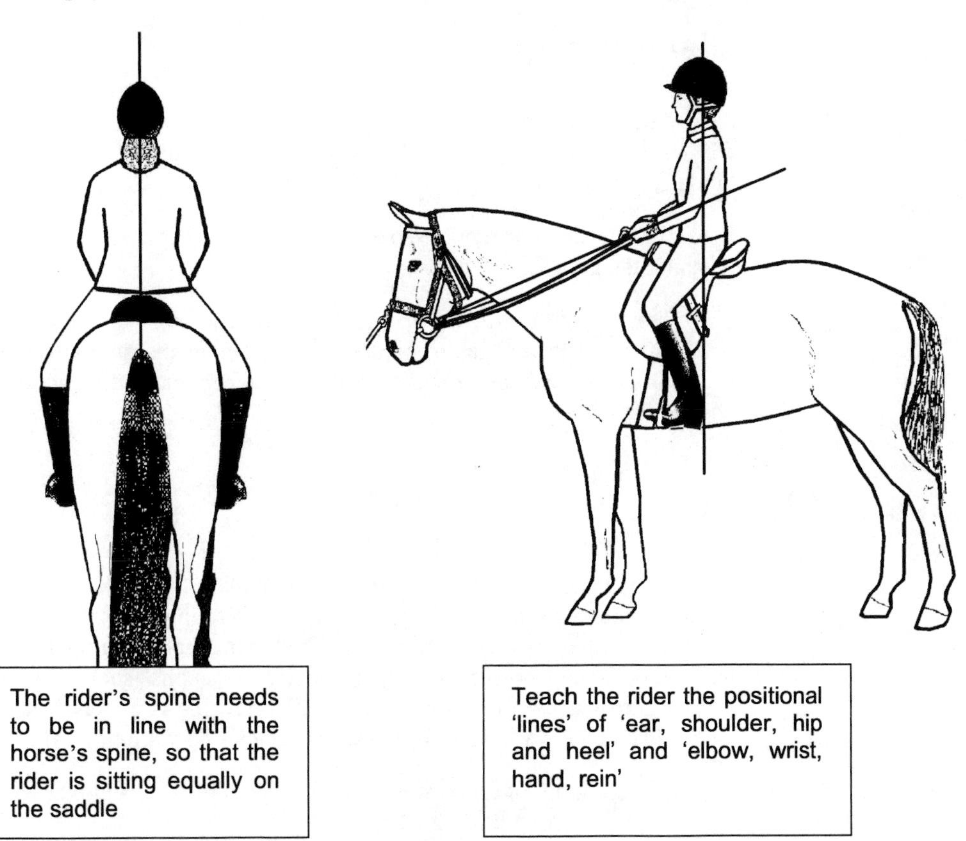

The rider's spine needs to be in line with the horse's spine, so that the rider is sitting equally on the saddle

Teach the rider the positional 'lines' of 'ear, shoulder, hip and heel' and 'elbow, wrist, hand, rein'

Teach the rider to carry the upper body, keep looking forward and in the direction of travel. Encourage the rider to relax the hips. The rider should be encouraged to 'feel' the horse's movement through the pelvic area.

Trot

After 15 to 20 minutes, depending on how the rider is coping at walk, a few paces of trot work may be introduced. The trot will be sitting trot as beginners normally find it difficult to cope with rising at this stage.

Explain about the transition, about the horse's change of pace and body movement, and warn the rider of the spring into the trot.

Lead the horse at first with the rider holding onto the front of the saddle. Instruct the rider to relax and go with the movement. The rider could count the '1-2' of the trot pace out loud. Concentrating on the horse's movement encourages the rider to relax and settle into a rhythm. Prepare the rider for the transition to walk and repeat the exercise on the other rein.

Dismounting

At the end of the lesson, repeat the explanations for dismounting, how to take both feet out of the stirrups first and how to bring the right leg across to clear the horse's hindquarters.

Stand beside the horse in preparation to steady the rider if he loses balance on reaching the ground.

Show how to put the stirrups up and bring the reins over the horse's head for leading. Lead the horse to the stable; explain about turning the horse in the box so that his head is facing the door. Escort the rider to reception so that another lesson can be booked.

Second Lesson

During this lesson the teaching can include leading the horse (with supervision) from the stable into the school. When checking and altering the girth the rider should again be made aware of how some horses dislike having their girth tightened. (Whilst those who work around horses develop instinctive reactions, such as watching the horse when tightening the girth, the beginner will have no experience of the horse's body language and the warnings this gives. Sometimes no warning at all!)

Explain the routine of mounting again; it is possible the beginner has forgotten some of the points raised in the last lesson.

The lesson content will be similar to the first, repeating the transitions halt to walk and walk to halt, and short periods of sitting trot with the rider holding onto the front of the saddle.

It may be possible to introduce a little work without stirrups, at walk only. Demonstrate how to cross the stirrups over in front of the saddle.

Exercises can be introduced to stretch and strengthen muscles and tendons. These should be simple exercises performed slowly and carefully. Avoid strenuous stretching, particularly in the hip area, which may cause cramp or pain.

At the conclusion of the lesson explain the dismount and assist the rider to lead the horse back into the box.

Third Lesson

Most of this lesson will be a revision of the first two lessons. Continue to correct the rider's basic position. Progress should be gradual keeping within the rider's limitations.

- *At halt* may begin careful exercises to strengthen and widen the hips, such as raising the knees to the pommel of the saddle.
- May introduce short periods of trot without stirrups. Instruct the rider to knot the reins, hold the buckle end and the front of the saddle with both hands.

Depending on the rider's progress, include some work off the lunge for about five minutes at the end of the lesson. Teach the rider how to turn the horse at walk using the natural aids and practise around the corners of the school or in a square shaped figure. Walk by the horse's neck for guidance and control.

The Rising Trot

The rising trot may be taught from the third lesson onwards depending entirely on the rider's progression and ability.

The function of the rising trot is to make the trot more comfortable for the horse and rider, and, by taking the weight off the horse's back on every alternate beat, help him to relax through his back.

First in sitting trot the beginner should learn to feel the rhythm. Explain about rising every alternate beat and about lowering the seat back into the saddle as gently as possible.

*The rider practises **at halt** first.*

- Incline the shoulders *slightly* forward.
- Think of the hip moving forwards and rising, then backwards and lowering with the horse's rhythm.
- Keep the body relatively still from the waist upwards allowing the hips to be propelled into rising by the horse's movement.
- Keep the lower leg relatively still and relaxed with the weight down the back of the leg into the heel.

Most beginners may find this difficult and attempt to rise by standing up in the stirrups and throwing the weight forwards. Continue to correct and assist the rider. Rising trot is one of those moves that, if learnt incorrectly, can become a difficult habit to break, limiting the rider's progress for years.

When the rider has achieved more balance and confidence, the 'rising' is practised at walk. The rider holds onto the neckstrap or a piece of mane.

Holding onto the reins will result in the rider losing balance, jabbing the horse in the mouth. Holding onto the pommel of the saddle prevents the rider from bringing the hip forward, encouraging the body to be launched straight upward. However, if holding onto the pommel makes the rider feel safer and more secure, this will be sufficient until more balance is achieved.

Remain near the horse and rider; it may help to hold onto one of the rider's ankles for steadiness and to prevent the lower leg from swinging forwards.

When ready the rider can practise at trot. Start with trotting on straight lines and stay close to the horse in preparation to steady the rider and to bring the horse to walk.

To practise the timing, call out the beat 'down and up'. (This prevents the rider launching out of the saddle on the strong upbeat of 'up and down'.)

If available, another more experienced rider could give a demonstration. *It is not necessary at this stage to explain the diagonals.*

Once the rider is more balanced and confident, the rising trot may be practised for short periods on the lunge.

Little and often is the key; this exercise can be strenuous on beginners who become tired and tense. Start with *short periods* of rising, gradually extending the time to develop the rider's balance.

Sitting Trot

Whilst it is essential for every beginner to learn rising trot, practice in the sitting trot should be continued. Sitting trot is a skill that is often overlooked. Practising sitting trot improves the rider's position and, by making the hips more supple, the rising trot.

With progression, the sitting trot becomes more important in flatwork and dressage. The rider in sitting trot has a greater ability of improving the horse's balance and of using the natural aids.

Progression

After the first few lessons, the length of the lesson time can be extended to 45 minutes and then an hour. This period can be split with some time spent on the lunge (or lead rein) and some off the lunge in a safe, enclosed environment.

Time spent working off the lunge, can be gradually increased from five, to ten and fifteen minutes.

As the rider increases in confidence, balance and ability, the teaching can include further work developing an understanding of the horse and the use of the natural aids.

- Teach the rider to develop feel with the hands with a soft light contact. The rider can learn how to keep the hands level on either side of the horse's neck whilst maintaining a contact through supple shoulders and elbows.
- Off the lunge, teach transitions and turns across the school.
- Explain the letters of the school, simple school figures, some of the more usual equestrian terms – 20 metre (20m) circles, diagonals across the school, centre line, changing rein, inside and outside of the horse, nearside and offside.
- Demonstrate how to put a head collar on the horse and how to tack up. Many riders do not learn this for years, turning up at the riding school where the horse is tacked and untacked for them.
- Show how to lead in hand, turning the horse correctly.
- In time the rider may practise the trot whilst holding the reins. Explain about keeping the hands fairly still, with the angle at the elbow increasing with the rise. This may take quite a few lessons to achieve depending on the rider's ability.
- Teach diagonals at trot and how to change diagonal when changing rein.

Continue to repeat the basic simple procedures until the rider knows and is familiar with the tasks such as leading the horse, mounting, adjusting the girth and stirrups, keeping a safe distance from other horses.

The rider will need time to mentally absorb each new aspect. Those who have been riding for years often do not appreciate that the simplest tasks can be quite a lot to learn for some beginners.

Continue also to correct the rider's basic position, helping the rider by noticing any physical difficulties and using exercises to overcome these.

Diagonals

When the rising trot is fairly established, the rider can be taught the diagonals. The rider sits when the horse's *inside hind leg is on the ground,* this supports the weight and helps the horse to keep in balance whilst working in a school, on circles and turns. When hacking, changing diagonals prevents the horse from developing stronger muscles on one side.

Explain the footfalls, the diagonal pairs, when the rider sits and rises. This can be demonstrated with another rider whose horse could have different coloured leg bandages to make it easier to observe.

As it takes time to develop enough feel to distinguish the 'correct' diagonal, the rider can check by momentarily glancing at the outside shoulder. When this shoulder is going backwards the rider sits, when the shoulder is forwards the rider rises.

Encourage the rider to make this a quick glance with the eyes only. A rider who brings the head forward to take a good, long look will compromise the position and balance. (Some riders find it easier to watch the inside shoulder; sometimes it depends on which side the horse's mane falls. The inside shoulder will be forward when the rider sits and vice versa.)

The beginner can also be taught how to change the diagonal, by sitting for two beats. The rider changes diagonals on the centre line when changing rein by a short or long diagonal. This does help to remind beginners to change diagonals. (As the rider progresses, possibly competing in dressage tests, the horse needs to be straight and in rhythm as he crosses the school. The diagonal is changed a stride or two before the horse reaches the opposite track. Changing the diagonal in the centre can break the rhythm of the trot and make the horse waver in direction.)

Canter Work

The introduction to canter can begin once the rider is **balanced and secure at trot,** both in sitting and rising. The sitting trot will be needed for the transition to canter.

Most riders will be ready to take a short canter after the fifth or sixth lesson, though this does **depend entirely on the rider's ability and fitness**. In some cases the rider may not be ready until several lessons later.

A demonstration of a horse in canter will allow the beginner to see and understand the difference in pace and rhythm. Describe the footfalls, the three-time beat; explain about the 'leading leg'. Describe the transition to canter showing how the rider sits to the trot for a few paces before the transition and then how the rider uses the leg aids.

The first canter work should be kept short; this will be physically and mentally demanding for the beginner. For the first few times it is easier and safer to canter down one long side of the school, in a straight line. Holding onto the lunge line, remain by the side of the horse and use the voice for the upward and downward transitions.

Talk through the transition, allowing the rider time to think and give the aids. The rider sits to the trot for four to six paces then applies the inside leg whilst using the outside leg slightly backwards behind the girth. At the same time command the horse to canter. The rider may need to hold onto the neckstrap or pommel of the saddle for security.

Instruct the rider to sit back and allow the movement through the hips. Encouraging the rider to feel the horse's movement does seem to soften the rider's hips.

If the rider does tip forward, or become unbalanced, instruct them to sit up and back, hold onto the pommel of the saddle; command the horse to trot and then walk.

When introducing canter work the rule should be – better safe than sorry. Short, safe canters will develop the beginner's confidence and physical fitness.

Group Lessons

Most adult beginners will need to continue on the lunge for six lessons. This will vary with individuals; some make progress quickly or are natural riders and can cope off the lunge after the third or fourth lesson. Others, who may not be as physically fit or who experience difficulties, may need to stay on the lunge for up to ten lessons.

Before joining a group lesson the rider should be able to:

- Mount and dismount safely.
- Lead the horse from the stable into the school and line up.
- Check the girth and stirrups from the ground and when mounted.
- Ride in walk and trot (sitting and rising).
- Ride school movements such as circles, turns, and diagonals.
- Ride changes of rein in walk and trot.
- Ride in canter on the track and on a 20m circle.

The group lesson adds variety to the work, giving the experience of riding with others. With increased physical fitness the rider will now be able to ride for an hour. Others in the group will be able to give demonstration from which the rider can learn and there will also be a sense of achievement at having advanced from the beginner private lesson.

Teaching Tips

Teaching beginners is one of the most important aspects of teaching horsemastership, yet many beginners are taught by instructors with the least experience. It is a credit to those instructors and the BHS training system that most beginners do enjoy their lessons and progress safely.

When teaching beginners be aware constantly of safety. It is easy to discourage a beginner by putting them into a dangerous situation or by having an accident.

Remember that everything is new. What you do automatically is completely new territory and the beginner needs to be told, sometimes repeatedly, about safety, the horse's reactions, the rules and regulations of riding in the school.

You will need patience and understanding, as well as enthusiasm and a desire to teach the basics. During the lessons remain observant, watch for the rider becoming tired. Some riders will not admit when they are tired or aching, through fear of showing weakness.

Never push a beginner beyond his capabilities. This is the sure way to have an accident.

Teaching beginners can be one of the most rewarding aspects of being an instructor. As the pupil learns and progresses their delight is obvious.

CHAPTER 5
Children's Lessons

Teaching children is a skill in itself and can be rewarding. Generally children are eager to learn and, having no preconceived ideas, are receptive to being taught.

The most important aspect of any lesson for children is safety, particularly as children have little concept of horses, ponies or danger. A child should never be put at risk. Though accidents do happen and children do fall off, the risk factor should be kept to an absolute minimum.

Children should always be supervised by competent staff, made aware of the dangers of handling and being around ponies, and organised responsibly whilst on the Centre's property.

Qualities for Teaching Children

When teaching children various skills and qualities are required.

- A different **language** is necessary, simple instructions and explanations, and more guidance. Children need to be taught correctly from the start; methods taught at a young age will remain for many years, possibly a lifetime. Incorrect methods once learnt are difficult to rectify in later life.
- Children also need **consistency** in teaching. Though there are alternative methods in riding, keeping the instruction correct and practical will ensure at least some uniformity. Inconsistent teaching causes confusion.
- Lessons for children need **variety**. Children have a short concentration span and can become bored quickly; they also need to learn, need to work, need to be kept active. Some children learn more quickly than others, but all are capable of being taught and understanding more than most adults believe. Most have a vivid imagination and can understand simple concepts if taught in a suitable way.
- An **understanding and rapport** with children is essential. Children differ enormously as individuals; some children desperately want to ride, others are pushed into it by parents, some start riding then lose enthusiasm. This is different for different children; girls can tend to be softer, boys more 'macho' (though not all boys are like this).

- **Discipline** is essential, especially around horses and ponies. Children do like discipline; it gives them boundaries, makes them feel secure and appeals to their sense of justice. The discipline, whilst being firm, should never descend to bullying.
- The learning should be **fun**. By keeping the lessons safe, progressive and interesting, both instructor and child will find the teaching enjoyable.

Requirements

Planning for the lesson requires careful consideration if the child or children are to learn in safety. The pony and tack, the school and the assistants are all prepared beforehand.

The Pony and Tack

Children will need a pony who is quiet, reliable, sensible and honest, possibly an older pony. The pony needs to have a reasonable conformation, be a suitable size, height and width for the child and should have even, balanced, steady paces. It does help, both rider and leader, if the pony is fairly responsive especially to the voice.

The saddle should be the right size for the child and fit the pony. The saddle may need a crupper to prevent it from slipping forwards.

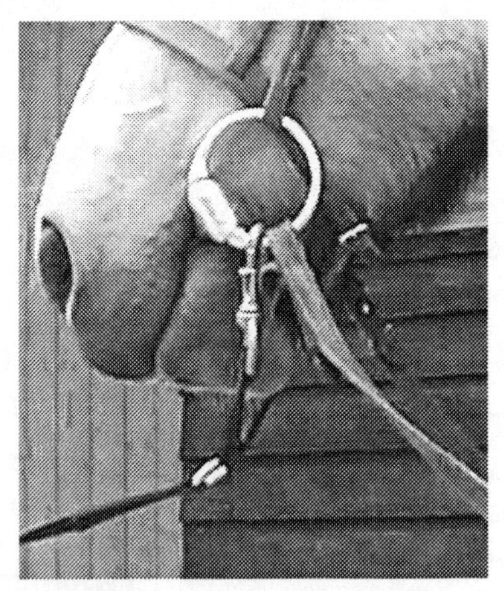

It is important that the stirrups are a correct size so that the child's feet do not slip through. Safety stirrups are excellent for children. The stirrup leathers should be sufficiently short without having to be twisted or having huge lengths of leather slapping the pony's sides.

The bridle will be a snaffle with thinner reins for small hands. The reins should be the **correct length** for pony and child. With long reins the excess loop often becomes wrapped around the child's foot and can be dangerous.

A neckstrap is essential for the child's security and safety.

The lead rope should be strong and in good condition. It is attached either to a head collar under the bridle, the noseband or a couplink that links the bits.

If fastened to the nearest bit ring this may pull the bit through the pony's mouth. When the lead rein is passed through the near ring and fastened on the outside ring, the pull increases the nutcracker action of the bit. Some ponies fight the bit if it becomes 'trapped' in the mouth. The rope also acts like a curb around the chin.

Riding Clothes

It can be difficult buying riding clothes for children especially for their first few lessons. Children grow quickly and expensive riding clothes may only last a matter of months. Younger children tend to fluctuate in their enthusiasm, which makes spending large amounts on clothing uneconomic.

A correctly fitting riding hat is vital. Trousers or jeans, that are not tight and do not have a seam inside the leg, are suitable.

Footwear is often the most difficult item for the child. Boots or wellingtons with a rough sole and no heel are not suitable, if the child's foot slips through the stirrup it may become stuck. Trainers can be dangerous and do not protect the child's ankle and leg. Parents should be informed of the dangers and advised that a good strong pair of boots with heels and smooth soles should be worn. A pair of children's 'long' riding boots, shorter in the leg, can double up as wellingtons and fortunately jodhpur type boots are now in fashion and can be worn at home or school.

Gloves should be worn; often children suffer from blisters or sores from the reins. If a jacket is worn, this should fit and be fastened securely.

The School

The school or menage should be safely enclosed and away from other classes. The gate or door should be shut and there should be no obstacles and jumps out unless using cones or poles.

Leaders

Having suitable and competent leaders for the ponies is vital for the safe and efficient running of the lesson. Sometimes lead rein pupils are led by children not much older or experienced than themselves. These will not have the knowledge, or the strength to deal with any problems.

Leaders need certain qualities.

- Physical ability and competence to put the child on the pony.
- Experience with ponies and the ability to hold the child if they are unbalanced.
- Strength to handle small but very strong ponies.
- Physical fitness to keep up with the pony at trot and short canters.
- A suitable age and size to lead correctly and safely.

Older teenagers, working pupils or students are ideal. If possible avoid using parents especially to lead their own child, as this can cause confusion as to authority.

Leaders can be briefed about the lesson plan prior to the lesson and requested to observe their riders and take care of them.

Leaders need suitable footwear to prevent injury if trodden on by a pony, with a sole that will not slip on grass or wet surfaces. Gloves are essential to prevent injury. Jackets should be fastened safely and a hat, if worn, should be secure. Long hair should be tied back and no jewellery worn.

Parents

Alas children do tend to be saddled with (excuse the pun) parents. Most parents want to watch their offspring as they are learning. Whilst most are understanding and sympathetic, there are some who should come with a health warning sticker.

Teaching children (and dealing with their parents) requires authority, discipline, diplomacy, patience and a thick skin. Keeping the children safe, creating an atmosphere of enjoyment and learning, and teaching the correct methods will offer a good lesson.

Lesson Format

Children generally begin on the lead rein, as they do not have the strength or height to cope with being lunged. Depending on the individual child, about six private lead rein lessons of 30 minutes each will be suitable at the start.

The First Lesson

The basic aim of the lesson is to develop the child's confidence, ability and interest. Explanations should be given for every movement and exercise; everything will be new to the child, they need to know the reasons and aims for each action.

Introduction

Once introduced escort the child to the stable and either lead the pony to the school or, if the child is able to lead, walk beside the child for safety.

Keep the child in sight. A child should never be left unattended with a pony.

The procedure for the first lesson can be similar to the adult beginner. Show how to approach and lead the pony correctly, how to enter the school, check the tack, tighten the girth and alter the stirrups. A small child may not be able to physically perform these tasks at first, but teaching the correct basics from the start provides a good foundation. It will also keep the child's attention focused.

When mounting, smaller children will have to be lifted on bodily. The pony should be held securely. Assist with altering the stirrups and girth.

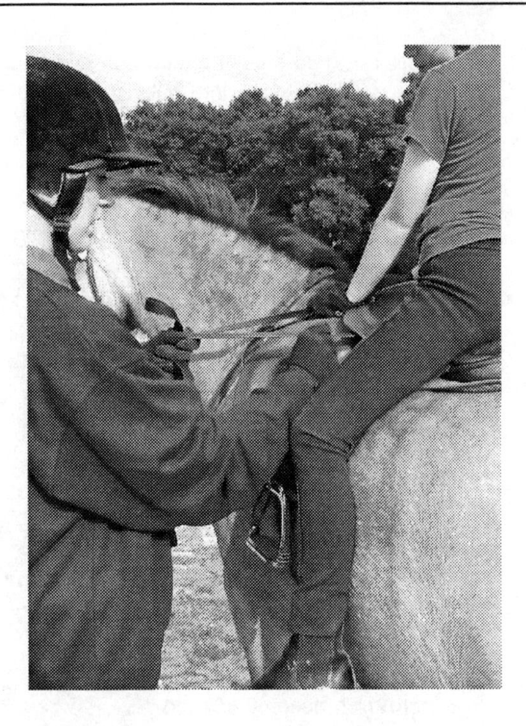

Content

During the first lesson the child is taught the basic procedures: the riding position, how to hold the reins, how to ask the pony to walk forwards and then to halt.

For the transition to walk, instruct the child to use the legs with a series of firm nudges; and command the pony to walk on. Try to avoid instructing the child to 'kick' the pony. Though this is tempting when a child is trying hard to move the pony without success, this term sticks in the mind for years and causes problems when the adult has learnt to raise the heels to kick the horse.

For a downward transition to halt instruct the child to sit up tall, keeping the legs on the pony's sides, and take a firmer contact with the reins. The child may ask the pony to stop by saying 'Whoa'; this encourages the child to breathe out and prevents tension.

Exercises

Some exercises can be included in the lesson. **The pony should be held securely**.

- ❖ At halt - arms circling one at a time (windmill), touching toes, turning around with the arms at shoulder height (aeroplane).
- ❖ At halt - co-ordination exercises such as tapping the head and rubbing the stomach (the child's).

Exercises build up the child's confidence on the pony as well as increasing suppleness and fitness. With complete beginners or small children avoid exercises that are too strenuous or dangerous, such as 'round the world' or 'threading the needle'.

Trot work

If the child is fairly balanced and confident a little trot may be introduced.

The trot should be slow and in a straight line, a few steps in sitting trot with the child holding onto the pommel of the saddle or the neckstrap. If the child is happy and fairly well balanced, a turn or half circle can be introduced. Make the curve large and gradual so that the pony does not change direction abruptly.

Some children become excited and giggle, losing their balance for a few seconds. Be vigilant and prepared to act by holding the back of the child's jacket or jumper if the child becomes unsteady.

Conclusion

During this stage the child can be encouraged to ask questions about the lesson. This will show what has been learnt and absorbed, as well as any areas that were not understood.

Children have amazing thoughts and ideas, possessing incredible insights through their fresh approach to life that we as adults miss. Occasionally, too, children misinterpret explanations or actions and it is a revelation when they express their views, which can often be astounding and humorous.

At the end of the lesson, explain the method of dismounting; take both feet out of the stirrups, hold onto the reins with the left hand, the pommel of the saddle with the right, then lift the right leg over the back of the pony without hitting him.

Smaller children, even medium sized ones, may find this difficult. Either lift the child down or be ready to give assistance. The child should then be escorted back to the yard.

Progression

The child's progress should be slow and steady but with variety and interest. Children need to be kept safe; they so easily lose their confidence. At the same time, they need to progress or they will soon become bored.

The lessons need to include repetition so that the correct procedures will remain in the child's mind. Variation on themes and new facts are introduced to retain the child's interest and enthusiasm, and to increase their knowledge.

Once the child has developed confidence and some balance, after the first three or four lessons, part of the time can be spent off the lead rein. Remain near to the pony and guide him when necessary, for instance on turns or circles, when the child finds it difficult to direct the pony.

During the first six lessons the teaching can include

- how to turn the horse around corners and across the school in walk from one marker to another
- transitions at different spots, walk to halt by a cone or marker on the wall
- weaving in and out of cones
- riding circles
- changing rein by long and short diagonals
- riding up the centre line
- simple points of the pony and the tack
- the letters of the school

Some children learn quickly and are eager to learn more, others are slower to learn and will need time to adjust. Progress should be tailored to the child's ability to learn. If overloaded with new information the child will either become confused or lose confidence and enthusiasm.

After the first six lessons on the private lead rein the child should be able to join the lead rein group. This will give a sense of achievement, accustom the child to riding with others, and increase confidence and experience with other ponies. It will also add variety with different types of lessons, different topics to learn.

Lead Rein Group Lesson

The lead rein group lesson may last from 45 minutes to an hour. There should be a maximum of six riders in the lesson, though this can increased to eight providing there is a competent leader for every rider and the lesson is run efficiently. A larger number can result in each child receiving less instruction and riding practice.

Depending on the abilities of each child, the warm-up phase may include a walk and trot on each rein around the school and a change of rein. The children can also do some stretching exercises.

Continue to work on improving the child's riding position. During a lead rein group lesson, with assistants leading, it is easier to check the child's position from the side and from the back for straightness in the saddle.

School figures, turns, circles, changes of rein and shallow loops can be introduced and props such as cones used for exercises in walk and trot.

Lead Rein Instructional Hack

Part of the child's progress will be to go on an instructional lead rein hack. This type of lesson is useful to children, adding variety and a different perspective to their learning. It will widen their experience and be stimulating for the ponies as well.

Safety is the important factor; competent and experienced leaders will be required.

The length of the hack should be from 30 to 45 minutes and kept at an even walk with short periods of trot, to prevent tiring the children and leaders.

As well as teaching riding ability, aids and positional work, facts about bridleways, riding around fields, the country code and how to ride up and down hills (keep hills gentle for the leaders) can be included.

Teaching Tips

Watching children's lessons or being an assistant during lessons can be valuable experience and a real eye opener.

It is often the training student or newly qualified PT who teaches the children's lessons, so any experience gained in this area of instruction will be of benefit.

Often with children's lesson, there is one child who will be apprehensive about riding, or about some aspect of the lesson. Use discretion and common sense in deciding whether or not to encourage the child to do the exercise. This is where experience with children is essential.

With some children it is beneficial to push them through their fear, at which point they will be proud of their achievement. With others pushing them beyond their own imagined ability can upset them.

Most importantly avoid placing the child in a situation that will be unsafe or destroy their confidence.

The teaching needs to be fun otherwise children quickly lose interest, become bored and will not learn. Using games such as I spy, (I spy ...something on the pony beginning with M) or Simon says (Simon says halt, now walk on. Simon says walk on) creates learning through enjoyment. One of the greatest rewards of teaching is to see (and hear) a child enjoying the pleasure of riding a pony.

CHAPTER 6

Group Lessons

A group lesson consists of three or more pupils having instruction on equitation or stable management. Though a group is a collection of individuals, each needing to be taught individually at times, the group is also a collective and needs to be compatible, that is work together harmoniously, for each individual to progress.

To be in harmony the group needs to have similar aims and objectives. Personalities, ages, standards, all affect the working capability of the group. Each individual is important to the group's integrity.

Teaching groups requires the ability to teach each pupil as an individual and also to teach the group as a whole. This takes control, organisation and planning.

Aims of the Group Lesson

The aims of teaching a group are

- To improve the individuals within the group
- To improve the group as a whole

To achieve these aims requires considerations such as group compatibility, standards, objectives and most importantly the quality of the instruction.

Group Compatibility

This depends on the standard of each individual and their aims. It also depends to some extent on the age range and the personalities within the group.

- Though often pupils of various standards within a group help each other, when the standards differ extensively this can be detrimental for individuals and for the group.
- The aims of the group need to be similar, for instance it would be difficult to teach those who wish to learn flatwork or dressage within a group wishing to practise jumping.

- Ages vary within a group but when some individuals are much younger or older the group may not relate as a whole. A young person in an older group may feel intimidated; an older person with a young group may feel awkward and possibly excluded.
- Personalities within a group can, and often do, influence each other. When the group mixes well the atmosphere is genial and conducive to learning.

Grading

Grading riders is important. Having a group of similar standard helps the group to be compatible; encourages the riders to learn from one another. They will be given corrections and advice at the same level.

Riders may discuss their own problems with each other and, if these are similar, offer each other help and support. A group consisting of riders at a similar standard is easier for the instructor to teach.

Riders of a better standard can provide demonstration, encouraging the others to imitate their riding and improve. However a group consisting of varying levels may be similar to teaching a number of private lessons at once.

Sometimes the lesson revolves around teaching the better rider or riders to the detriment of the less able or vice versa. Also if one or two riders are below the standard they may feel intimidated and demoralised. Those riders who are far above the standard of the class may become bored.

Most groups will have a core of regular riders but there will always be new riders joining. Even the most static of groups does change over time. The standard of new riders should be clearly assessed so that the group remains compatible.

The horses should be of a standard and ability suitable to the group so that no horse is pushed beyond his capabilities.

Types of Group Lessons

The various types of lessons include; lead rein groups for children; adult beginner groups; novice, intermediate and advanced, flatwork and jumping, instructional group hacks and stable management lectures.

Pupils vary: there are beginners, adults and children; the 'once a week' rider and the more serious rider who rides three or four times a week; students and working pupils studying for Exams, livery owners on their own horses for pleasure or to compete.

Riders who hack exclusively, if the weather is bad and hacking is restricted, may be encouraged to take lessons. This can add variety to their riding, may improve their skills and consequently their enjoyment of hacking.

Group Size

The number of pupils within a group is a relevant factor.

- ❖ The establishment needs to make a profit to continue trading.
- ❖ The pupil needs to obtain value and a portion of the instructor's time.
- ❖ For safety the number in a group should be limited to avoid placing any pupil or horse in danger.
- ❖ The instructor needs to control the group and to teach each pupil in the lesson.
- ❖ Beginner classes (adults or children off the lead rein) may be limited to between four and six persons. The instructor may spend more time with each individual and the riders may need more room to maintain their horses at a safe distance from others.
- ❖ Children's groups are normally limited to between six and eight. Larger groups may result in problems, as children are not always able to maintain control.
- ❖ Jumping classes ideally have a lower number of riders to avoid standing around for long periods whilst the others are jumping.

In most groups the size is limited to eight riders, sufficient for a normal indoor or outdoor school and for an instructor to teach comfortably. Sometimes in a group lesson the number is less than eight and obviously for the pupils this offers more value for money.

Groups do occasionally number up to ten, but this is excessive for riders and the instructor. Riders may feel that they are not obtaining value for money, leave the group or change riding establishments.

It is in the centre's interest to limit the numbers in each class.

Teaching the Group

To create good quality lessons, organisation of the group is essential. The group needs to be controlled and the lesson arranged appropriately to the theme if the riders are to have the space and time to perform each movement to their best ability.

Achieving this needs planning and preparation so that the group is organised, stage-managed, almost like choreography in a dance.

One of the structures by which the group is controlled is by the words of command.

Words of Command

Specific words and phrases have evolved to allow control over the riders in as efficient a manner as possible during a lesson in the school. These standard commands are listed here with their meanings.

'Whole ride' the group performs the movements either following the lead rider or together.

Working as a ride
the group works together keeping one horse's distance from the horse in front.

In open order the group works around the school keeping the space of three to four horses between each rider.

Working as individuals
the group works as individuals doing their own exercises whilst watching out for and keeping a safe distance from one another.

Going large working around the outside track of the school.

Working on an inner track
riding on a track about one metre in from the outer track.

Whole ride turning across the school in single file, leading file turn left (or right)
the group as a ride follow the leading file to turn across the school.

Whole ride turning across the school as a ride, whole ride left (or right) turn
the group working as a ride turn across the school together at the same time.

Come onto a 20m circle
the ride starts to ride a circle from a school letter.

Cease the exercise and go large
the ride stops the exercise they are performing and rides onto the outer track. Could specify a point such as '*cease the exercise at A and go large*'.

Change the rein across the diagonal from…to….
the ride follows the leading rider to change the rein via a diagonal.

Down the centre line from A to C and at C track left (or right)
this command can be used to change the rein or as an exercise to check straightness.

Leading file only **or** ***Leading file in succession***
only the first rider in the group. Used to work the ride as individuals, for instance 'leading file only at A go forwards to canter and canter to the rear of the ride'.

Rear file only the rider at the back of the ride only will perform the exercise, for instance 'rear file only go forward to walk'.

Preparation Time

It is important that before any command the ride is always instructed to **'prepare'**, for example 'whole ride prepare to walk; whole ride prepare to change the rein across the diagonal M to K'. This allows the riders time to think, apply the aids, prepare the horse and act. It prevents confusion, sudden or dramatic actions.

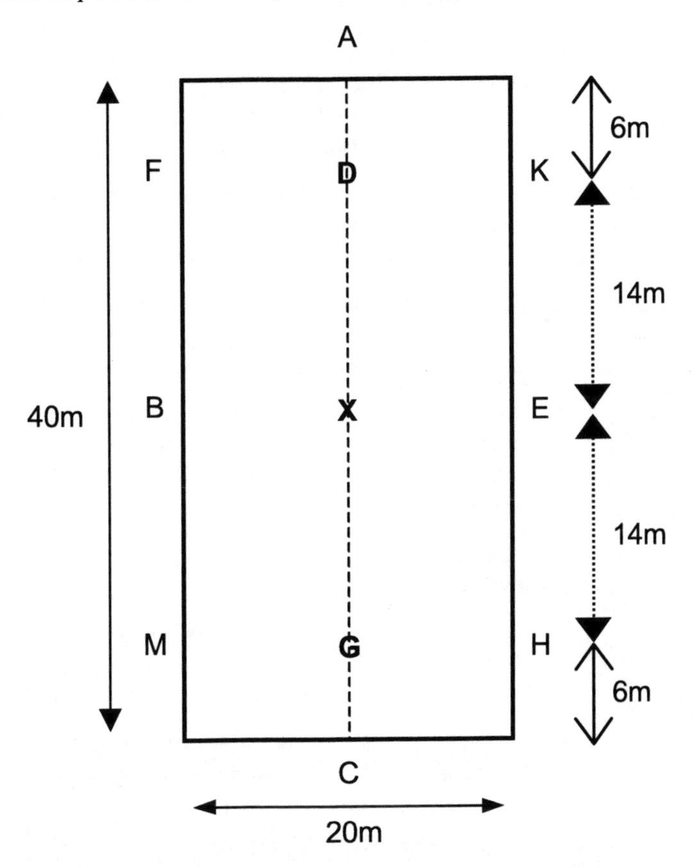

For transitions the preparation needs careful timing, on average about four to six strides before the change. If given too short a time the rider will not be able to prepare; the transition will be abrupt. If given too long either the horse will anticipate or the rider will become irritated waiting for the command.

For school movements or figures such as a change of rein, coming onto a circle or leg yield, the ride will need preparing at least two to three markers in advance.

For instance, if the ride is to change the rein from the left to right rein from H to F they will need to be warned before M, ideally around B to give sufficient time to think, look, prepare, adjust, give the aids and perform the turn.

School Rules

These rules are necessary for the safety of the riders and horses.

- Before entering a school, if someone is teaching or riding in the school, knock on the door or wait by the gate and ask for permission to enter. In an outdoor arena warn that the gate is about to be opened so that riders can avoid that area.

- Lead the horse quietly into the middle of the school and turn to stand the horse across the centre line parallel to A. It can be dangerous and is inefficient if the horses are stood anywhere in the school, particularly if the riders start to tighten the girths.

- The first rider to lead the horse into the school should proceed to the far end before halting on the centre line. This allows the other riders to lead their horses in without having to pass behind the other halted horses.

- Keep a safe distance between the horses whilst standing, especially when tightening girths and mounting. Horses can fidget or kick out at this point and, if close to another horse, can cause injury.

- Keep a safe distance between the horses throughout the ride, at least one horse's length between a horse and the one in front. When passing a horse keep sufficient distance to the side to prevent any horse feeling threatened and kicking.

- Avoid cutting up another horse and rider, that is, cutting in close either to the side or the front.

- Avoid making downward transitions directly in front of another horse. Depending on the exercises being performed, downward transitions are safer if made away from the track or across the centre line.

- When the ride is working in different paces, depending on the exercise, those in walk should be on the inner track giving sufficient room for those at a faster pace on the outer track.

- Riders give way to those doing more advanced movements such as lateral work.

- Pass left to left when working on different reins.

- At the conclusion of the lesson, all the horses should be brought to halt across the centre line parallel to A, at a safe distance from each other.

- If leaving the school whilst others remain inside, ask permission first and warn that the door or gate is going to be opened.

Vantage Points

There are points within the school from which the ride is visible most of the time. This prevents moving about constantly, which is tiring, confusing to the riders and could make commands, explanations and instructions breathless and muffled.

With the ride going large, stand near to one corner; this gives a view of practically the whole school. This point can also be used for some school movements such as serpentines or leg yield.

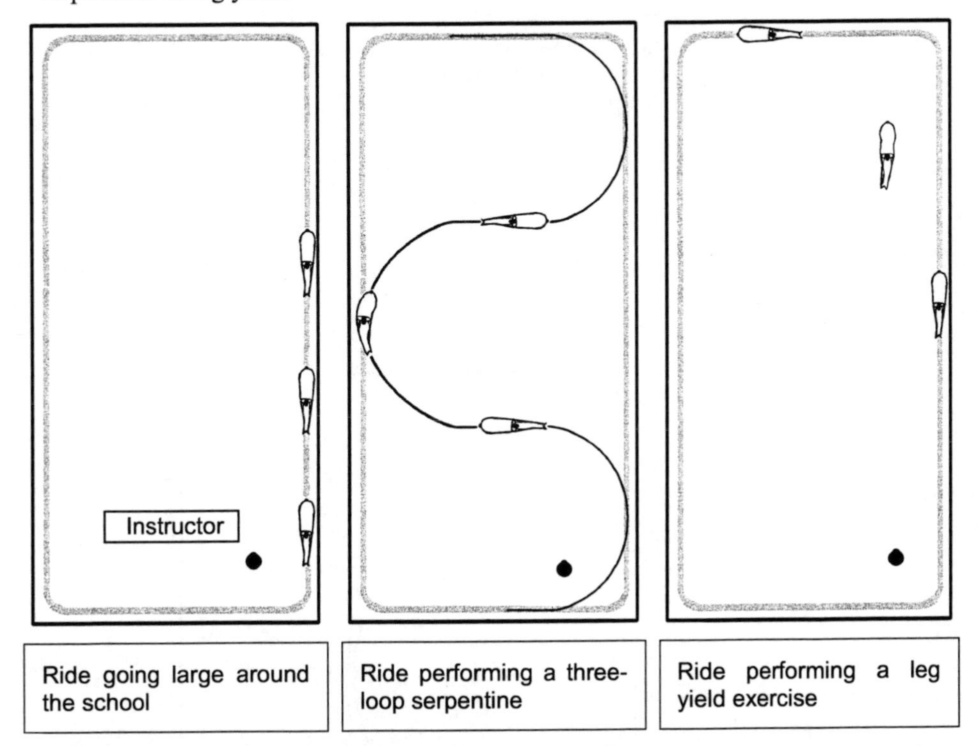

Ride going large around the school

Ride performing a three-loop serpentine

Ride performing a leg yield exercise

There are times when it is necessary to move to a point from which the rider can be seen more easily or observed from a different angle. For instance, watching a rider from behind can show if the horse is working straight or crooked. When teaching a jumping lesson, the vantage point will be close to a fence.

For instance, watching a rider from behind can show if the horse is working straight or crooked. When the riders are working on a straight line down the centre line, the best vantage point is to stand at A or C to check if the line is straight, if the horses are straight or crooked.

When teaching a jumping lesson, for a single fence the vantage point will be near to the fence. If the riders are jumping over a number of fences or a course, the best point will be in a safe position where the riders can be observed over every fence.

For a 20m circle, a vantage point just inside the circle near the circumference is the best place to see all the riders. This will encourage the riders to ride a more accurate circle.

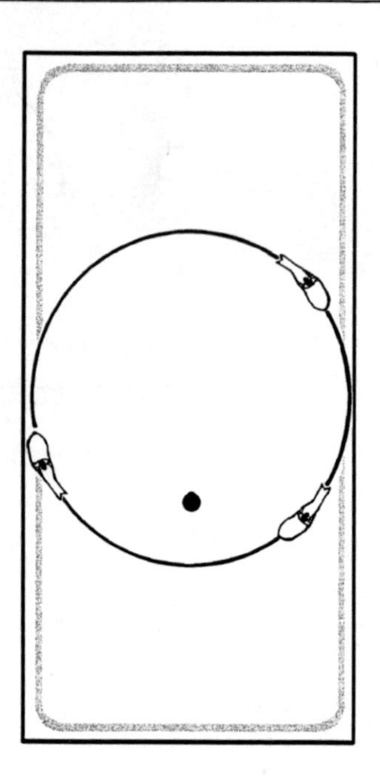

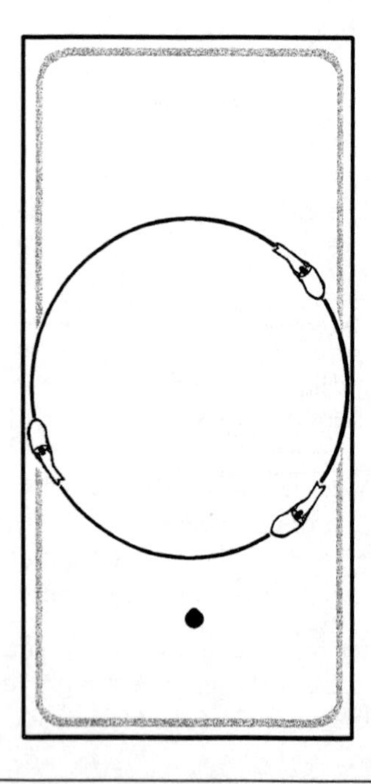

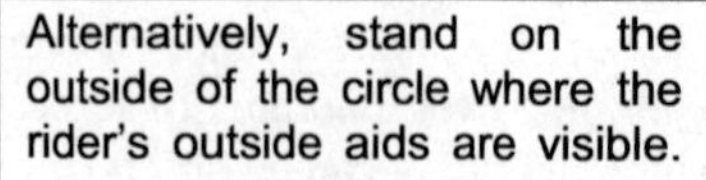

Alternatively, stand on the outside of the circle where the rider's outside aids are visible.

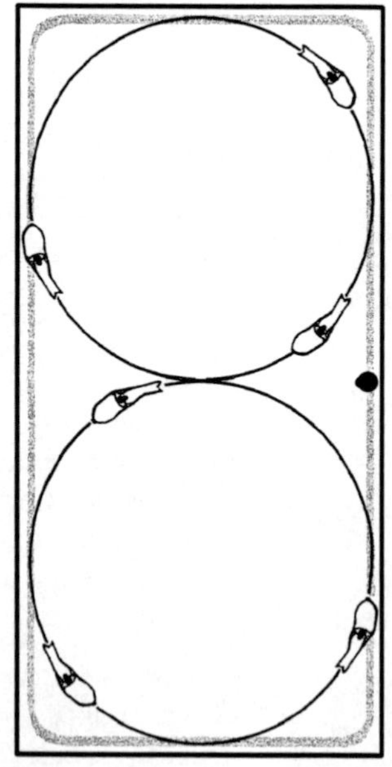

Where a group is organised into two circles, stand at the side of the school for maximum visibility.

Teaching Individuals

It is as important that each individual within the group receives attention and teaching, as it is for the whole group to be organised efficiently.

When a group is working as a ride there may be a tendency to concentrate on the leader to the detriment of the other riders. One method of avoiding this is to alternate, teaching from the front to the back of the ride and then from the back to the front, this will ensure that everyone receives a fair amount of time.

Often too the teaching centres on the weakest person in the group. Whilst this may help their ability it may make them feel conspicuous and emphasise their lack of skill. The other riders may feel ignored.

Stable Management Lectures

For lectures too, the group needs organisation and control. The aims will be similar, to learn about managing and handling horses. The lecture could be planned to assist pupils learn general points about stable management, or aimed at students studying towards their exams.

In a lecture room too there will be a vantage point. Ideally the pupils should sit with their backs to the window. This will provide light for writing and keep them from being distracted by events in the yard. If the pupils sit in a semi-circle, this will increase their attention, rather than sitting in conventional 'classroom' positions.

During the lecture, have eye contact with individuals in the group. Keep observing the pupils to assess if all are attentive and understand the subject of the lecture.

Pupil's Records

For both riding and stable management group lessons, each pupil should have their own record so that progress can be monitored. The record should include the pupil's aims, standards, any particular problems, physical ailments, the horses they have ridden or lectures attended.

The reports need to be kept up to date so that current information is available, particularly when other instructors may need to occasionally take the lesson. This will also prevent any repetition of the same subject and keep continuity in subject matter and standard of achievement.

Teaching Tips

The skill of teaching groups is achieved by learning the techniques and through experience. You need to know how to control the group through the words of command, where to stand for the best visibility.

Watch groups of various standards. Notice how different standards of riders need a different type of organisation and control, beginners need a different lesson from advanced riders. Watch how flat lessons are run as opposed to jumping lessons.

Watch instructors and notice how they use the school to the best advantage, by standing in the most efficient place, by organising the riders and the horses, and by planning the school movements in various parts of the school.

Then practise as much as possible so that you become familiar not only with controlling riders but also just speaking to a group of people.

Practise organising a group to perform different school figures and movements, circles, straight lines, leg yield. You will soon become aware of the best places for these figures and movements and of how the group needs to be organised to perform these efficiently and safely.

Experience is invaluable when teaching group lessons. If you are unable to teach groups, ask some friends with their own horses or people at your yard if you can practise with them. Riders are usually willing to help and you may receive some interesting and useful feedback that will help to expand your knowledge.

CHAPTER 7
Lunge Lessons

Being taught on the lunge is one of the greatest aids to improving riding technique. It is beneficial for riders from beginner up to advanced levels. This type of training is often under-valued but many top establishments use lungeing as the foundation of their teaching throughout the rider's whole career. Teaching a rider on the lunge needs skill, technical expertise, observation and knowledge.

Aims of the Lunge Lesson

The aims of teaching a rider on the lunge are:

- to improve the rider's position
- to improve suppleness and balance
- to deepen the seat
- to create an independent seat
- to develop an awareness of the horse's paces and transitions

To achieve these aims the primary requirement is the ability to lunge a horse effectively. Through the use of the voice, body language, lunge line and whip, the horse is controlled so that he works with impulsion, rhythm and balance.

The use of the lungeing equipment should be almost second nature, so that the concentration is on teaching the rider. The rider then does not need to guide the horse but can concentrate on improving their position, balance, suppleness and co-ordination.

The second requirement is knowledge of the rider's position; the ability to recognise faults and, more importantly, the root of the faults; of correcting these to improve the rider.

The ultimate objective is for the rider to develop a secure, independent seat with balance and suppleness so that he can harmonise his body movements with the horse's movements. Then the natural aids can be used effectively to influence the horse in all paces and transitions.

The Horse

The horse should be suitable for lungeing with a good temperament, paces and conformation; obedient on the lunge, quiet, reliable, sensible and fit, as lungeing is strenuous. Sharp, sensitive or 'hot' horses may discourage a rider or result in a loss of confidence. The horse does need to be active though; able to go forward, well schooled, responsive to the voice and to the rider's aids.

The horse should be six years old or over, but not too aged, with steady, rhythmical, balanced paces and lateral suppleness. Being lunged on a stiff, unbalanced horse is uncomfortable and may encourage an incorrect riding position.

The horse needs to be able to work in a comfortable outline, not too deep but not hollow. The horse should accept the use of the side reins. If the horse is 'on the forehand' giving a 'downhill' ride, the rider may feel unbalanced and anxious; particularly beginners who can tend to tip forwards and feel insecure.

The horse should be the right size for the rider. A horse with a strong, medium length back with a medium length stride is ideal for most riders, particularly beginners. Attempting to learn rising trot on a horse with a short or long stride can prove difficult.

The horse should be appropriate for the rider's standard. Beginners should preferably have the same horse for their lunge lessons, this will help them to relax and improve. The horse should have a temperament that is able to cope with loss of balance and mistakes. Different types of horses with varying paces can be used for advancing riders; this helps them to increase their experience and feel.

Tack

The tack includes a lunge cavesson, lunge line, side reins, bridle, saddle, brushing boots.

- ❖ Beginners and novices will need a neckstrap or breastplate. A breastplate is ideal, as it is fixed, allowing more security. Neckstraps can have a tendency to move around if the rider is very unbalanced.
- ❖ The bit should be as mild as possible, a snaffle.
- ❖ The bridle reins need to be a reasonable thickness, easy to hold. Narrow reins encourage the rider to grip too tightly; thick reins may not fit into smaller hands.
- ❖ For beginners a GP saddle is ideal. A dressage saddle is suitable for experienced riders. A jumping saddle is not advisable, as it is difficult for a rider to maintain sufficient balance.
- ❖ The saddle needs to fit the horse and the rider. The stirrups should be the right size, and the stirrup leathers the right length, with sufficient holes to avoid twists.
- ❖ The use of a numnah or saddlecloth, particularly for beginner riders, will in some way help to protect the horse's back, relieving tension.

Clothing

For safety and protection suitable clothing is required when lungeing a horse: a riding hat, gloves, jodhpurs or jeans, a long-sleeved jacket or shirt, and strong boots that will not slip. Spurs should not be worn; neither should jewellery.

The rider needs to wear the normal riding clothes; a whip is not carried on the lunge.

Environment

The lungeing area should be safe and secure. Lungeing in an indoor school is ideal. An outside menage should be enclosed by a fence. The lunge area needs to be as quiet as possible, distractions and noise may result in the horse being inattentive and disobedient.

The arena should be sufficiently large for a 20m circle. Being lunged constantly on a small, tight circle is difficult for riders and tiring for the horse. The centrifugal force will be greater; the rider may lose balance and sit incorrectly.

Ideally there should be no other riders in the school though it is possible to lunge two riders in a 20m x 40m or 20m x 60m arena in safety. There should be no group lessons taking place, certainly not children's lessons, in the same area as lungeing. This is dangerous.

Revision

Stage II Reasons for lungeing, lungeing equipment and fitting, basic methods of lungeing. Using the lunge equipment, lungeing aids. Fitting the side reins, functions of the side reins, use of body language. Basic assessment of the horse on the lunge.

Stage III Use of equipment. The lunger's stance, body language, voice, feel. How to control the horse's paces, working the horse correctly. Changing the rein, transitions.

Lungeing the Horse

To achieve the full benefit of being taught on the lunge, the rider needs to be able to concentrate on his own riding position. The horse needs to be working forward actively, at a constant rhythmical pace, making smooth and balanced transitions. Lungeing a horse is a skill learnt through instruction, practice and experience. Body language, voice, eye contact, feel on the lunge line and the subtle use of the whip are used to control the horse.

The Lunge Line

The line should be held firmly but softly just as a bridle rein maintaining a contact. The horse needs to be worked into this lunge line contact.

The Whip

The whip is used in place of the leg aids, to ask the horse for activity, to work him into the lunge line contact and to maintain the correct bend on the circle. The whip can be used in various ways.

- As a 'soft' driving aid when pointed at the hocks.
- As a firmer driving aid when moved in a circular action.
- To ask for bend when pointed towards the girth.
- As a restraining aid when pointed at the shoulder.

If the horse does not respect the whip, flicking him above the hocks will teach him to respond.

When near to the horse the whip should be safely tucked under the arm to prevent threatening and frightening the horse.

The Side Reins

These are used to accustom the horse to a rein contact, to work him into a more correct outline, for a steadier head carriage, for straightness and for control.

The side reins are fastened to the girth slightly above the lower edge of the saddle flap. When fitting the side reins to the horse's bit, they should be parallel with the ground, and of a sufficient length to make a contact.

The horse's head should be in a naturally flexed position, his neck curved but relaxed. His face should be just in front of the vertical. The reins should never be used to force the horse's head down, to fix his head carriage. This will only restrict forward movement and in some cases can panic the horse.

Though at the beginning of the lunge period the reins can be fairly loose to allow the horse to stretch, they should never be too long or slack. Once the horse is warmed up the reins can be shortened to encourage the horse to work along his back and neck.

The Voice

The voice is used to instruct, command and control the horse through the use of language (correct commands), flexion and tone. The voice needs to be clear, audible, firm and authoritative to keep the horse's attention and obedience. A weak, whispering, unsure voice can be ignored or not heard.

Body Language and Posture

Body language is used for control. Standing in the centre of the circle, moving as little as possible, subtle changes of body position can drive the horse forward or steady his pace.

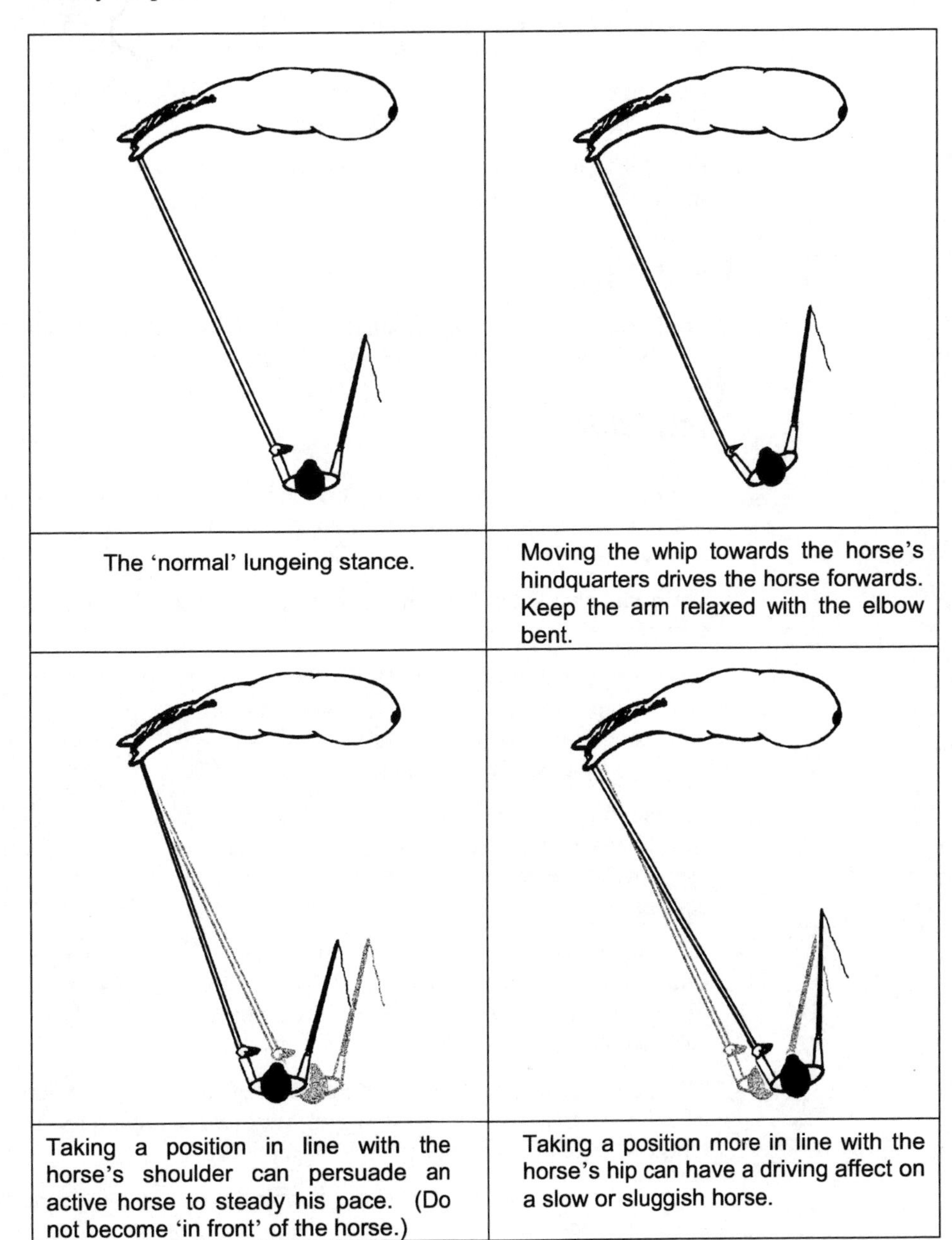

The 'normal' lungeing stance.

Moving the whip towards the horse's hindquarters drives the horse forwards. Keep the arm relaxed with the elbow bent.

Taking a position in line with the horse's shoulder can persuade an active horse to steady his pace. (Do not become 'in front' of the horse.)

Taking a position more in line with the horse's hip can have a driving affect on a slow or sluggish horse.

The posture is similar to riding, head up, neck and shoulders relaxed, upper arms by the sides, elbows bent, back straight, knees slightly bent, the weight down into the heels and feet. This posture is important for voice projection, balance and control of the horse.

Practice and experience develops 'feel', knowing how to work the horse through the use of the voice and body language, almost instinctively knowing what the horse is thinking, what action he is about to perform and being able to control it.

For instance, a subtle change in the horse's trot is a sign that he is about to break into walk. Just at that second a slight movement of the whip will send the horse onwards.

It is this ability that is required to give a good lunge lesson, controlling the horse whilst at the same time, observing the rider and making corrections.

The Lesson

The lunge lesson lasts approximately 30 minutes and, as with normal lessons, should be planned and structured to suit the standard of the pupil.

Introduction

The horse is lunged first without the side reins for a short warm-up period. Then the side reins can be connected to the bit and the horse lunged again. This will encourage the horse to loosen the correct muscles and accept the contact.

The bridle reins should be twisted round and the throatlash threaded through to secure them.

The stirrups should be made safe for lungeing with the stirrup leather looped through the iron, preventing the irons from sliding down and banging against the horse's sides.

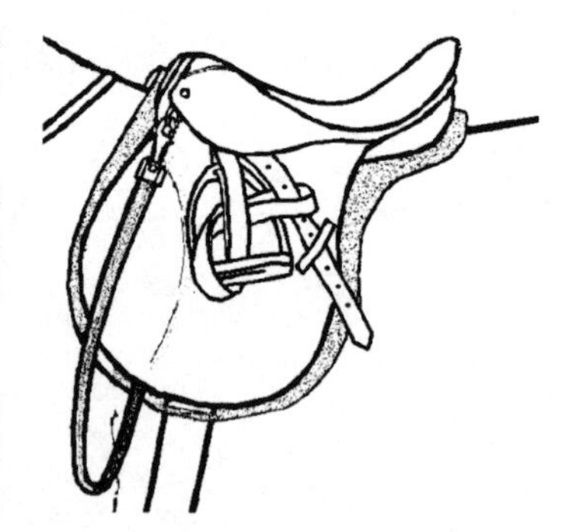

Use this time to assess the horse, making sure that he is obedient and going forward actively. This is the time to assert authority if necessary and demand obedience.

After this initial warm-up the rider can mount. The side reins are unfastened first; they may restrict and panic the horse, particularly if the rider becomes unbalanced whilst mounting.

The girth is checked, the bridle reins unfastened from the throatlash and the stirrups taken down from their secure lungeing position, being altered if required. The side reins can be refastened once the rider is mounted.

The rider should be given a short warming up period with the reins and stirrups. Assess the rider and explain about the lesson content.

Content

Lunge lessons can be based around any one of several themes.

- Beginners will be taught the basic riding position; develop balance and fitness.
- Novice riders will work without stirrups to improve their position, increasing the security and independence of the seat.
- More advanced riders will also work without stirrups to lengthen the leg position, deepen the seat, increase balance and suppleness.
- The rider may need to improve the suppleness of the upper body, loosen the hip, thigh and knee areas. Exercises will be used to increase fitness and suppleness.

Working without Stirrups

Beginners should not work without stirrups until they are confident to do so and have developed some balance, fitness and security. Novice riders will work part of the lesson without stirrups whilst advanced riders may do this type of work most of the lesson.

- The horse is brought to and remains at halt whilst the rider quits the stirrups and crosses them over in front of the saddle, the right stirrup first.

- The reins are knotted and the rider holds onto the loop. This keeps the reins safe, preventing them from slipping down the horse's neck.

- To start, the rider should hold onto the pommel of the saddle with both hands. More advanced and balanced riders can eventually hold on with the outside hand only; this gives the correct body position when working on a circle. Holding on with the inside hand only will encourage the rider to twist the body to the outside.
- The rider should be encouraged to hold onto the pommel as lightly as possible, with finger and thumb, or at least to lighten the hold progressively throughout the lesson.

Paces

For beginners most of the work will be in walk with short periods of trot. For novices and advanced riders most of the work will be in trot, with and without stirrups.

More experienced riders benefit from doing some sitting trot with stirrups. Many pupils, especially those who have lunge lessons regularly, are excellent without stirrups but need practice riding in balance with stirrups.

It is not advisable to canter on the lunge. Beginners and novices can be apprehensive at the faster pace and through the transitions. Also many horses are not sufficiently balanced in canter on the lunge to be of benefit to the rider.

Changes of Rein

Change the rein regularly so that the horse and rider work both sides equally, but not too frequently to unsettle the rider. Three or four changes within a 30 minute lesson are sufficient. A little more time may be spent on the rider's weaker side.

The side reins can remain fastened for changes of rein providing the horse is led in a wide arc and is not asked to bend excessively in his neck when he will feel the restriction of the side rein.

Transitions

The transitions need to be in rhythm and balance so that the rider can maintain his own balance during the change.

Always prepare the rider first before any transition. Some horses on hearing a command do change pace abruptly, unbalancing the rider. In these cases, change the tone of the voice, making it quieter or even spelling out the transition command.

Exercises

Use two or three physical exercises during the lesson to loosen and stretch the rider but only if these are appropriate to the rider's needs.

The exercises should not be continued for too long; a tired rider will tense and start to grip. Watch the rider's face and body language, if the rider is grimacing and tensing this indicates tiredness. Cease the exercise and allow a short rest period at walk or halt.

Teaching on the Lunge

When making corrections in the rider's position, start with the seat, then the leg position, upper body, head and then hands. The body posture needs to be learnt and developed through increasing the suppleness of the back. The rider needs to avoid either stiffening the back through holding the body too rigidly or collapsing the back when instructed to relax.

Teach only that which is relevant to the rider. Avoid stock phrases that have little meaning or exercises that have no purpose. Use positive corrections; inform the rider of the problems then give the corrections.

Ask the rider if they feel a difference; this develops self-criticism, a thinking rider. Praise the rider when they achieve the result or when they try to achieve. The lesson should progress smoothly with the rider knowing that they have improved.

Conclusion

Towards the end of the lesson, the rider should take back the reins and stirrups to work in walk and trot for a few minutes. The rider may need to lengthen the stirrups by at least one hole.

Assess the improvements, give advice for future progress and encourage the rider to ask questions if necessary.

Before the rider dismounts, the side reins are unfastened. The rider takes up the reins and dismounts as normal.

Teaching Tips

Lungeing is such an excellent method of teaching a rider. To develop this expertise you will need to practise lungeing a horse, and teaching a rider on the lunge. This will build up your confidence and ability.

Observe as many lunge lessons as possible, assessing the quality of instruction, checking that the exercises given are appropriate.

If possible, have some lunge lessons yourself. Being taught on the lunge will help you understand how the rider feels.

The lungeing does need to be organised in safety. Make sure that both rider and horse are lunged within their abilities and not beyond. For instance, trotting on the circle for too long a period without stirrups will tire the rider who will then stiffen, tense and lose balance. It may strain the horse's back.

The horse will certainly tense and stiffen in an attempt to protect himself against discomfort and pain.

The rider does need to feel secure. Part of the reason for lungeing is to increase the rider's confidence. If the lunge horse is allowed to be disobedient, the rider could lose confidence in the horse and the instructor.

You will need to be positive in your control of the horse and in your teaching, so that you can create confidence in the rider and make real corrections to improve the rider's ability.

CHAPTER 8
Teaching Flatwork

The next chapters are designed specifically to explain the basic principles of teaching equitation, flatwork and jumping, in a clear, direct and concise language.

The power of teaching is in simplicity, having the communication skills to impart knowledge to others in such a way that this creates comprehension and thus improvement.

The information contained within these chapters follows a logical, practical and simple (uncomplicated) pattern. The definitions and explanations are written to assist with teaching, to increase the level of communication.

Flatwork

Teaching the basic flatwork position from beginner to novice so that the rider achieves a secure basic position is vital to the rider's progress. The rider needs to develop the correct balance, fitness and suppleness to maintain this position.

The rider's position influences the horse's 'way of going'. The rider needs to sit straight, in balance and in his own self-carriage to allow the horse to be straight, in balance and in his self-carriage.

If the rider is crooked, holding onto the reins, gripping with the legs, body slumped in the saddle it is difficult for the horse to work efficiently and correctly.

The Rider's Position

The aim of the rider's position is to maintain balance and harmony with the horse and, through 'controlled relaxation', to use the aids effectively.

When teaching the rider's position start by explaining the seat and body position first, followed by the position of the legs and the hands.

Revision

Stage I, II and III - Basic riding position, position of the pelvis, the seat, upper body, legs and hands. Weight and lightness from beginner level to Stage III standard.

Seat - should be level in the saddle with an **equal weight** on both seat bones. The whole pelvic area, whilst maintaining an upright position, should be relaxed, free of tension. The hips should be supple and capable of movement so that the horse's energy and motion is allowed to come through his back.

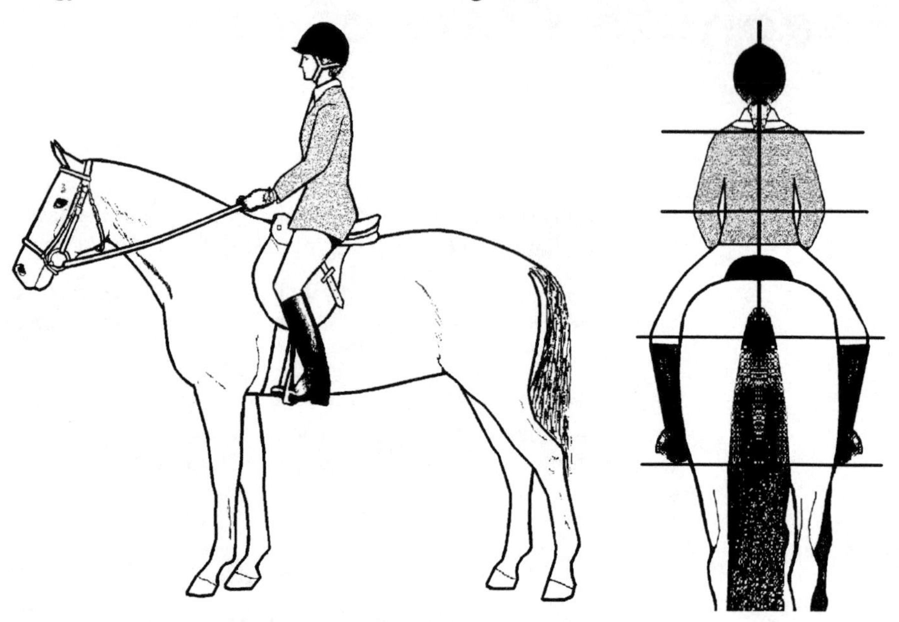

When viewed from behind the rider's spine should be in line with the horse's spine.

The rider's shoulders, elbows, hips, knees and feet should be level.

Body - the body should be carried upright in a relaxed way with the head raised and looking forwards. Shoulders should be relaxed, back and down. The upper arms should remain against the body with the elbows bent. The lower arm should also be relaxed without tension in the muscles.

Legs - The thighs and knees should be in a relaxed contact with the saddle, the knees bent. Relaxed thighs and knees will help the lower legs to stay in contact with the horse's sides, making it easier to give the leg aids. The feet should be pointing forwards with the heel slightly lower than the toe.

Hands - The hands should be held on either side of the horse's neck just in front of the withers, approximately the width of the horse's mouth apart.

The hands should maintain a soft, light contact with the horse's mouth, conversing with the horse by squeeze and release movements on the rein.

- ❖ Check the lines from the elbow through the lower arm, hands and reins to the horse's mouth, viewed both from the side and from above.

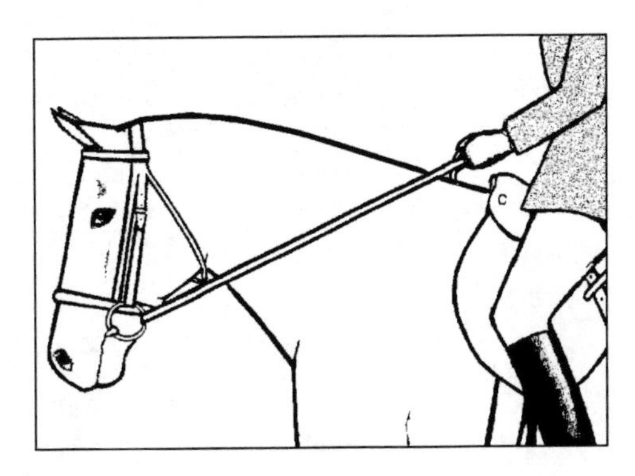

Faults, Causes and Corrections

For the beginner and novice improving their position on the horse, developing balance and the correct fitness takes time and practice. Constantly and consistently correcting faults is essential; otherwise riders develop the wrong muscles.

Seat and Body

Most problems start with the seat; if the seat is incorrect in the saddle, the rest of the body will be incorrect.

The 'Armchair' or 'Slouch' Position

The rider sits slouched in the saddle with the body too far back, the legs brought forward, the ribcage collapsed, the back and shoulders rounded. The rider's head is poked forward and the neck muscles stiff and tense.

The hips are not in the correct position, the top of the pelvis is too far back and the seat bones too far forward.

Correct the rider's seat position by bringing the top of the pelvis forward slightly. This will correct the upper body and enable the rider's head to be carried straight. The rider can bring the lower leg back, increase the bend of the knee.

The 'Forked' Position

The rider's upper body tips forwards with the legs too far back. The heels will probably be raised. In this position the rider is 'perched' that is sat on top of the saddle rather than into it.

The pelvis is incorrect, with the top of the hips tipped forward. This gives a forward, unbalanced seat, and makes the rider's back hollow.

Correct the rider's position. Here the top of the pelvis needs to go slightly backwards. The upper body and lower leg positions should then be corrected. The rider needs to practise sitting deeper in the saddle. Lunge lessons and riding without stirrups should help.

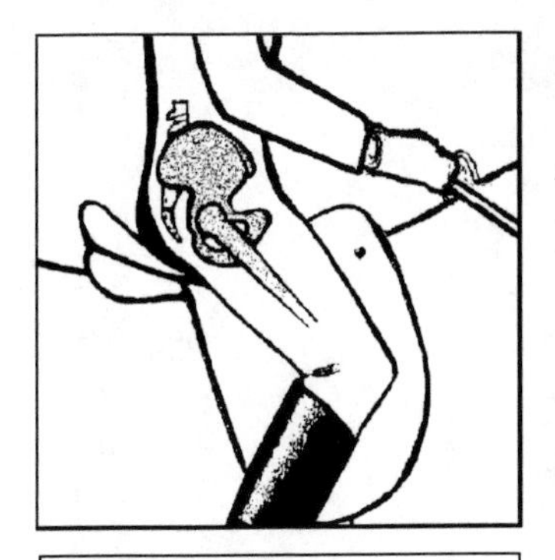

Correct alignment of pelvis

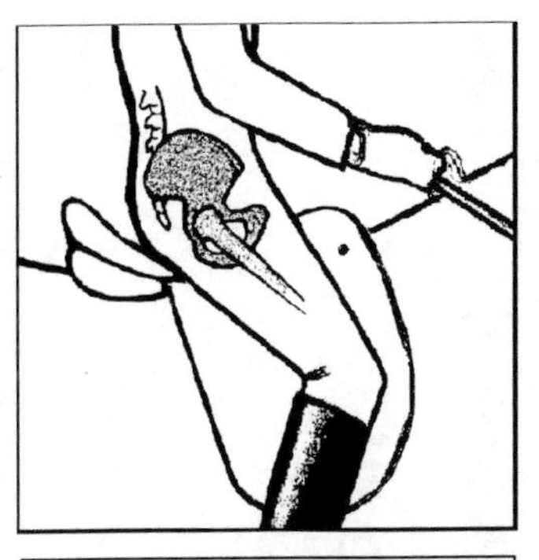

Top of pelvis tipped back as in the armchair position

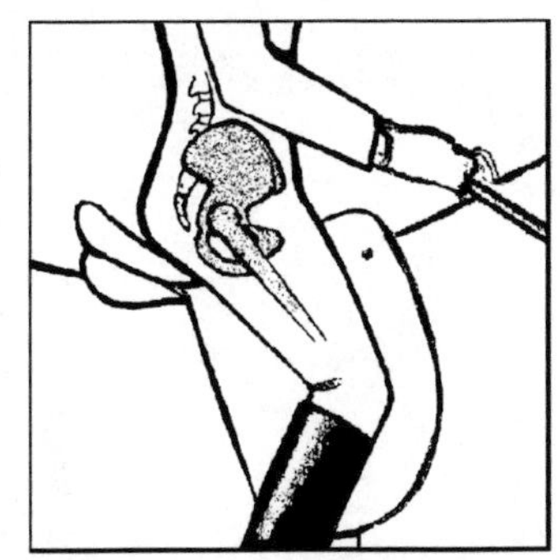

Top of pelvis tipped forward as in the fork position

The 'Twisted' and the 'Leaning' Position

The rider's body is twisted, with one shoulder further back than the other and one hip further back than the other. Often the hands reflect this 'twist', either becoming unlevel or one in front of the other.

In the lean position, the rider leans over to one side. This can vary from a slight, subtle lean to an obvious lean when the rider's head is tilted in an attempt to counterbalance the body. The rider's seat is not level in the saddle.

Often these faults are more evident viewing from behind. The pelvis is crooked and the seat bones will be uneven.

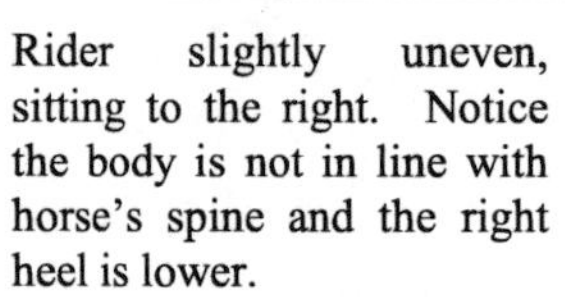

Rider slightly uneven, sitting to the right. Notice the body is not in line with horse's spine and the right heel is lower.

Rider sitting to the right. The head is tilted to the left; the right shoulder is higher than the left shoulder.

Rider uneven in weight and balance; seat to the right. The rider is collapsing the left hip to try to keep in balance.

The rider is twisted, the left hip is collapsed and the seat and body weight is over to the right. The rider is leaning his head to the left to try and counterbalance the body weight.

Correct the position, by observing the rider from the back. The rider needs to sit straight in the saddle, his spine in line with the horse's spine. The body weight needs to be shifted; the head position will then be corrected.

The 'Rigid' Position

The whole body is tense and rigid, the arms straight, elbows locked. The thighs and knees are tense, tight against the saddle. Often the lower legs are held away from the horse's sides, making the leg aids difficult to apply. The rider may be sat 'perched' more on top of the saddle than sitting into it.

Often originates in the hip area where the muscles and tendons are tense through lack of relaxation or stiff through lack of suppleness and fitness. The rider may be trying too hard.

Correct the rider's position by bringing the top of the hips further forward. The rider now needs to relax, bend the knee, bend the elbow, look up, and breathe. The stirrups may need shortening if the rider is tending to reach for them. Lunge lessons and work without stirrups would increase the suppleness of the seat.

After making these corrections to the seat and the body position, the ride may feel awkward and slightly uncomfortable at first. With practice the correct muscles will develop and the rider will be able to sit correctly in balance.

The Legs

Most of the problems with the legs originate from the seat and body region, in particular the hips. If the lower legs are too far forward or too far back this could be a result of an incorrect hip position. Tense thighs and knees, with the rider perched on the saddle can be caused by a lack of suppleness and fitness in the hip and back areas.

Feet Pointing Outwards

Quite a common problem particularly with beginners and novices. One or both feet point outwards; the knees point outwards and the lower legs are normally clamped tightly to the horse's sides.

If the rider wears spurs this becomes painful to the horse and can cause physical injury. Originates in the hip joints. The hips are incorrectly positioned.

Correct the source of the problem.

Instruct the rider to gently rotate the hip joints by taking hold of the back of each thigh and rolling it outwards so that the thigh, knee and foot point forwards.

Support this correction with gentle exercises to develop fitness and suppleness in the hips and legs. Periods riding without stirrups may help. The rider will need time to practise and develop the correct muscles.

The Hands

Good hands are developed as a result of an improved seat position, good teaching, the rider's thought, practice and experience. The hands are influenced by, and should be thought as part of, the shoulders, the upper arms, elbows, lower arms and wrists.

Faults, Causes and Corrections

a. *Unsteady hands, where the rider's hands are continuously moving up and down, particularly in the rising trot.* A result of an insecure, unbalanced position. The seat is not sufficiently deep and the rider needs to use the reins for balance.

   The rider needs to improve the whole body posture to acquire a deeper seat. Begin by encouraging the rider to sit up straight, bend the elbows, relax the shoulders, and the upper and lower arms.

b. *The rider holds the hands low around the horse's shoulders. The rider is constantly moving the hands, often using a 'see-saw' action through the reins to the bit.* The rider may be attempting to 'get the horse on the bit', trying to work the horse in a more 'correct' outline, with the horse's head lowered. Some riders will try to force the horse's head down by using the hands.

Teach the rider to keep the hands 'quiet', the contact consistent and equal, soft and elastic. The rider needs to understand that the horse's outline is achieved by creating energy with the legs and by allowing this energy to flow through a relaxed body and seat. The horse should be encouraged to relax; then he can begin to accept the bit.

c. *Rigid hands combined with straight arms and locked elbows.* Stiff, tense shoulders and elbows, often originating from a stiff, tense back and seat position. Possibly an attempt to get the horse into an outline again.

The rider needs to improve the position and balance, then to relax the shoulders, the arms and to bend the elbows. Teach the rider to understand the rein contact, the 'give and feel' with the hands.

d. *The reins are an incorrect length. If too short, the rider's body will be tipped forward. With too long a rein, the rider's arms are pulled back, the elbows will be behind the body.* The rider does not understand the feel of the contact with the reins and bit to the horse's mouth.

Correct the body position, the arms by the rider's side, elbows bent, hands in front of the saddle.

Encourage the rider to alter the reins until they are a comfortable length, that is, so that the rider can relax and sit up. The rider may need to relax and stop trying too hard. The elbows should be bent and the rider should be taught to feel the bit and the horse's mouth.

Gradually the rider can learn to use the leg aids for activity, this will encourage the horse to use his hindquarters more, stretch and seek the bit contact. The rider may then, whilst maintaining the body position, gradually and sympathetically shorten the reins to regain a soft contact.

The Wrists

The rider bends the wrists turning the hands inwards.

In most cases this is caused by the reins being too long. The rider may be afraid to take up a contact.

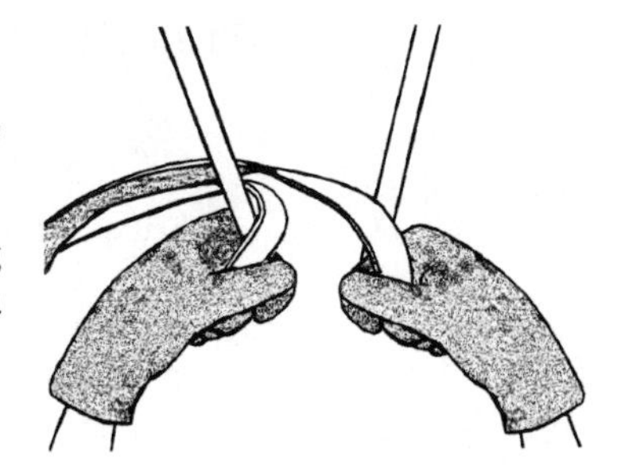

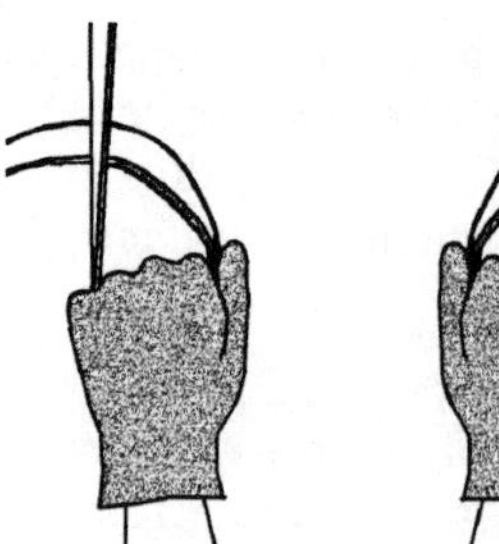
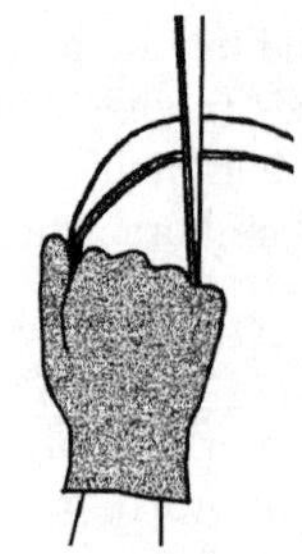

The hands may be held incorrectly with the palm down as in 'piano hands'.

This is caused by the rider twisting the wrists and holding the reins incorrectly.

Piano hands result in stiff, tense arms and wrists; this tension is consequently passed on through the reins to the bit.

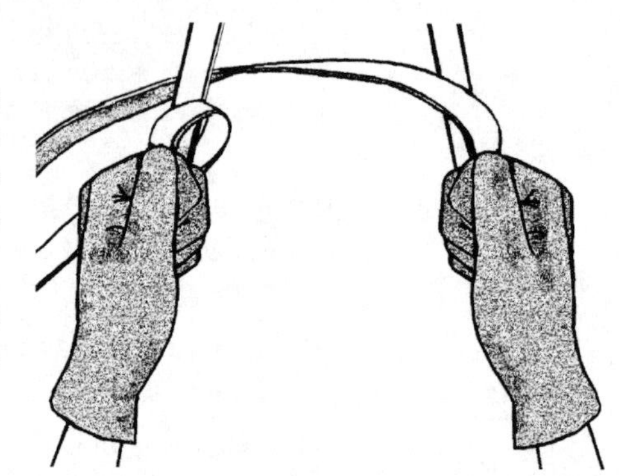

Correct the hand position. Instruct the rider to straighten the wrists and to keep the thumbs on top of the reins so that the line from elbow to bit is maintained.

The reins need shortening to maintain the contact. Allowing too long a rein is not necessarily 'kind' to the horse.

The rider needs to gain confidence in his own ability and feel, to maintain a contact through the reins and bit with a constant, light, mobile, subtle feel through the shoulders, arms and hands.

The Head

The head is the heaviest part of the rider's body; it does influence the rest of the posture.

Faults, Causes and Corrections

a. *The rider constantly looks down.* Often whilst concentrating on the horse's head and neck position the rider will look down. This can be a difficult habit to stop.

   The rider does need to keep the head up, looking in the direction of travel. The rider needs to learn to feel how the horse is working without looking, as when driving a car the driver cannot look down to change gear, use the brake or accelerator.

b. *The rider pokes the head forward particularly through transitions. The neck is stiff and tense.* Poking the head forward is caused by an incorrect body position, by stiffness and tension and by a loss of balance through transitions.

   Correct the body position, the hips may need slight correction possibly by bringing the top of the hip slightly forward so that the shoulders come forwards and allow the head to be carried.

These are the basic, common faults and difficulties experienced when teaching up to novice level (and beyond). Often a fault is a symptom of another underlying cause, and the root of the problem needs to be corrected. The first principle should be to teach and achieve the basics, that is, a balanced, independent seat, relaxed legs, shoulders, arms and hands.

The Rider's Position in Motion

The seat should be relaxed and supple so that when the horse moves the rider can feel and allow the movement through his hips and lower back.

The upper body, whilst remaining relaxed, should be carried in an upright posture, that is the head is held up with the chin parallel to the ground, held naturally from the shoulders so that the neck muscles are soft and relaxed. The chest is 'open', the ribcage raised. In this way, through 'controlled relaxation' the rider carries his own body weight.

The rider's thighs and knees, whilst lying in soft contact with the saddle and horse, are relaxed to allow the horse's energy through. The lower legs remain around and in contact with the horse, almost as if gently 'cuddling' him.

The shoulder and upper arm muscles maintain their control through an elastic, almost 'spongy' feeling. To achieve this the elbow must be bent and the lower arms and wrists kept relaxed.

The rider maintains a constant contact with the horse's mouth through the hands, that is, the rider should be able to 'feel' the horse's mouth and keep the feeling constant. At the same time the hands, through **slight** and **subtle** movements, allow and follow the horse's head movement.

The key word is 'relaxation' but in such a controlled manner that the rider maintains the position through the balance of the seat and body. This is the result of correct training, the development of the suppleness and fitness necessary to keep the seat deep in the saddle whilst maintaining the body posture.

Teaching Tips

Riders first need to be taught the basic riding position; this will influence their riding, use of aids, their effectiveness up to the highest levels. Teaching involves correcting the rider consistently so that this position becomes automatic; the rider's muscles, balance and fitness need to develop correctly so that progress can be achieved.

All riders are individuals having different shapes, sizes, ages and degrees of fitness and suppleness. You need to develop the ability to teach each rider the correct position and balance. This requires knowledge, adaptability and understanding.

In any lesson there will rarely be the time to correct all the rider's problems, particularly as most lessons also include teaching other subjects, school movements, figures or jumping. So practise watching for the most important correction you can make that will help the rider.

Also practise watching for the source of the problem rather than the symptom. A rider may have tried for years to correct the lower leg position, you then instruct them to slightly alter their body position and the lower leg will come naturally into place.

Watching and assessing other instructors, reading magazines and books, watching videos, and having lessons yourself will increase your experience, expand your knowledge and consequently your expertise at teaching.

CHAPTER 9
Teaching Jumping

Teaching a rider to jump takes knowledge, skill and confidence. Having the knowledge of the basic techniques of jumping and the skill to communicate this to the rider will create the confidence. This is vital to gain the rider's trust.

The Balanced Jumping Seat

The balanced jumping seat is the position the rider adopts to keep in balance with the horse during the stages of the jump, whilst allowing the horse complete freedom of movement through his back.

The rider is aiming to achieve three basic qualities:

1. **Balance**
2. **Harmony**
3. **Effectiveness**

Balance the foundation of **balance** is the **security of the rider's lower legs,** keeping the base of the body relatively static so that the rider's upper body is able to move and retain the centre of gravity with the horse.

Harmony a horse is a living creature with a mind, emotions and instincts of his own. Through instruction, practice and experience the rider learns and increases his harmony with the horse. The rider's security of seat and balance is the foundation of this harmony.

Effectiveness to ride the horse to his maximum potential the rider needs to use the natural aids effectively. This comes from the rider's security of seat, which in turn keeps the rider in balance and allows control.

In all disciplines, the riding position is never absolutely static. The rider constantly changes the position to influence the horse or to stay in balance with him. In flatwork and dressage these changes are eventually so subtle that they are almost imperceptible. When jumping, the changes of position and balance are more visible.

To understand how and why the rider needs to alter the position it is essential to know how the horse uses himself over a jump. This is divided into six stages: the track, the approach, the take off, in flight, the landing and the recovery.

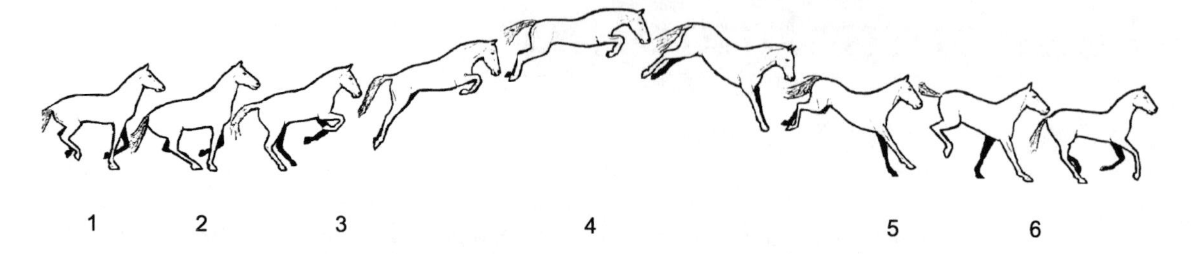

1. The track - is the path ridden to, from and between the fences including the turn into the approach.
2. The approach - the horse prepares for the fence and in the last stride lightens his forehand bringing his hindlegs underneath him.
3. The take-off - the horse lifts his forelegs and pushes off with his hindlegs.
4. In flight - the horse bascules, that is he raises his shoulders, tucks up his forelegs and stretches his neck forwards to give the feeling of arching his back.
5. The landing - the horse lands on one foreleg absorbing most of the concussion through his leg and shoulder.
6. The recovery - the horse regains his balance transferring some weight from the forelegs to the hindlegs.

During these stages, the rider modifies the balanced jumping seat.

1. On the track the rider takes the light seat keeping in harmony with the horse's movements.
2. On the approach the rider sits slightly more upright allowing the horse to lighten his forehand.
3. For take off the rider begins to fold from the hips, allows with the hands and reins.

4. During flight the rider stays in balance by folding from the hips to allow the horse freedom through his back, head and neck.
5. On landing the rider begins to unfold to keep the weight off the horse's forehand.
6. The rider adopts a slightly more upright position to help the horse regain balance.

To achieve this manoeuvrable but secure position the rider needs to be taught and to develop:

❖ **A secure lower leg** - the *anchor*

The rider's weight is pressed down the leg, through supple knee and ankle joints, into the heel.

❖ **Supple hips** - the *hinge point*

The rider decreases and increases the angle of the hip to alter the point of balance, allowing manoeuvrability of the upper body whilst keeping the legs relatively stable.

❖ **Supple knee and ankle joints** - the *shock absorbers*

These joints need to be supple and flexible to absorb the movement of the horse and concussion of landing.

First the rider needs to physically change the length of leg by shortening the stirrups.

Reasons for Shortened Stirrups

The length of the stirrup is shortened to close the angles at the hip, knee and ankle joints, increasing stability and security whilst allowing more flexibility of movement.

1. **Balance**: the decreased angles at the knee and ankle joints, through suppleness and spring, allow the rider to absorb the horse's movement to remain in balance.
2. **Security**: decreasing the angles of these joints allows the rider's weight to be pressed down into the heel to provide security.
3. **Stability**: the thighs and knees are placed further to the front of the saddle and the hips further back to increase stability.
4. **Flexibility**: with this security and stability the rider can increase and decrease the angle of the hip joints altering the upper body position when required.
5. **Contact**: through this flexibility of movement the rider can move the hands and arms to maintain a light contact allowing the horse to stretch his head and neck.

The number of holes by which each rider shortens the length of the stirrups will vary depending on the rider's flatwork length. Occasionally riders shorten the length by four or more holes but generally the length is decreased by two holes.

This may feel uncomfortable at first, particularly for riders who are not accustomed to shorter stirrups. The rider may need time to build up the fitness and suppleness required. If this length does prove to be uncomfortable, the rider may lengthen the stirrups, shortening them again later when the muscles and joints are more supple.

When shortening the stirrups the rider keeps both feet in the irons, taking one foot out of the stirrups whilst altering the length is unsafe, especially if the horse moves. If for some reason the rider needs to take his foot out of the stirrup to change the length, for instance if the stirrup leather is difficult to alter, then both feet should be taken out of the stirrups. This will offer the rider more balance should the horse move.

Variations of Position

Though the rider varies the balanced jumping seat in many subtle ways, three main positions are taught to help the rider understand the main differences in the upper body movement. These are the **light seat**, the **upright seat** and the **fold position**.

The Light Seat

The light seat (often termed the forward position or the poised position) is used around the track, on the approach to the fence and after the recovery. For riders starting to learn to jump, the light seat is taught and practised first.

The rider's seat is placed slightly further back in the saddle, the shoulders further forward in line with the knee joint and the ball of the foot. The back is kept straight; the rider looks up and forwards.

This position offers the rider more security, helps to encourage the weight into the legs and heels until balance and fitness has been developed. It is also sufficient to maintain the balance of both rider and horse over small jumps.

The Upright Seat

At times the rider uses a more upright position. The most influential of the rider's aids is the body weight; from this position the rider can control and rebalance the horse.

This may be necessary on the approach to a fence or on the track, for instance when negotiating corners or turns.

The rider lowers the seat into the saddle and sitting up straighter brings the shoulder to just in front of the hip line. Though the rider will be in contact with the saddle, the weight should still remain pressed down the legs into the heels through supple ankle joints.

The rider, when using this position in combination with the other aids, is in effect applying a half-halt. Through practice and experience the rider will begin to feel when the upright seat is required.

The Fold Position

The fold position is used specifically over the fence. The rider decreases (closes) the angle of the hip joint, moves the seat slightly backwards, the upper body forwards. The weight is maintained through the legs into the heel, so that the rider's position is secure, stable and in balance with the horse. The rider should look up, over and beyond the fence so that the back is kept straight, the shoulders level.

With a secure, balanced position the rider can, whilst keeping a light contact, allow with the hands and reins so that the horse stretches his head and neck over the fence. As a general rule, the hands give in the direction of the rein towards the mouth, halfway down the neck.

The fold position is modified depending on the height and design of the fence. For smaller fences or drop jumps the rider folds only slightly, for higher fences the rider will adopt a more forward position.

❖ During the initial stages of training, the fold position should be used only as an exercise to help increase the suppleness of the hips and stretch the muscles and tendons of the legs. **This should be done with the horse at halt.** Until the rider has developed a more established, secure seat and balance, this position is not used when the horse is moving as it throws the rider's weight too far forward.

  This can cause problems over small jumps. With the weight on the forehand the horse may stumble over the jump or even stop and refuse. The rider being too far forward may exit by the front door. Other riders whose hips are not supple will tend to stand in the stirrups in an attempt to 'fold'.

Introducing Jumping

It is important that before being taught to jump the rider is ready both physically and mentally. Physically the rider needs to have a relatively secure and balanced seat when working on the flat. When the rider is able to maintain a balanced position at walk, trot and canter, confidently control the horse on turns and circles, and use the natural aids with effect, the jumping lessons can begin.

Mentally the rider should want to learn jumping and be confident on the flat. Some riders are nervous or apprehensive, some are reluctant, but with safe, well-structured and planned lessons, most riders do enjoy learning to jump. Though the rider who steadfastly refuses to jump should never be forced, learning and practising the jumping balance on the flat and over ground poles will increase fitness, suppleness and co-ordination.

Creating confidence is essential when introducing jumping; start the process by preparing the pupils before their first practical jumping lesson.

Preparation

Prepare the rider by giving a couple of lectures, explaining the mechanics of jumping, the basic techniques of the jumping balance and the rider's position. Explanations should be kept simple at this point. The subject of jumping should be presented as safe and enjoyable, a natural stage in the rider's progress. Overloading the rider with too advanced or complicated information will cause confusion.

The lectures can be supported by visual aids such as videos, photographs and by a practical demonstration, observing other riders in a jumping lesson.

The rider will benefit from riding outside, in a field or on hacks to experience the more forward going pace and the difference in the horse's attitude. The rider can also practise with shortened stirrups, (even one hole shorter to begin with) for part of flatwork lessons and when hacking. This will begin to exercise the muscles, increase the suppleness of the joints.

Teaching the Jumping Seat

Teach the rider the light seat initially on the horse at halt, explaining the position step by step:

- Move the hips slightly backwards.
- Incline the upper body forward bringing the shoulders in front of the hips and in line with the knee joint and the ball of the foot.
- Keep the head up, look ahead.
- Keep the back straight, the shoulders level and relaxed.

- ❖ Keep the elbows close to the sides.
- ❖ Position the hands either side (but not resting on) the neck, maintaining the 'line' elbow, lower arm, hands, reins to the bit.
- ❖ Keep the thighs lightly in contact with the saddle.
- ❖ Place the lower leg in the region of the girth.
- ❖ Press the weight down the leg through supple knee and ankle joints into the heel.
- ❖ Fractionally more weight can be placed onto the inside of the stirrup iron. The rider should not force the toe out; this will result in a stiff and rigid ankle joint.

The thigh and knees remain in contact with the saddle, supple and relaxed, so that the lower leg can come into contact with the horse to give the leg aids. The rider should avoid gripping tightly with the thigh and knee; this impedes the horse's movement and makes it difficult to give the leg aids.

Whilst the weight is pressed down the legs into the heel, the ankle joint should remain supple, flexible and relaxed to absorb the concussion of the horse's movements. The rider should feel the action of the ankle joints as they subtly move with the pace.

The Rider's Aids

The rider uses the natural aids as in flatwork, this is one reason why flatwork is so important to jumping. Another reason is that the rider will be asking the horse for the same quality of work, impulsion, balance, rhythm and straightness; it is important that the rider is taught and understands these concept.

The leg aids are used for forward movement, for transitions and to maintain the balance on circles and turns; the horse should not lean or cut in around turns.

The hands are used with discretion guiding the horse and controlling the speed. For the first few lessons, or until some security in the position has been achieved, the rider may need to hold onto a neckstrap, breastplate or some of the horse's mane. This will help to prevent the rider losing stability and using the reins for balance.

Practice

The riders practise the light seat at walk first around the school and doing school figures such as circles, and changing rein across the diagonals.

When the rider is more balanced teach the light seat at trot. At this level the trot should be in rising. Once the leg position is more secure, with more weight being placed into the heels, the ankles more supple, the rider should be able to 'hover' or remain 'poised' just above the saddle.

Note: the rider at first will find it difficult to hold this position for long periods. At frequent intervals the rider should be given time to rest and take the strain off the legs by sitting up straighter with the seat in the saddle.

For instance the rider could perform the school movement in the light seat, returning to an upright position around the track. This will also give the rider practise at changing the positions, help to develop the swing between the light and upright seats.

The rider can then progress, at the appropriate time, to working over ground poles. Pole work will increase the rider's confidence, ability and experience. The instructor can make use of the poles to introduce, explain and demonstrate the stages of the jump.

The Stages of the Jump

As well as teaching the rider the different positions, the stages of the jump can also be used to teach control of the horse's pace, balance, activity, and the preparation necessary to judge the correct approach as a preliminary to jumping fences and courses. The rider needs to be taught how to guide the horse to, away from and between fences.

The Track

Most of the success of presenting a horse at a fence is achieved by riding a good track. The rider needs to keep the horse balanced, active, going forward with impulsion. Then the rider needs to judge the turn before the approach so that the line to the fence is straight.

The Approach

The rider aims at the centre of the fence keeping the horse straight. The horse should be prepared before the last three strides, so that he can concentrate and use himself over the fence without interference. There is a horsy cliché that 'the last three strides before the jump belong to the horse'.

Take Off

At this standard it is better for the rider to keep in balance with the horse allowing him to negotiate the fence, rather than attempting to calculate strides and take off point.

In Flight

The rider maintains his own balance allowing the horse to use his body effectively.

Landing

The rider brings the shoulders back a little, taking the weight off the horse's forehand. This will help the horse regain his balance. A more upright position is also more secure should the horse stumble or 'peck' on landing.

Recovery

The rider comes into the light seat again to keep the balance and to control the horse around the track.

In all jumping lessons the objectives should be safety and gradual progression.

Progression

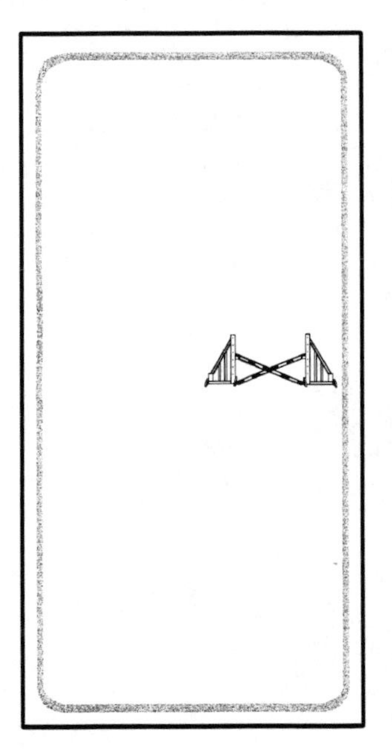

Once the seat and balance are more established, the rider can progress to work over a small jump. A cross-pole helps the approach as it naturally guides the rider's eye to the centre and the horse normally wishes to jump the lowest part. The jump should be positioned encouraging a straight approach.

Ideally the jump can be placed on the long side of the school at right angles to the wall, slightly in, on the three-quarter line.

Cones can be placed on the track and used to help the approach.

A small upright fence can be used after the rider has jumped the cross pole successfully and confidently.

This type of fence may encourage the horse to make a more pronounced jump.

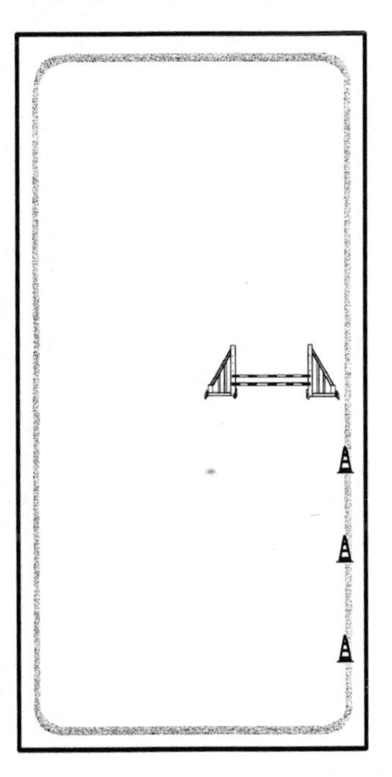

As the horse is quiet and sensible the rider can jump towards home or towards the rest of the ride. This will encourage the horse forward.

With progression as the rider begins to ride more forward-going horses, the horse can be jumped away from home or the ride.

Faults, Causes and Corrections

Teaching jumping involves teaching the basic position first, giving the rider time to practise and develop fitness, suppleness and balance. Once the rider starts to jump fences, most of the teaching will be making corrections to the rider's position.

a. *The rider comes too far forward, looking down and leaning over the horse's forehand. The lower legs tend to swing backwards.*

The rider has lost the security of the lower leg. The rider is trying to fold too much. To practise in a more folded position without sufficient suppleness or fitness will make the rider lose balance and fall forward.

The rider needs to practise the light seat to develop the required fitness and balance and to increase the security of the lower leg

b. *The rider tends to sit too upright and become 'left behind' the movement of the horse. The rider may hold onto the reins for balance pulling the horse in the mouth.*

The rider loses balance and is left behind sitting on the saddle. This happens through lack of fitness, suppleness, and experience or because of a sudden leap from the horse.

The rider needs more practice in timing. Also needs to increase the suppleness in the hips.

c. *The rider stands up in the stirrups, does not fold from the hip at all.*

The rider has not developed sufficient suppleness in the hip area to fold correctly.

The rider needs to increase the suppleness of the hips; more practice on the flat and over poles is needed.

d. *The elbows stick out, the shoulders hunch, the rider may lean to one side.* The rider tries to keep in balance by raising the shoulders, the arms and elbows. Lack of fitness, suppleness, confidence, possibly concentrating too much on the pole or fence. Sometimes it is through the rider trying too hard, almost 'making the horse jump' through raising the shoulders.

Encourage the rider to look up at a point beyond the jump, perhaps a letter or mark on the wall at the end of the school. The position of the head will influence the rest of the body. The rider needs to learn to 'feel' the horse going over the fence.

Though corrections are essential, avoid making too many corrections in the early stages of a beginner's development. Sometimes it is better that they learn the basic position then practise to find their own balance.

It is more important that the rider learns to 'go with' the horse, experiences and then 'feels' the correct balance over the fence, without interfering with the horse.

At the end of the lesson the result should be that the rider has increased in ability, in fitness and confidence. Both rider and horse should finish the lesson with feelings of enjoyment and achievement.

Teaching Tips

When teaching jumping at any standard the most important point is safety. Though the horses, certainly at beginner and novice level, should be safe, honest and quiet, any horse can behave unpredictably. You need to prepare and structure the lesson so that the possibilities of incidents are minimal.

Never overestimate a horse or rider; never push them beyond their capabilities. Avoid at any standard, fences or courses that are too complicated. Some horses are not as athletic as they appear (nor are the riders).

Know when to stop. If a horse is jumping well and the rider is enjoying the lesson, there is sometimes a temptation to keep on jumping. It is better to finish on a good jump creating confidence in both rider and horse than to continue jumping until the horse refuses or runs out. Quality is better than quantity.

For beginners their preparation lessons are vital; they should not be asked to jump too soon. They need to develop fitness, suppleness and confidence before starting to jump fences. Then make the fences small, inviting and easy to jump.

The basis of jumping is good quality flatwork; this ability is then continued as a natural progression into jumping. You will need to assess first, particularly with beginners, their quality of flatwork and perhaps improve on this prior to jumping.

Riders are created in all shapes and sizes so you will need to be observant and adaptable in your teaching to achieve improvement for different physical (and mental) problems.

The track and the approach are the most vital areas of the fence. Encourage the rider to maintain the pace, to keep the horse active, going forward but in rhythm and balance before and also after the fence. Convey as near as possible that feeling of the horse going forward with a steady rhythm, light in the hand but feeling eager to jump.

Pole work is just as important as fences. Working over poles can really teach the rider about the quality of the horse's paces on the track, on the approach and over the poles. Poles can be versatile, rolling poles slightly further apart or closer together can teach the horse to alter his stride, teach the rider about control, as a preliminary to combination fences or gymnastic jumping.

CHAPTER 10
Jumping Lessons

Planning and preparation are an important part of the jumping lesson if the rider is to progress in safety, increase in confidence and consequently in ability. There is a fine balance between keeping the lesson safe and increasing the rider's ability and experience.

Aims of Jumping

Riders have different aims for taking jumping lessons.

- ❖ Beginners learn to jump to expand their riding skills.
- ❖ Some riders have a desire to jump competently to compete or to take exams.
- ❖ For jumping when out hacking.
- ❖ As a challenge or for fun; can be more exciting than flatwork and some riders enjoy it more.
- ❖ Some riders jump to regain confidence; not having jumped for some time.

There are several benefits to jumping; it creates fun, increases rider confidence, improves the rider's fitness, balance and suppleness, and adds variety to the schoolwork.

Planning the Lesson

Preparing and planning for the lesson will be based on these aims and on information about the riders.

- ❖ Number of riders.
- ❖ Standards and levels.
- ❖ Reasons for jumping.
- ❖ Approximate age range.

The plan for the lesson will include deciding on the number and types of fences, the position of the fences and the horses for each rider.

The Horse

Choosing a suitable horse is vital, particularly for beginners or nervous riders. The horse should have a good temperament, be honest, fairly quiet yet sufficiently forward to jump easily from trot. The paces need to be balanced, rhythmical; a horse with smooth, short strides is preferable to one with long, bounding strides.

Generally Cobs, Cob crosses or Irish Draught crosses are excellent for learning to jump. For more experienced riders a forward going horse possibly a Thoroughbred or Thoroughbred cross can also be used. The horse should still be honest with good paces and rhythm; even for competent riders building confidence is important.

Assistants

If assistants are available to help, they will need briefing before the lesson, so that their jobs are clear.

They should know how to move poles and wings safely, efficiently and quietly. Wings should be moved carefully as they can be heavy and difficult to move. They should be lifted clear off the ground; dragging a wing along the ground makes it more awkward to manoeuvre and could damage it.

The cups should be removed first in case they catch the assistant or fall out and cause injury. Jumpkins are light and easier to carry; often one person can carry two.

Each pole should be carried by being balanced in the centre, clear of the ground. Care should be taken not to swing the pole around causing injury to anyone. Ideally, when two poles need carrying, two assistants should do this. If there is no alternative, one person can hold them at one end and drag the other end across the ground.

Equipment

When not in use, wings, poles, cups and pegs should ideally be stored out of the school area. As preparation for a lesson they can be placed in the school if kept in a safe position.

Cups and pegs should always be put in a safe place, preferably outside the arena or school until required.

Alternatively, they can be placed by the foot of the wings ready for use, but never on the floor where a horse could tread on them. *They should never be left in the wing of a jump.* If a horse is being ridden through the wings for practice, this could easily cause injury.

All jumping equipment should be put away safely after use, to avoid an accident and injury, and also to preserve them. Poles and wings can be expensive to buy.

Lesson Structure

The jumping lesson is structured as every other lesson.

- Introduction (with warm-up phase)
- Lesson content (the theme)
- Conclusion (with cooling down phase)

Introduction

Always begin by checking the tack. The saddle should be a GP saddle, correct size and fit for both horse and rider. Though this type of saddle is preferable for most riders, for some, particularly those who are tall or have longer legs, a jumping saddle may be more suitable. The stirrups should be the correct size for the rider; the rider's foot may become stuck if the stirrups are too narrow or slip right through if too wide.

For beginners, who may need to hold on for security, a neckstrap or breastplate is essential. A hunting breastplate is preferable being more securely fastened to the saddle.

Warm-up

The 'warm-up' phase is crucial; horses and riders should never be expected to jump 'cold'; this may cause muscle cramps, strains and sprains. During this time assess the class; even with familiar pupils this is necessary; one rider may be stiff today.

The horses should also be assessed, for unlevelness, activity and general way of going. The riders should warm up in all three paces and, depending on their ability, include some lengthening and shortening of the trot or canter.

Content

Depending on the standard of the class, the content will include teaching the riders the balanced jumping seat and allowing them to practise with shortened stirrups. Pole work may be included. The lesson will lead progressively to jumping a fence or fences.

The plan for the content should cover the ground plans for the fences, the types of fences to be used and their positioning in the school. It may also cover positioning the riders for safety whilst others are jumping and possibly how many times each rider will be able to jump. Timing is important, as riders should not be left waiting too long for their turn. Both horses and riders can lose interest and enthusiasm.

The types of fences to be used, the number and their situation in the school or menage will be related to the abilities of the riders.

Types of Fences

The different types of fences are designed to create variety, to encourage the horse to jump in a different way. Some fences are more inviting than others; there are various fillers making the fences more interesting, different kinds of wings or jumpkins, to vary the height of the fence.

The Cross Pole

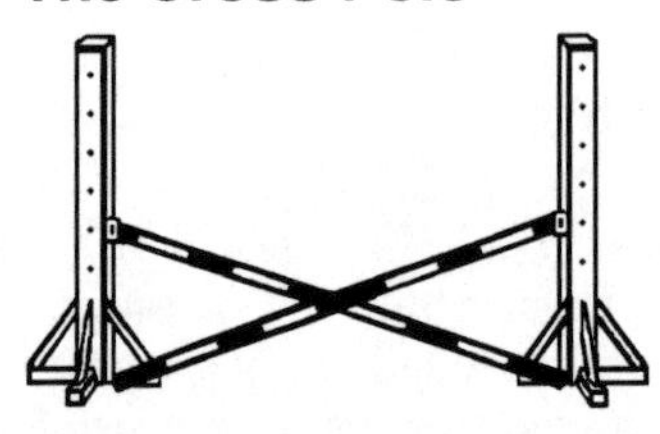

This type of fence is inviting for both rider and horse; the low point in the centre naturally brings the rider's eye to the middle of the jump influencing the approach. The cross pole is easy to vary in height.

- If the cross pole is fairly small, many larger horses take it in their stride, giving the rider little 'feel' for a jump.

A ground pole at the bottom on the fence, or even placed a few inches in front, can be added creating width and encouraging the horse to make a more pronounced jump.

The Straight Bar, Upright or Vertical

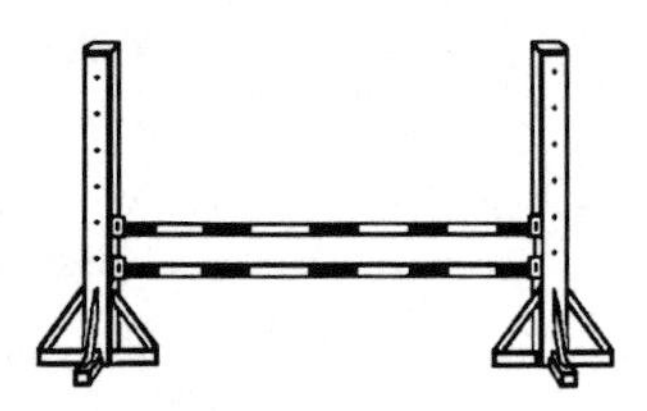

Poles or similar elements, such as planks or fillers, are placed straight between two wings.

This type of fence offers more variation in height than the cross pole. The poles can be raised according to the height of the wings.

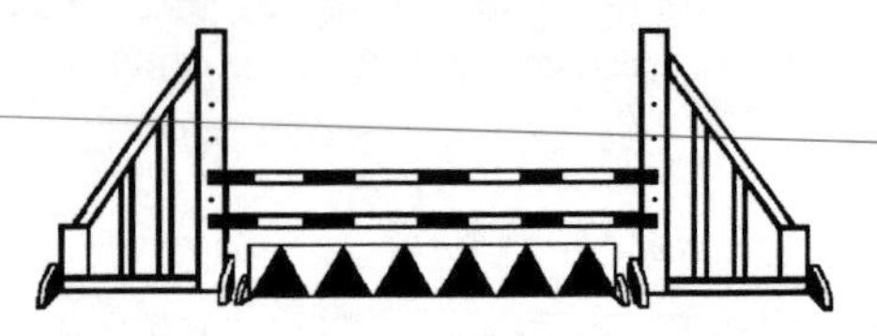

More demanding a fence, the approach needs to be ridden accurately.

- The horse may jump off centre, 'stand off' or 'get below' this type of fence.

The Spread Fence

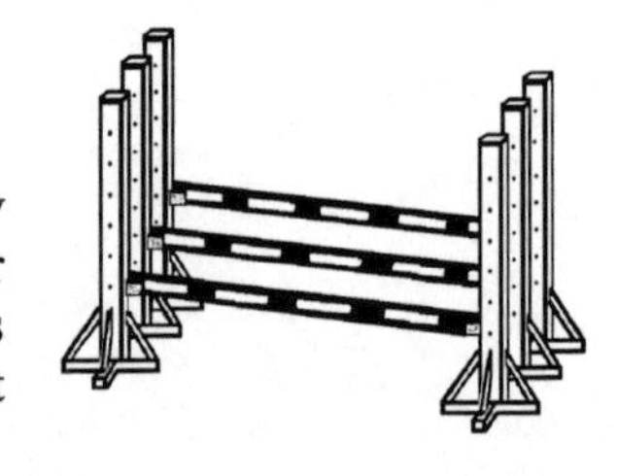

Though there are a variety of designs, there are basically two types of spread fence: the ascending oxer or staircase spread and the parallel spread. The 'spread' is measured from the front of the front pole to the farthest edge of the back pole.

The ascending spread has lower elements at the front and a higher element or pole at the back. Horses and riders tend to find this type of fence inviting because the slope leads the eye to the highest element.

The parallel spread is an upright fence with a bar at the back, at the same height as the front element, giving the fence depth.

- This fence is less inviting and can encourage the horse to stand off or get underneath unless the approach and take off are accurate.

Both types of spread fence offer a good variation in height, depth and design using different elements, poles, planks and fillers.

Position of the Jumps

The fences within the school or menage need to be placed for optimum advantage to cater for the standards and abilities of the riders, and for the eventual lesson plan. For instance one fence will need positioning so that other fences can be built at the appropriate places. Starting with the single fence near to E or B, this can be expanded to

* two single fences on the three-quarter track near to E and B
* three fences, one on the diagonal around X between the other two

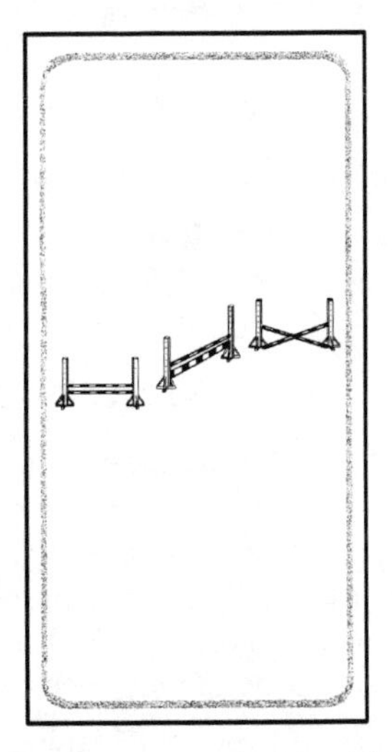

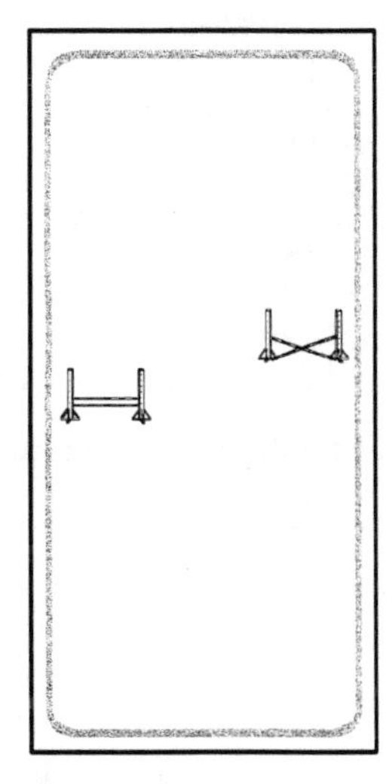

Additional fences can be placed in different areas of the school, for more experienced riders. Avoid placing a fence in a corner of the school, on the short sides for novice riders and in situations that make the approach or get away difficult.

As the riders advance and increase in confidence, they will want to progress, expanding their ability, skill and experience. Fences can be raised in height, widened, be of different types and designs, poles, planks, gates and 'walls'. Fences can also be grouped together, as combinations related by the distance between them.

Related Distances

Combination fences are built at specific distances apart. These distances are calculated and depend on the pace at which the horse approaches the fences and the number of strides between each fence.

The distance is named for the number of strides the horse takes between the fences, or *non-jumping strides.* Fences can be two non-jumping strides apart or one non-jumping stride apart. Where the horse lands from one fence and immediately has to take off for the next, this is called a bounce fence.

Distances

	Approach in Trot		Approach in Canter	
Type of fences	**Ponies**	**Horses**	**Ponies**	**Horses**
Bounce fence (no stride in between fences) Approx. metre, feet and human strides	**2.7 - 3m** **9 - 10 feet** **3 strides**	**3 - 3.3m** **10 - 11 feet** **3½ strides**	**3 - 3.6m** **10 - 12 feet** **4 strides**	**3.3 - 4.3m** **11 - 14 feet** **5 strides**
One non-jumping stride between fences Approx. metre, feet and human strides	**4.9 - 5.5m** **16 - 18 feet** **6 strides**	**5.5 - 6.4m** **18 -21 feet** **7 strides**	**6.1 - 7 m** **20 - 23 feet** **7 strides**	**7 - 7.6m** **23 - 25 feet** **8 strides**
Two non-jumping strides between fences Approx. metre, feet and human strides	**7.3 - 8.2m** **24 - 27 feet** **9 strides**	**8.5 - 9.5m** **28 - 31 feet** **10 strides**	**9.5 - 10.4m** **31 - 34 feet** **11 strides**	**10.4 - 11m** **34 - 36 feet** **12 strides**

- The distances have been calculated to be as simple and practical as possible even though metres do not exactly match up to imperial feet, nor do metres and feet precisely match up to human strides. These distances though will give a good approximate guide when measuring out distances between fences.
- Distances based on fences up to 1 metre in height.
- Distances based on an average sized school horse 15.2/16 hands. For competition horses, larger or longer striding horses, the distances will need lengthening.
- Distances can vary depending on certain conditions, state of ground, the weather, the environment. For instance horses and ponies generally have a longer stride when jumping outside. This needs to be assessed on the day and the distances altered appropriately.

For novice and less experienced riders related fences should be simple combinations, until the riders have increased their ability and confidence.

As riders progress and increase their ability, fences can be combined to form a gymnastic jumping exercise, known as a grid work.

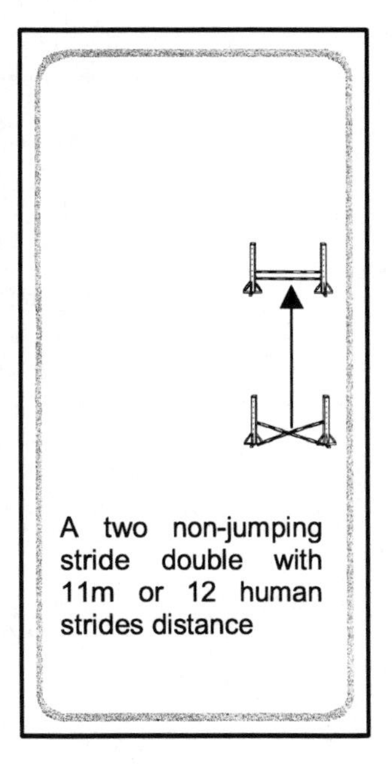

A two non-jumping stride double with 11m or 12 human strides distance

Gymnastic jumping - Grid Work

A grid is made up of a number of fences, normally three to five, with related distances between them. The vital point is that the distance between each fence is suitable for the horses or ponies and for the pace at which they approach the grid. Another important point is to keep the grid simple, the fences inviting. Over-facing a rider and horse will definitely lead to problems.

Grid work is extremely useful for riders wanting to improve their ability. This type of exercise does have its advantages and disadvantages.

Advantages

- Increases concentration.
- Improves the rider's position.
- Athletic exercise builds up the strength of both rider and horse.
- Increases balance, rhythm and co-ordination.
- Sharpens the horse and rider's responses when jumping.
- Encourages the horse to bascule when jumping, increases suppleness.

Disadvantages

- Demands a lot of energy from the horse, fitness and physical strength. Too much grid work can tire the horse, resulting in muscle, tendon and ligament injury.
- More risk involved with this type of jumping both to horse and rider.
- If the horse is not ridden actively through the grid the horse may stop or run out.
- The rider needs to be fairly competent at jumping; this is not an exercise for beginners or inexperienced novices.

To build a grid start with a single fence and place wings where the second and subsequent fences are planned.

Observe and assess how the horses jump the first fence and their stride to the second. This will give a good guide as to whether the distances are suitable. After the horses have jumped the single fence, continue by building the second fence and after the horses have jumped this, the third and so on.

The fences in a grid can vary in design. Cross poles are useful particularly for less experienced riders and small uprights or ascending spreads. The first fence is more inviting as a cross pole, followed by another cross pole or small upright, the last fence could be a small spread.

This diagram shows three fences, the first is a cross-pole, the second and third uprights. The approach to the first fence is in trot. Distances for an average sized horse 15 - 16 hh.

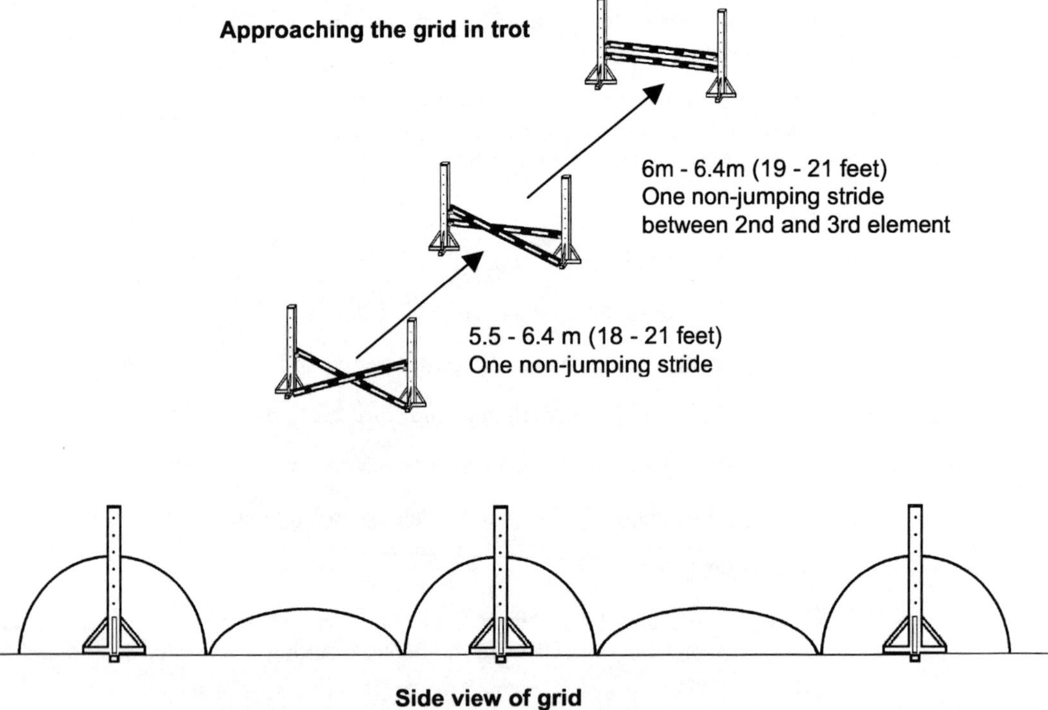

Side view of grid

When the approach is in trot, the distances between the fences will vary; the distance between fences 2 and 3 needs to be slightly longer than between fences 1 and 2 as the horse will be taking a longer stride at this point. The distance could be 0.3 to 0.6 metres (1 to 2 feet) longer.

This diagram illustrates approach in canter, one non-jumping stride between fences 1 and 2, and two non-jumping strides between fences 2 and 3.

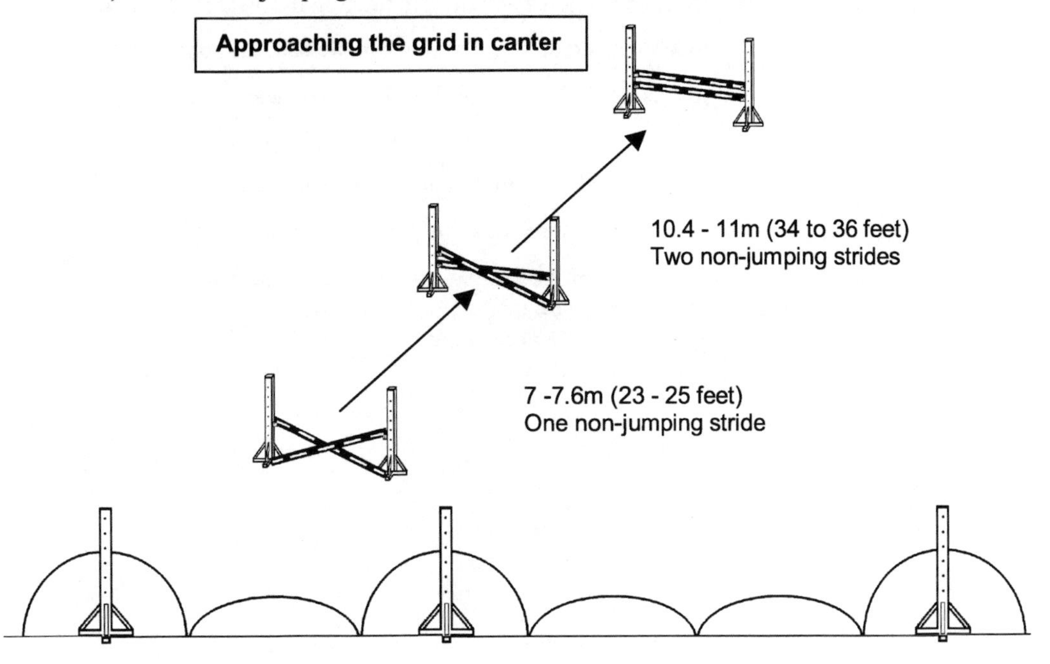

Ground Line

The 'ground line' is the solid part of the fence nearest to the ground. A true ground line, such as a pole laid on the ground in front of the fence, encourages a good take off.

For a horse who takes off too near or underneath the fence the ground pole can be placed about 15 to 30cms (6 - 12 inches) away from the jump.

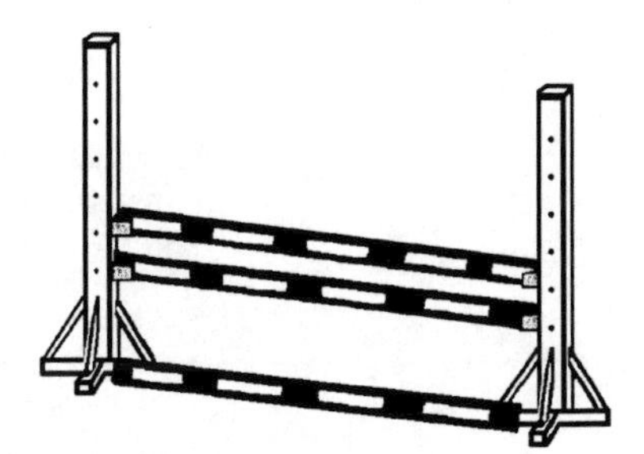

Placing Poles

These are poles placed at certain distances in front of a fence. The number of poles can vary from one single pole to three, four or more. The distances vary depending on the pace of the approach and the number of strides between poles or between pole and fence.

Placing poles should not be used for beginners.

For novice riders it is advisable to place only one pole in front of the jump, laying down more can confuse the horse and rider at this stage.

The functions of the placing pole are

- to assist the horse and rider in judging the distance from the jump
- to help the horse arrive at the suitable take off point
- to encourage the horse to lower his head and neck
- to help the rider to judge the speed and rhythm
- to help the rider learn to control or regulate the speed and rhythm
- helps the horse regulate his pace, teaches him to balance and collect

The pole is placed on the ground on the take off side of the fence. The distance is measured from the centre of the jump at its base, or ground line, either by tape or in the more practical manner of pacing.

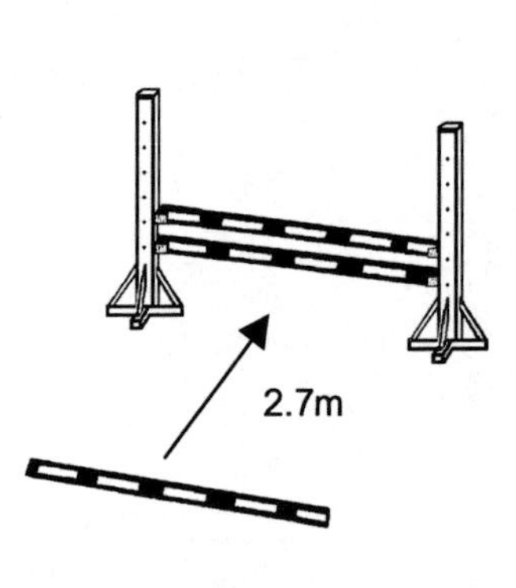

Approach in trot, for an average sized horse, the pole is placed 2.7 metres (9 feet).

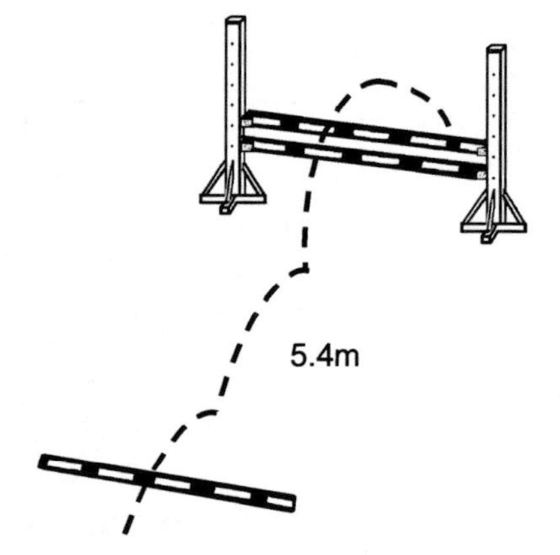

Approach in canter, for an average sized horse, the pole is placed 5.4 metres (18 feet away) - one canter stride.

These distances are suitable for novice riders on experienced horses. The pole can be moved slightly nearer or further away from the jump to suit a horse with a different length of stride or to regulate his pace and rhythm.

Courses

The natural progression for the rider is to learn to ride a course of fences. A course will consist of different designs of fences with a range of heights, positioned in different areas around the school, menage or in an outside area. Riding the course will include changing direction, making turns, looking and planning ahead. The course needs to be considered as a whole, not just as a collection of single fences or even combinations.

Teaching course work involves teaching the rider to plan the best line of approach to each fence, to ride the track accurately and actively. The track is one of the most important parts of riding a course. (Jumping consists mostly of flatwork.) This is where the rider's ability to ride the horse straight, around turns and corners whilst maintaining balance, rhythm and pace come into effect.

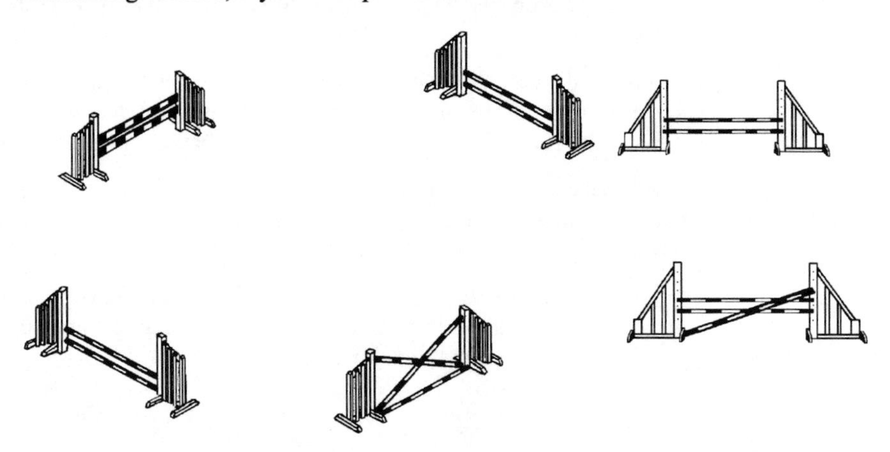

In normal lessons, the course work will be built up gradually, with riders jumping one then two fences, progressing on to jumping over another two fences and so on. The fences will then be jumped as a course.

Alternatively the fences may be built using one or two fences at first, and positioning wings possibly with ground poles where the other fences are to be placed. This will help the rider to memorise the route around the course.

If problems do occur such as the rider's loss of balance, forgetting the route, the horse becomes too fast, instruct the rider calmly to return to trot, circle, ask for canter and continue with the course.

Conclusion

At the end of the lesson, all the riders and horses should be allowed time to 'cool down' and relax. Allowing the horses to walk on a long rein gives them time to stretch and mentally unwind, as well as allowing the riders to ask questions if required.

Teaching Tips

When you start to teach riders to jump you may be a little apprehensive, plan and prepare the lesson beforehand as much as you can. With practice and experience you will build a repertoire of lessons for different pupils.

You will also be able to recognise which riders are capable and which need to keep within a limit.

Always give the riders and horses a warm-up period, this can include riding in all three paces with shortened stirrups. Riding on the flat is important for jumping; riders need to build up the muscle, suppleness, fitness and balance before they work over fences.

Learn the distances between related fences. These cannot be absolute because even horses of a similar height and build can have varying length of stride. Horses too, can differ from day to day and depending where they are jumping, inside or out in a field.

The distances do need to be as accurate as possible though. Measure your stride so that you will know approximately how many of your own strides you need between fences.

In practice begin with the recommended distances. Then observe each horse, if one does find a distance difficult, too short or too long, do not continue, alter the fence and distance as required to suit his stride.

CHAPTER 11
Exercises

There are many types of exercises designed to help the rider improve the position. At every level of riding, from beginner to advanced, exercises are beneficial to eliminate physical faults, increase fitness and suppleness, relaxation and confidence.

Exercises should be taught with discretion, used only when they will be effective, and performed in such a way to improve the rider without causing strain.

Aims of Exercises

Improving the rider through exercises has several aims and benefits.

- Develops the rider's muscle strength.
- Increases fitness by stretching and loosening ligaments and tendons.
- Increases the suppleness of the joints.
- Increases balance, confidence and co-ordination.
- Improves the rider's position.
- Useful as a warm-up at the beginning of the working session.
- Adds variety and fun to a lesson (children).

The body is made up of various bones, muscles, tendons, ligaments and joints. All these are connected and work together to create a whole.

Any misalignment, stiffness, tension or injury in one part of the body can and does affect another part or even the entire posture.

For instance tense, fixed hands could be a result of stiff elbows or rigid shoulders.

Types of exercise used specifically for certain parts of the body not only benefit that area they also improve the general position as a whole.

Head and Neck

Exercises for the head and neck areas are certainly of benefit yet these areas are often ignored. The head influences the whole posture.

Many riders suffer from looking down, this develops into a difficult habit to break (even for advanced riders). Looking down unbalances the body, shifts the weight subtly forward rather than being down the back into the seat and through the legs into the heels. It also causes tension around the face and neck areas.

Most importantly the head houses the brain; tension in the muscles may reduce blood flow and possibly cause headaches.

Aims

To release tension in the rider's head and neck area, creating relaxation of muscles and improving blood flow to the brain. To improve body posture.

Exercises

1. Instruct the rider to gently bring the head up straight, then to slowly allow the chin to drop towards the chest, bring the head up and straight again. This exercise should be done with the horse at halt or walk only; at a faster pace the rider's head may be jerked backwards.
2. The rider gently and slowly moves the head from side to side, keeping the neck straight. This exercise should be done with the horse at halt or walk only.
3. To release the tension in the jaw and neck, instruct the rider to *allow* the mouth to drop open slightly, not forcing or pushing it open, but allowing the jaw to drop. Then to close it gently. (Interestingly, in some cases, the moment the rider relaxes the jaw, the horse relaxes and lowers his head.)

   This exercise is useful whenever there is tension around the face and neck but the rider need not constantly have the mouth wide open. If the rider tends to clamp the jaw, just having the lips slightly parted should help. This exercise can be done at any pace.

Avoid

Never allow the rider to push the head backwards, this crunches the neck bones.

When doing these exercises instruct the rider to move slowly and gently, never to use forced or jerky movements.

Shoulders and Arms

Shoulder and arm exercises improve the upper body and the whole posture.

Aims

To release tension in the muscles around the shoulders, back, upper and lower arms, as well as in the joints. Used for riders on the lunge or in a lesson with the horse at halt or walk.

Exercises

1. Shoulder shrugs; the rider brings the shoulders up slowly towards the ears, then rotates them backwards and down. The rest of the body including the hand should remain fairly still. Encourage the rider at the end of the exercise to keep the shoulders back and down; this will expand the chest area.

2. Arm circling: the rider circles one arm at a time from the shoulder, keeping the palm uppermost when the arm is behind the body. Instruct the rider to stretch the arm out as far as possible. The body should stay relaxed without too much movement of the seat.

   For a crooked rider who sits with the inside shoulder forward on a circle, rotating the inside arm will help to bring the shoulder into a more correct position.

Avoid

The rider should not make any exaggerated movements; the exercises should be smooth with a slow stretching action.

Waist and Back

The waist is the pivot point between the upper and lower body. The rider needs a supple waist to slightly 'swivel' the upper and lower body in different directions, particularly on turns and circles when the inside shoulder needs to be further back and the inside hip slightly forward.

Aims

To stretch and supple the waist area, the muscles in the top of the hip and lower back.

Exercises

1. At halt without stirrups the rider slowly raises the knees to the pommel of the saddle (jockey style). This brings the seat bones underneath the body encouraging the rider to sit deeper into the saddle.

   Now the rider gently returns the legs down into position. This stretches the lower back, the inner thigh and widens the hips. The rider may hold the pommel of the saddle for balance.

2. With arms straight out at shoulder level, or hands on the waist, the rider slowly moves the body from the waist round from one side to another.

   The shoulders remain level so that whilst the back is rotated it is not twisted as well.

   The lower body and legs should remain as still as possible.

   Performed at halt or walk only with the horse securely held or on the lunge.

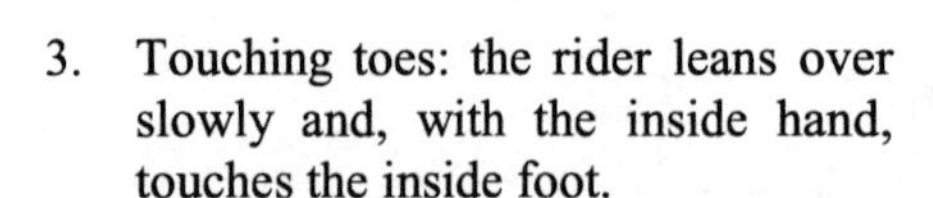

3. Touching toes: the rider leans over slowly and, with the inside hand, touches the inside foot.

   The rider should keep the seat as near to the saddle as possible and maintain the leg position. This exercise stretches the spine.

   Used on the lunge, lead rein or in the school with an assistant holding the horse. Performed at halt only.

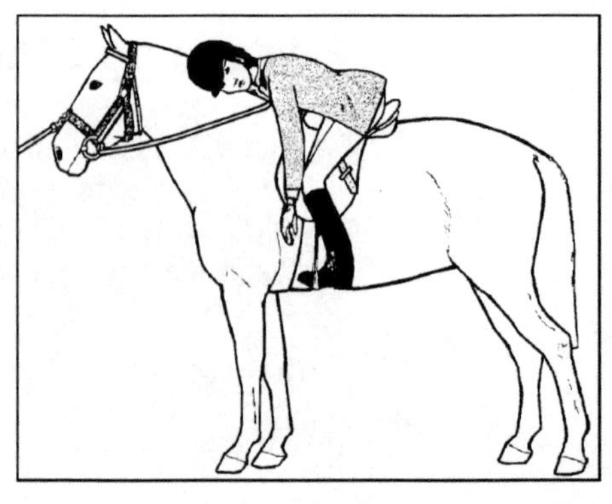

Avoid

Never instruct the rider to lean over and touch the opposite toe, for example the right toe with the left hand. This twists the vertebrae in the back crookedly, crunching the bones, twisting the muscles and ligaments in a way that could result in muscle, tendon and ligament strain, sprain and spasms.

(This exercise does not benefit the rider; the rider strains to do it and in some cases the leg shoots back kicking the horse.)

Prevent the rider forcing the body down to the toe, this could tear muscles in the back. *The rider should only go down as far as is comfortable*, feeling a stretching of the muscle, not pain. Gradually over a period of time the rider will be able to go lower. The toe should not be brought up to the hand.

Hips and Legs

The hip area is vital to the whole position and the horse's movements. There are numerous muscles around the pelvis connecting the back and legs, the upper and lower body. A tense, stiff hip and seat is uncomfortable for the horse and restricts movement coming through from the hindquarters. For these exercises the rider quits the stirrups.

Aims

Develops suppleness in the muscles and joints in the legs. Stretches the ligaments around the pelvis and the inside of the upper thigh and lower abdomen. Improves balance and co-ordination.

Exercises

1. The rider moves the lower leg only, from the knee down, slowly backwards and **into position again**. Alternating the legs, taking one back then the other helps to loosen the knee joints and improve co-ordination.

2. The rider rotates the feet from the ankle joints, preferably in towards the horse, that is the right foot turns anti-clockwise, the left foot clockwise. Loosens the ankle joints and encourages the rider to keep the feet to the front.

3. Legs away: instruct the rider to *carefully and gently* move one leg from the hip sideways away from the horse, keeping the body upright, the seat in position. Some riders find it easier to move both legs at the same time. *Use this exercise with discretion; some riders find this difficult and painful.*

Used on the lunge or lead rein with the horse at halt or walk; the rider holds onto the pommel for balance.

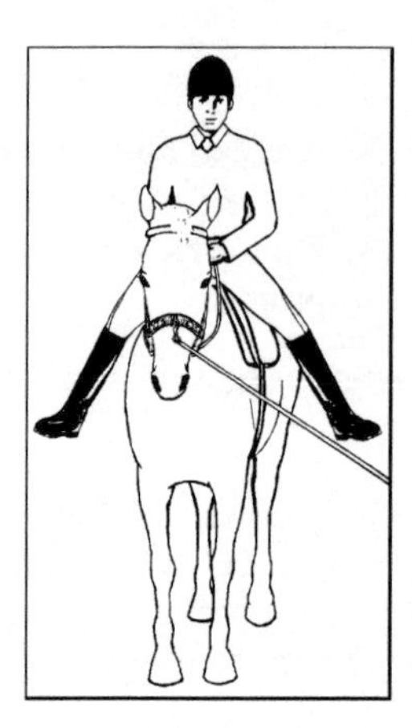

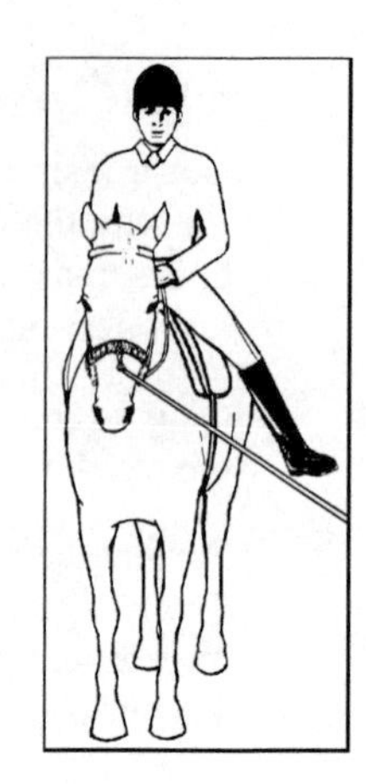

Avoid

The rider should never, ever force or push the body beyond its capabilities, particularly with the hip exercises. The area around the pelvis is prone to strain and damage. Slow and sure is ideal, gradually over time the rider will be able to stretch this area further. The 'legs away' exercise should be avoided for beginners.

Breathing Exercises

Strange as it may seem, breathing does make a difference when riding! How often others must hear my trainer exclaiming loudly, 'That's good. Now all you have to do is breathe!' It is amazing how many riders hold their breath through concentration, tension or fear.

Aims

To expand the chest cavity, improve the posture and increase relaxation.

Exercises

1. Instruct the rider to breathe in through the nose for a count of four seconds and out through the mouth for the count of four. This exercise is useful at any pace.
2. Whilst doing all the exercises mentioned the rider could breathe in and out slowly.

Taking in air not only helps the blood circulation and increases energy it also increases relaxation and posture.

Avoid

The rider should not take quick short gasps; the breathing needs to be deep and slow.

Working without Stirrups

Working without stirrups is excellent for improving the rider's whole position.

- Stretches the leg muscles.
- Increases suppleness in the pelvic and hip areas.
- Increases the rider's balance.
- Increases the rider's fitness and stamina.
- Helps to develop an understanding for the horse's paces and rhythm.
- Increases the rider's confidence.

Less fit riders should perform this type of work for a short period only, five or ten minutes, gradually increasing with ability.

Quitting and Crossing the Stirrups

It is important for safety that the rider quits and crosses the stirrups correctly. *Both feet* are taken out of the stirrups at the same time. The rider should never have one foot in the stirrup and one foot out. If the horse spooks, the rider, being out of balance, may be jolted and injured.

To prevent the buckle bruising the rider's thigh, the stirrup leather is pulled down so that the buckle comes a short distance away from the stirrup bar. The leather is placed onto the horse's neck in front of the pommel with the right or offside stirrup crossed over first. Then, if the rider dismounts, the left or nearside stirrup is conveniently at hand.

Exercises

Work without stirrups begins in walk to relax and stretch the rider's joints and tissues gently, whilst establishing balance and security. The rider gently stretches the legs down, letting the feet and ankles relax. The rider may then bend the knees slightly and raise the toes of the feet.

The rider keeps the posture through the upper body, ribcage raised, sitting tall with the shoulders back and down, and looking forward, head and neck relaxed.

Once the rider has relaxed, the exercise can progress into trot.

- The trot should be steady, in rhythm and balance, so that the rider can stay in relaxed harmony with the movement.
- The trot should be active though; a horse constantly stopping and starting will throw the rider out of balance - leg aids followed by a half-halt to regulate movement.
- The rider allows the legs to drop down, relaxing the knee and ankle joints.
- Instruct the rider to allow the hips to relax, go 'soft' and, feeling the horse's movement, go with him.

Working without stirrups needs careful control. Safety is the prime factor; be observant and discriminating as to how much and what type of work the rider can physically do. Short periods are more beneficial than creating tiredness, tension, pain and strain through excessive work. The riders can be given short rest periods in which they can perform exercises at halt or walk.

Children's Exercises and Games

Children's physiques tend to be flexible and pliable but even with children, exercises should be carefully performed, slowly and gently, without strain. Often, in an effort to please, children will attempt to do an exercise quickly and jerkily.

- ❖ Make the exercises safe - vital in children's lessons.
- ❖ Make the exercises fun.
- ❖ Use imagination to create images.
- ❖ Vary the exercises; repeat two or three times then alternate with some other activity. For instance, do one exercise then a school figure such as turns or circles, then another exercise. Children will concentrate completely, but only for a short span of time, then their attention wanders.
- ❖ Always praise children, they love it.

Some of the exercises mentioned are suitable for children, with exciting names such as the 'Windmill' (arm circling), the Aeroplane (arms out and turn round from side to side).

Children can touch their toes; they can also lean forward to touch the pony's ears.

Other images can be used such as growing tall, imagine a balloon fixed to the top of the hat and it is pulling the child taller. Who can grow the tallest? Imagine the legs are growing longer and try to touch the ground, with both legs at the same time.

Adapt these exercises according to the ages and abilities of the children, using suitable exercises for the type of class. Do not forget or ignore the child who is shy, quiet or not as knowledgeable; use simpler questions and answers and lots of praise to build self-confidence.

Considerations

There are some important points to remember when teaching exercises.

- The rider should not exercise quickly with a jerky action. The most vital aspect of exercising is to do every action **slowly and gently**. It is rather like gradually stretching an elastic band, rather than snapping it open. Combining the breathing exercise with all the other exercises will create a smooth, relaxing movement, a yoga-type action.
- Never repeat an exercise too often or to excess. This will tire the rider, possibly resulting in cramp and injury. Better to do an exercise that stretches a little, then, over time, the fitness will develop.
- Never continue with an exercise that causes pain.
- Never request an exercise that contorts the body unnaturally, particularly crunching or twisting the spine. Stretching the spine along its length or gently rotating on one axis is beneficial. Twisting, curving, pulling, contracting the muscles and tissues does not improve the rider.
- Never put a rider or horse in danger. Exercises should be performed on a quiet horse who is accustomed to the rider's movements and in a safe environment. If at all unsure avoid the exercise. The last thing the rider needs is to be swinging his legs free of the stirrups and the horse dashes off. This may cause an injury, for example whiplash.
- Avoid doing exercises that are not appropriate or relevant to that rider. Explain to the rider the aim of the exercise, how it influences the rider's body and position. Though all exercises will benefit most riders, some actions cause tension. For instance the 'legs away' exercise for a complete beginner may be difficult and result in some pain.

When doing exercises the rider maintains the seat position. For instance movements of the arms or legs should not move other parts of the body. If one part cannot move without affecting another, this indicates stiffness or tension within the body.

Teaching Tips

Though exercises can be taught to practically all riders at any time and result in improvement, choosing a specific, relevant exercise appropriate to that rider at that time will be of much more benefit to the rider, the horse and your teaching reputation.

Develop the ability to recognise a rider's problem areas, the source or root of the faults. It is of little use doing an exercise that loosens the knee joints if the rider's shoulders are stiff and tense. Also one particular exercise may improve the root of many problems. Loosening and fittening the hip area may help the rider to release tension throughout the back, neck and head area, or help to release tense thighs.

Avoid doing too many exercises in one lesson. Apart from causing pain or strain, the rider may become bored, may feel they have not progressed as much as they would wish. The rider will not wish to spend most of the lesson doing exercises no matter how much they may be needed, so choose the areas where two or three exercises will be most productive.

Observe, observe, observe; watch lessons, ask questions of other instructors, increase your knowledge and awareness. Learn to recognise problem areas in the rider, stiff shoulder blades, a tense hip area, a rigid neck. Observation and knowledge is vital when teaching exercises.

CHAPTER 12
Ground Poles

Poles are a useful training aid. They provide a different aspect for teaching and can be used in a variety of ways for flatwork and jumping lessons.

Placed around the school at strategic positions, ground poles are used in two main ways: by working the horse over them at different paces and as a guide when performing school figures.

Ground Poles

Poles are versatile in their use and offer an aid for improvement in both the rider and the horse. They have several functions:

- Increases the rider's **awareness of the horse's rhythm, balance, impulsion** and **straightness**.
- Improves **the rider's co-ordination**.
- Adds **variety** to the lesson.
- As an **introduction to jumping**.
- Increases the awareness and **ability to control** and **guide the horse**.
- Develops the horse's **rhythm, balance, suppleness** and **co-ordination**.
- Improves the horse's **physical fitness, develops** his **muscles**.
- Improves the horse's **paces** encouraging him to take **more care over his footfalls**.
- **As training** to **lengthen** and **shorten the strides**.
- Encourages the horse to **stretch** and **round his back** and **topline,** to **bend his hocks**.
- Useful **warm-up exercise** for dressage and jumping.

Distances

When poles are used in combination with other poles, as with trotting poles, the poles have to be a specific distance apart. This varies depending on

- ❖ Size of the horse or pony. In relation to their size, horses and ponies have different lengths of stride.
- ❖ Pace. Horses and ponies in faster paces have a longer stride.

The distance between poles is initially based on the average length of stride to which most horses and ponies conform.

Length of stride

	Walk	**Trot**
Average pony	0.85 m (2ft 9ins)	1.1 m (3ft 6ins)
Average horse	0.90 m (3 feet)	1.4 m (4ft 6ins)

In classes that include a selection of horses and ponies, the distance between the poles will be based on the distance for a horse. It is easier for ponies to adapt their length of stride or put in an extra stride.

The distances do need to be correct for the horses and ponies to work over the poles in safety and with confidence. Poles can be hazardous, if the distances are incorrect the horse may step on a pole, roll it, stumble over it, fall, and become anxious. The horse may even attempt to jump the poles or refuse to work over them.

Measuring Distances

To measure the distance between the poles, the instructor normally takes the appropriate number of strides.

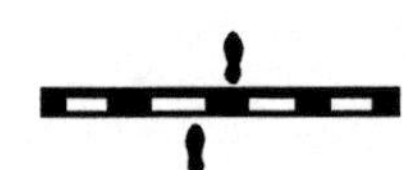

Most people's stride measures around 1m or 3 feet, small ladies may need to stretch a little, tall men will need to shorten their stride slightly.

The approximate measurements are:

Poles to be used at **walk** have **one stride** between poles.

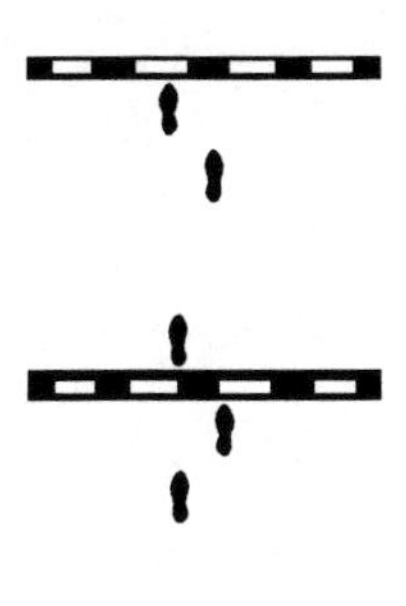

Poles used for **trot** have **one and a half strides** between poles.

Take one stride then place one foot so that the heel is about 0.1m (6 inches) in front of the other foot. This gives a fairly accurate measurement.

Method of Using Poles

Poles need to be introduced in a progressive way throughout the lesson.

- ❖ Start with a single pole placed across the **three-quarter line** near E or B. Do not place the pole over the track; the rider will find it difficult to keep the horse straight on the approach and to aim for the centre of the pole.
- ❖ Instruct the rider to ride over the pole in walk.
- ❖ A second pole can be placed at a distance of 2.7m (9 feet) from the first pole.
- ❖ This distance allows the poles to be used for walk and trot. The rider can walk over these poles and then proceed to work in trot.

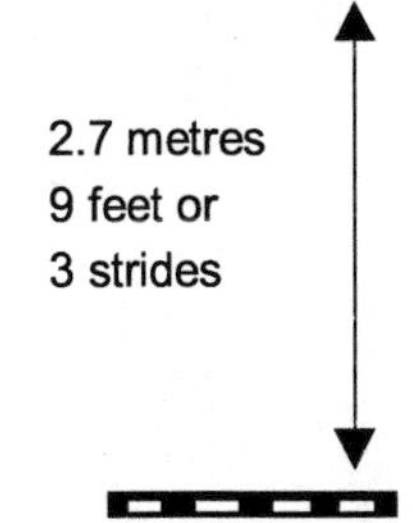

Do not position two poles close together (0.90m or 1.4m) this may encourage the horse to jump the poles.

Trot Poles

Most of the work over poles is performed at trot. Though riders practise first at walk to assess the horse's response, the real benefit comes from working in trot.

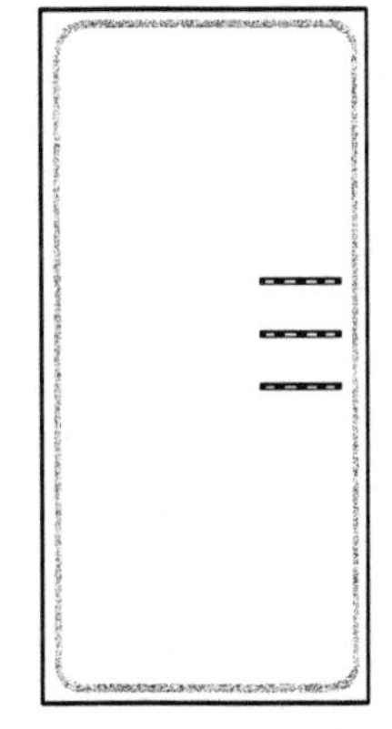

- ❖ A third pole is placed in the centre of the two poles that is 1.4 metres (4ft 6ins) from each pole. These are now used as trotting poles only.
- ❖ Three poles are the usual number for novice or inexperienced riders to work over. If the rider cannot keep the horse active, the horse may lose impulsion and stumble over too many poles.

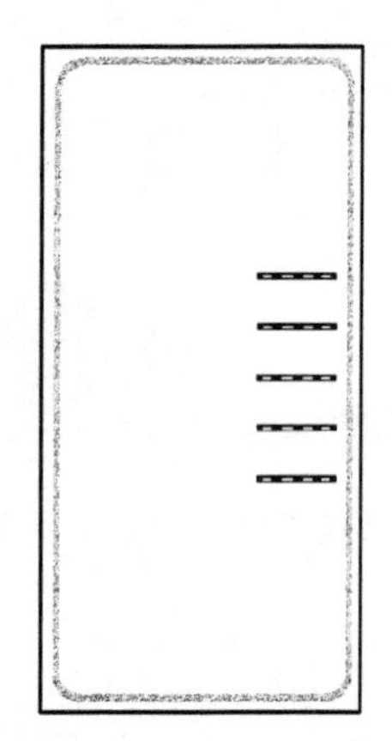

- For more experienced riders the number can be increased up to five poles. A fourth and then fifth pole is added at 1.4m away from the other poles.
- There is no difference between using an odd or even number of poles, though an odd number is normally preferred. If the first pole is placed halfway down the school at E or B, an odd number of poles will be an equal distance from both ends of the school.

Variations

Though the length of stride for similar sized horses is normally relatively the same, there can be differences in stride length even between horses of the same height. The length of stride can be effected by:

- Conformation. Some horses have a short stride, some a long stride.
- The horse's or pony's stage of training. Fitter, more supple horses may take a longer stride.
- The horse's or pony's way of going. This varies with individual horses and ponies on different days and in different environments.

To compensate for these variations, assess the horses on the flat first before they work over poles.

Place the poles to suit the horses with the shorter strides; those with longer strides can normally shorten their stride more easily.

The Rider's Position

Teach the rider to keep the body position when working over the poles.

- Keep the back straight with the shoulders relaxed.
- Look up and beyond the poles.
- Legs remain in contact with the horse's side ready to ask for more activity and energy if needed.
- Hands remain soft with a light contact on the rein ready to allow by giving slightly when the horse stretches forwards and down over the poles.
- When working in trot over trot poles with the stirrups at flatwork length, the rider should be in **rising trot** so that the horse can lift and round his back.

Working over Ground Poles

Teaching the rider how to work over the ground poles accurately does cover various aspects such as control of the horse, the independent and co-ordinated use of the aids.

Teach the rider to ride the horse in an active, forward pace, in rhythm and balance on the track before the poles. This requires leg aids and half-halts to achieve activity, balance and rhythm.

The rider needs to judge the turn before the approach and ride into a straight-line approach.

On the approach the rider should ride the horse in a straight line towards the centre of the poles. For this the rider needs to use the aids to maintain the straightness. If the horse starts to pull away from the centre of the poles the rider will need to use the opposite leg aid for correction. This will teach the rider to use the aids independently.

The pace should be kept active but controlled. This teaches the rider to use the aids with discretion. Too much leg and the horse may rush the poles, losing balance and rhythm. Too much hand or not enough leg and the horse will slow down either making a downward transition or knocking the poles through lack of impulsion.

The rider maintains the riding position over the poles keeping the legs in contact with the horse's sides to maintain the pace and activity.

After the poles the rider should guide the horse in a straight line, aiming towards the track at the end of the school.

Teaching with Ground Poles

The skill of teaching a rider and horse to work over poles takes certain qualities:

❖ **Observation**

Observe each horse and rider as they work over the poles. Ideally the horse should step into the centre of the distance between the poles, that is, place one forefoot in the centre of the space between the first two poles and the other forefoot into the centre between the next poles.

❖ **Assessment**

Assess the quality of the work, the horse's activity, straightness, balance and rhythm on the approach, over and beyond the poles. The horse should be 'tracking up', the appropriate hind foot stepping into the centre of the distance between the two poles, almost the same spot where the forefoot was placed.

❖ **Correction**

Make corrections as and when necessary. Avoid too many corrections that may confuse or discourage the rider. Avoid making too many comments whilst the rider is working over the poles as this can be distracting. Watch for the horse's pace before the poles, this needs to be active but not fast. Watch that the rider accurately rides the turn and the approach to the poles.

❖ **Adaptability**

Always be adaptable. If a horse is working at an active pace yet constantly hits a pole because he has a short stride, the distance between the poles needs to be reduced. Most of the time if a horse does hit a pole this is a result of the horse not working actively or rider error. Correct the rider but be discriminating, an inexperienced rider will be unable to alter, that is shorten or lengthen, the horse's stride to any great degree. If the horse still continually raps the poles then alter the distances.

Progression

To maintain the improvement and progression, the horse should be ridden over the trotting poles only two or three times in both directions. Other work can be introduced to keep the horse's (and rider's) attention.

The poles can be arranged in sets:

- ❖ two sets of three down one side 11m distance in between each set
- ❖ three poles either side of the school
- ❖ one additional set across the diagonal

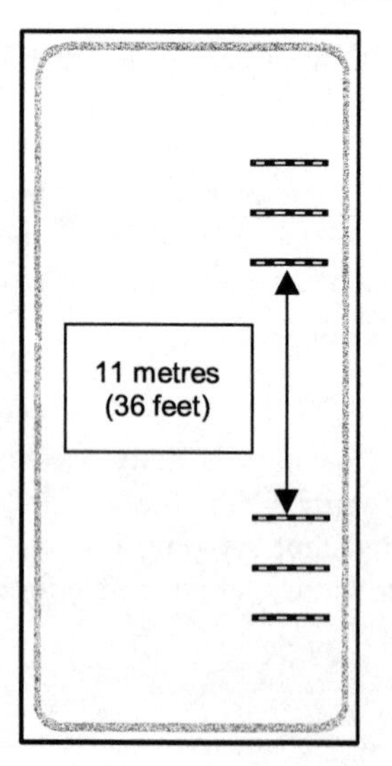

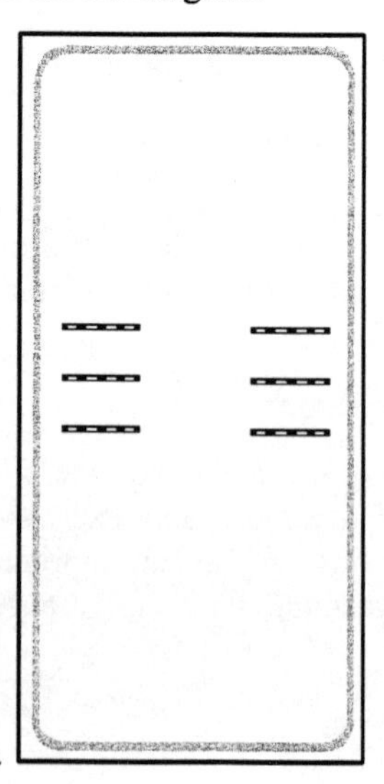

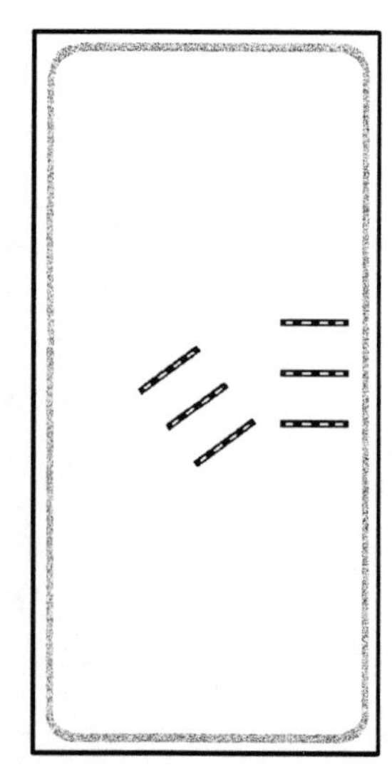

School Figures

Poles are often used as a training aid to improve the rider's accuracy and control on school figures.

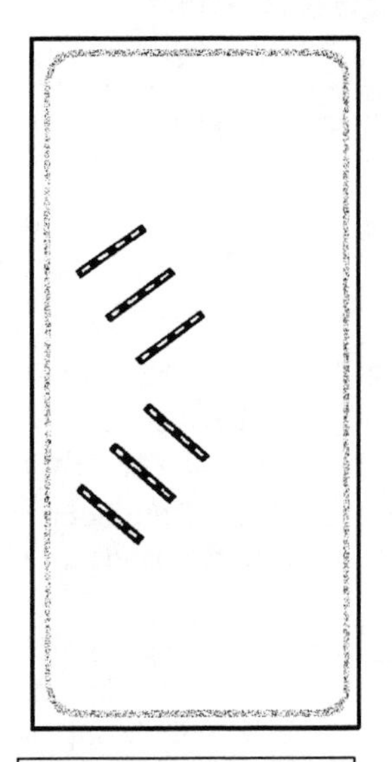

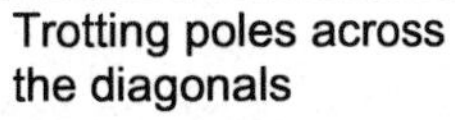

Trotting poles across the diagonals

Poles across both diagonals placed 2.7 metres or 9 feet apart

Serpentines and Circles

Poles positioned at points in the school encourages the riders to make good turns and to ride straight lines

Poles can be used for serpentines to help the pupils ride the loops accurately and to guide the horse in straight lines between the loops

Poles are used on a circle to help with accuracy

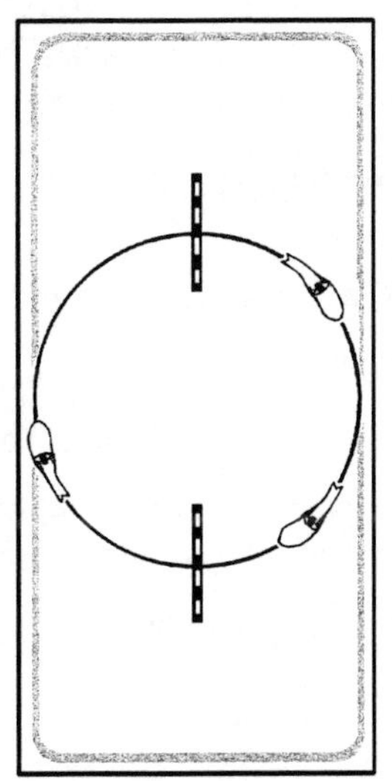

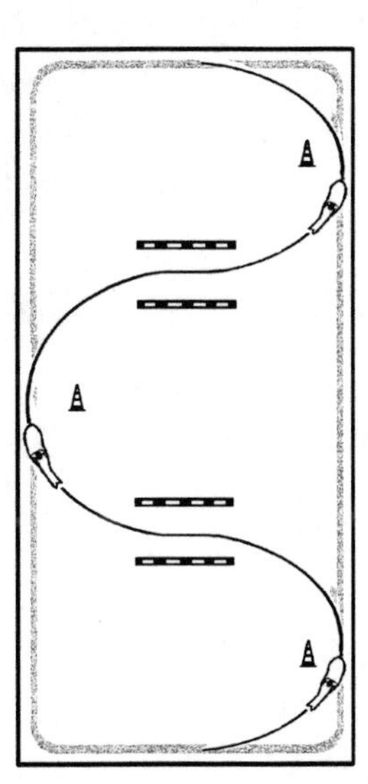

Working over poles during school figures offers a different dimension to flatwork and an alternative method of training horses.

Introduction to Jumping

Working over ground poles is useful as a preparation for jumping either to help beginners develop their fitness and confidence or, in a jumping lesson, as a warm-up to increase the suppleness of both rider and horse.

The rider can shorten the stirrups by one or two holes then practice in the light seat over the poles. This is an excellent method of improving and increasing the rider's balance, suppleness and strengthening the leg muscles.

- It teaches the rider how to guide and control the horse towards and over a fence.
- Gives the rider the 'feel' of the horse going over an obstacle, how the horse's action, his rhythm and balance can alter.
- Gives the feel of the horse stretching forward and down; the rider can practise allowing with the hands to follow the horse's stretch, whilst maintaining the light position.
- The rider can be shown and given explanations about where to place the hands. Initially beginners should practise whilst holding onto the neckstrap or breastplate to avoid losing balance and pulling on the reins and bit.

For all work over poles, ground poles, trotting poles or as an introduction to jumping, progress should be slow and steady. It is better that the rider develops the fitness and suppleness slowly, and learns to work the horse over the poles.

Other Training Aids

There are other training aids that can be useful in lessons, such as cones. Music adds another dimension to riding, creating relaxation as well as being a good training aid for rhythm and balance. Mirrors and videos offer excellent mediums for self-assessment and improvement.

Cones

Cones are an extremely useful training accessory, often undervalued. They have several advantages.

- Can be placed anywhere in the school, on corners, down the long sides, down the centre line.
- Easily moved, lightweight to carry.
- Will not injure or hurt the horses should the cones be knocked.
- Can be used for a variety of exercises and games.
- Can be used in conjunction with poles and jumps.

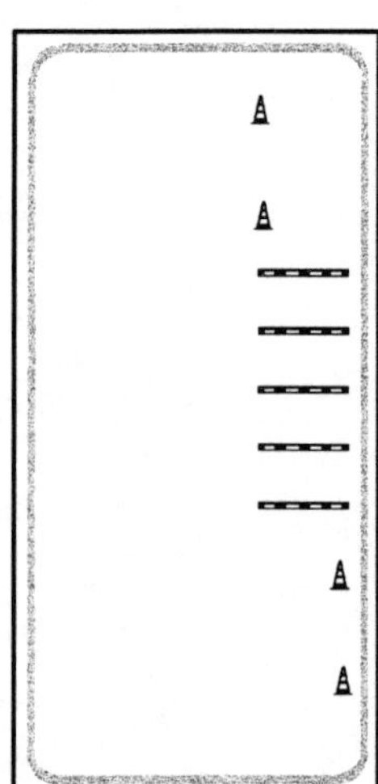

- Easily stacked and stored.
- Almost indestructible, rot proof.

The only disadvantage is that often horses (and riders) do not respect cones and will ride over or through them with ease.

Using Cones

Cones can be used for different types of lesson, such as group, private, flatwork, jumping, beginners and children's lessons.

- Used to encourage the rider to ride into the corners correctly, preventing them from cutting the corners.
- Used to mark a straight line down the inner track or centre line to encourage the rider to keep the horse straight.
- Used in a line to teach beginners and children how to steer by weaving in and out of the cones.
- Used in gymkhana events as markers in races.
- Used to mark out circles, serpentines and other school figures for accuracy.
- Used as a guide to jumps, on the turns and for a straight approach.

Cones are useful in the school, the menage, the field and in an outdoor jumping arena.

Mirrors

Mirrors placed on the walls around the school are a useful training aid, provided they are kept clean and clear. The rider is able to observe his own position and make adjustments. The horse can be observed and an assessment made on how he is working, how he is using himself, whether he is straight or crooked, or how he moves in lateral work.

Mirrors are particularly useful because they show at the precise moment exactly how the rider and horse are working. Improvements and corrections can be made immediately.

Videos

On the same theme, a video recording of a single rider, or of the group, is another method by which the rider may achieve improvement. Self-assessment is a vital part of improving, progressing and advancing.

Good instruction is of prime importance but there are times when the rider needs to observe his own position to understand the corrections or advice given by the instructor.

Videos do not give the rider the ability to correct immediately, but by being slowed down they provide a view not normally available. Many slight and subtle aspects of riding can be seen and comparisons made with better riders, giving an example to work towards.

Videos are extremely important as training tools to observe and understand the horse's actions. How the horse moves, how he jumps a fence, or makes a transition. Once the rider can understand the horse's movements, riding takes on a whole new dimension and meaning.

Watching videos of top riders will often inspire the rider and result in improvements.

Music

Music can improve rhythm and balance dramatically. It provides relaxation; riders are often seen to visibly relax when riding to a piece of music. Dressage to music is a growing sport and inspiring to watch. Music is a medium used for other types of riding such as drill rides.

Music adds variety to lessons and achieves one of the most vital aims; it makes riding fun.

All these training aids are of tremendous benefit to the rider and horse. Their use expands the scope of teaching and adds to the enjoyment of learning.

Teaching Tips

Using poles takes practice. Keep the plan simple, such as poles on the three-quarter line down the long side of the school. It is of more benefit for inexperienced riders to practise over a simple layout than to attempt a more difficult plan. You can then concentrate on the rider's position and ability to control the horse rather than trying to explain and guide them through a complicated design.

Starting off with two poles at 2.7 metres (about 9 feet or 3 human strides) is good. This design is quite versatile. Two more poles can be inserted at 0.90m and 1.8m (3 and 6 feet) to make walk poles, then one pole removed and the other rolled to mid-distance 1.4m (4 feet 6 inches) for trot poles.

If one rider and horse only is working over the poles, position the other riders in the school away from the poles so that they do not encourage the horse to run out or veer over towards them.

Make use of the training aids as much as possible, they add another dimension to teaching, offering variety and interest.

CHAPTER 13
School Figures

This chapter covers information on school figures; circles, turns, straight lines, and explains how to teach riders the methods of riding these figures with accuracy. To achieve this the riders first need to know exactly how to apply the natural aids, when and in what combination.

Though most of the information contained in this chapter will be familiar, it is the manner in which this information is presented that is important. It is mostly *written from the teaching point of view.* It is a different perspective learning information to teach others rather than learning the information for yourself, to increase your knowledge.

The art of teaching is possessing the knowledge then having the ability to communicate this to others. It is transforming lengthy, complicated information into brief, clear explanations that pupils can understand.

The Aids

The **aids** are the **language** by which the **rider communicates with the horse**. There are two types: **natural** and **artificial**. The natural aids are the seat and body, the legs, hands and the voice; the artificial aids include the whip and spurs.

- ❖ The foundation of the seat and body aid is a **secure and independent seat**. The seat is deep but light in the saddle, soft and relaxed. The upper body is carried and the legs, though in contact with the horse's sides, are relaxed, free to move. Secure and independent means that the whole body position is in balance and can move in harmony with the horse's movement, without having to grip with the thighs and knees or hold onto the reins for stability.
- ❖ 'Controlled relaxation' is the key, the body is carried and under control yet the muscles are free of tension. Relaxation does not mean drooping.
- ❖ The seat and body aid can then be used tactfully and subtly, by sitting up and strengthening the muscles of the lower back. This aid is used in combination with the legs and hands to balance the horse or as a restraining aid.
- ❖ The **inside leg asks** for **impulsion**, to encourage the horse to **bend** through his body and, when required, for sideways or **lateral movements**.

- The **outside leg controls** this **bend**, is used in **transitions** and **lateral movements**.
- The **inside hand guides the horse** and is used for **direction** and to ask for **bend**.
- The **outside hand controls** and **regulates speed, pace and bend**.
- The hands are used with a slightly resisting but **elastic feel** from the shoulders through the arms and by slight movements, 'spongy feelings', of the fingers. They should only act in conjunction with the other aids.
- The voice is used to praise or to correct when necessary. (The use of the voice aid is not allowed in Dressage competitions.)
- The whip is normally carried in the inside hand and used when required to support the inside leg.
- Spurs should only be worn when the rider can effectively apply the leg aids; they are then used as a refined aid. They are not used to strengthen the leg aid.

The Mind Aid

There is one more aid and that is the mind or 'thought' aid. This is where the whole process starts, the mind thinks, the will determines and the body reacts. The mind is powerful; 'it's all in the mind', mind and thought control the other aids and in consequence the horse.

To progress requires determination, a desire to improve, self-confidence, an ability for self-criticism, an ability to assess, to listen to and understand the horse's body language.

Co-ordination of the Aids

At first the aids are used simply and singly, one at a time, rather like learning the alphabet and then small words. With progress, the aids begin to be used in conjunction with each other, rather like putting words together to make a sentence.

Eventually the aids are used in co-ordination with each other in a harmonious way; each aid is applied separately but in combination with the other aids - the seat and body aid, then the legs, then the hands.

If all the aids were used together, all at the same time, the horse would be confused, rather like when driving a car using the accelerator whilst applying the brake.

To use one aid on its own makes this aid strong; for example, to use the hand aid only causes the horse to pull back, hollow, stop or, if in pain, bolt.

The Half-Halt

The half-halt is used to balance the horse, to engage his hindquarters, to lighten his forehand and to prepare him before a change of pace, a school figure or movement. It also keeps the horse attentive, listening and obedient.

The half-halt is used frequently when schooling and working the horse, for instance before every corner of the school, before every transition.

Aids

Straighten the seat and body momentarily by sitting up a little taller and strengthening the back muscles. Apply the leg aids. Then squeeze and release with the hands; if necessary use a slight resistance then release. This may be on both reins, though sometimes using the outside rein only is more effective.

Think of asking the horse for a downward transition but only for a second then just before the horse makes the transition ask for forward movement.

There are degrees of half-halt, sometimes giving a softer, lighter half-halt or a series of softer, lighter half-halts is effective. At other times the horse will need a stronger half-halt to respond. Almost like giving quarter-halts or three-quarter halts.

Release

An important point about the aids is that they should be applied and then **released**. A constant, continuous aid makes this aid strong, tenses the horse and can also cause pain. If a firmer aid is required this should be given with a little more strength and determination, then released.

Transitions

A transition is a change from one pace to another or a variation within a pace.

- A **progressive** transition is a change from one pace to another in sequence, for example from walk to trot or from trot to canter.
- A **direct** transition is a change from one pace to another out of sequence; walk to canter, halt to trot.

There is also the **transition within a pace**, for instance from medium walk to free walk on a long rein.

Aim

The aim of a good transition is to change the pace maintaining the horse's activity and balance throughout.

Preparation

Preparation for all transitions is essential:

- think ahead and plan the transition
- keep the current pace active and forward
- a few strides before, prepare the horse with half-halts
- then, at the moment of transition, apply the correct aids

Upward Transitions

For the upward transition halt to walk, sit a little straighter in the saddle, then apply the leg aids with both legs equally, at the same time allow the forward movement by giving slightly with the hands.

For walk to trot, first make sure the walk is active, not fast, but with energy. Apply a half-halt a few strides before the transition. At the moment of transition apply the legs equally and then give slightly with the hands.

For trot to canter prepare by sitting to the trot for a few strides and balance the pace with a half-halt. Apply the inside leg in the region of the girth. This is the important aid asking for forward movement and strike off.

Stroke the outside leg *back slightly* behind the girth. Avoid bringing the leg too far back or using too strong an aid; this will encourage the horse to swing his hindquarters in, away from that leg.

Ask for *slight* flexion of the horse's head to the inside with the inside hand and, at the moment of strike off, give *slightly* with this hand to encourage a free, forward transition.

Keep the contact with the outside hand and rein but allow the slight flexion to the inside.

Downward Transitions

The transition from a faster pace to a slower pace needs good preparation to make a smooth, balanced change.

Prepare the horse first with a half-halt, yet keep the pace active. (May possibly require a series of small half-halts.)

Maintain the leg contact, to encourage the horse forward into the transition. It is important to create forward movement with the legs, containing this energy with the body and seat, and the hands. Without the leg aids the horse will change abruptly, fall onto the forehand and lose impulsion, balance and rhythm.

School Figures

School figures are manoeuvres performed around the school, such as straight lines, circles, turns and changes of rein.

Circles and Turns

Circles are a useful exercise to improve flexibility and suppleness in the horse, for improving the paces, straightness, balance, rhythm and obedience.

Turns are important to make a change of direction and as preparation for riding a straight line.

Aims

To guide the horse around the turn or circle keeping his bodyline bent uniformly from poll to tail. The horse's hind feet should follow the same line as the fore feet.

Maintain the horse's balance and rhythm throughout the turn or circle.

Method

- Prepare the horse by maintaining the activity and rhythm of the pace.
- Balance the horse with half-halts.
- Look around the circle or turn.
- Keep the seat level in the saddle.
- Apply the inside leg aid to ask for bend and forward movement.
- Keep the outside leg in contact, slightly behind the girth, to contain the hindquarters, preventing them from swinging out.
- Keeping the hands level at the same height on each side of the horse's neck, with the inside hand invite the horse around the curve in the direction of travel.
- Maintain the contact with the outside hand. This controls the horse's neck so that he does not bend his neck more than the rest of his body and allow his outside shoulder to fall out of the curve. At the same time give slightly to allow the horse to bend around the arc of the circle. The horse's inside eyebrow should just be visible.

Faults, Causes and Corrections

a. *The horse 'falls out of' the turn or circle through his outside shoulder. He has too much neck bend.*

The rider's body may be twisted, the inside shoulder further forward than the outside shoulder. This allows the horse to be crooked and fall out through the shoulder. The rider may be applying the aids incorrectly, asking too much with the inside hand.

Start by correcting the rider's position. Instruct the rider to ride the turns and circles at a walk to practise the co-ordination of aids until these are understood.

The rider is twisted with the right shoulder in front of the left shoulder

The rider needs to give more with the inside rein and take more control of the outside rein to prevent the horse falling out.

The rider is leaning in with the shoulder, collapsing the hip

b. *The horse 'falls into' the circle, leans in making the circle smaller or cuts the corner of a turn.*

The rider may be leaning into the circle. The inside hip 'collapses', the inside shoulder drops and consequently the inside hand is lower than the outside hand. The rider is not using sufficient inside leg aid.

The rider needs to use more inside leg, to insist that the horse obeys this leg aid and bends his body around the curve.

c. *The horse's hindquarters swing out.* The rider is not applying the outside leg to control the horse's hindquarters.

The rider's needs a firmer outside leg aid to control the quarters.

Straight lines

Straight lines are used to judge the horse's straightness or crookedness and the accurate, effective use of the aids.

Aim

Ride the horse on a completely straight line. This is normally performed across the long diagonal, down the centre line of the school or along the three-quarter line down each long side.

Method

Prepare the horse before the turn into the straight line. Ride him forward with activity, then steady and balance the pace with a half-halt. The turn before the straight line is vital; this needs to be judged and ridden accurately.

- ❖ Ride the turn with a clear inside leg aid, a series of firm nudges, to ask the horse for bend; use the outside leg to control his hindquarters. Guide the horse around the turn with the inside hand. Control the pace and bend with the outside hand.
- ❖ Look round the turn, down the straight line guiding the horse onto the line.
- ❖ Keep the seat level in the saddle, body upright and relaxed, and look directly ahead down the line. Keep a contact with the legs and keep them still except when asking for forward movement when the leg aids are given with an equal amount of pressure. Keep the hands level with an equal contact.
- ❖ One good hint is to ride the horse forward with activity and energy; this helps to keep the horse straight on the line.

Faults, Causes and Corrections

a. *The horse under or over shoots the line.* Poor preparation and turn before the straight line.

The rider needs to practise judging when the horse has to be turned onto the line. Some horses are less supple and need turning sooner. Others can turn on the proverbial sixpence and need controlling in the turn.

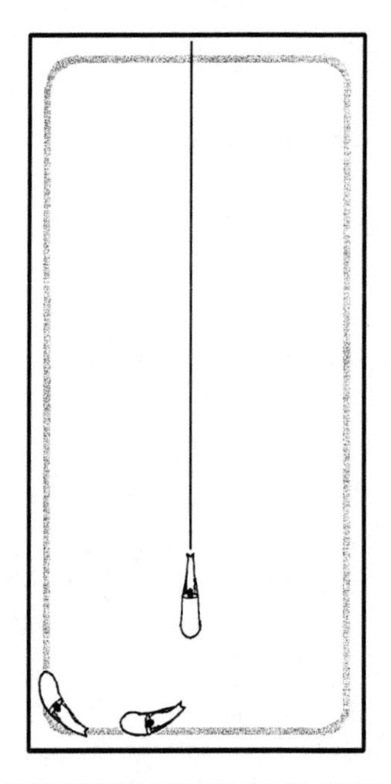

Making a good turn helps to ride a straight centre line

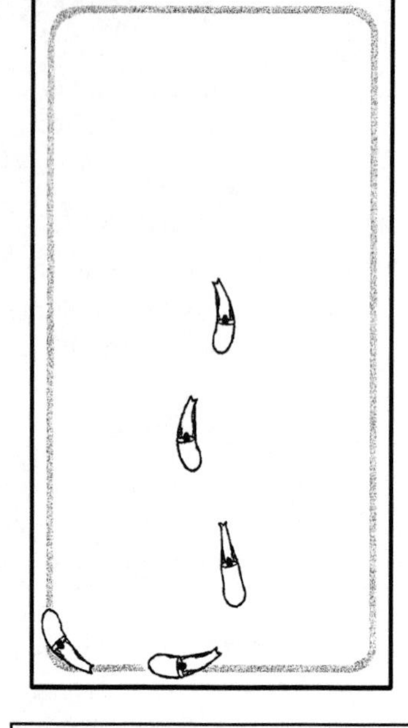

Misjudging the turn will result in a crooked line

b. *The horse wavers down the line, may drift one way or waver first one way then another.* The horse may not be going forwards and so loses the balance on the turn. The rider's weight may be slightly to one side, or one leg aid may be applied more strongly than the other.

The rider needs to be aware of the body weight and the aids. The image of riding on a narrow causeway between two steep cliffs either side concentrates the mind on the line.

Accuracy of School Figures

Teaching riders to ride school figures accurately is important; this is the basis of all school movements. Accuracy demands discipline from both rider and horse, encouraging the horse to be obedient and responsive. Riders learn preparation, control and the independent but co-ordinated use of the aids.

The dimensions of the school, including the markers, need to be learnt and memorised. One useful rhyme to remember the markers by is

'**A**ll **K**ing **E**dward's **H**orses **C**an **M**ake **B**ig **F**ences.'

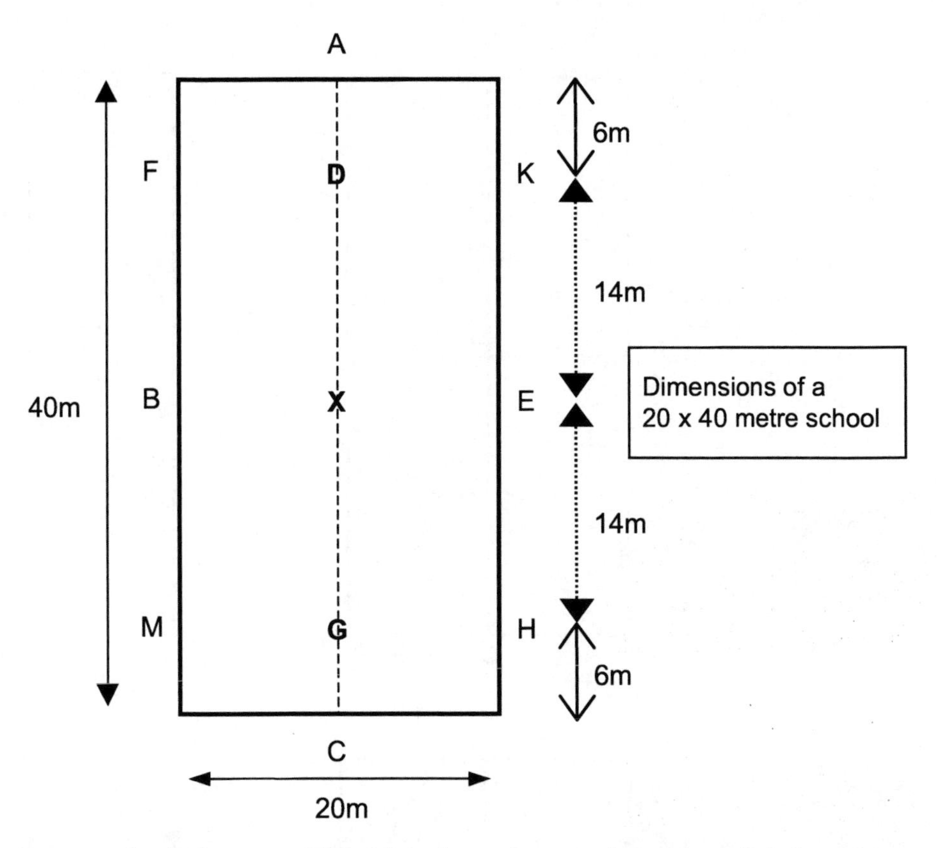

In most schools there are additional markers: shapes such as coloured circles, squares or triangles. These indicate the tangent points for figures such as circles. Though most schools do not measure exactly 20m by 40m, using these tangent points as guides, riders can calculate and ride fairly accurate school figures.

Circles

Circles in the school are normally commenced at the markers, A or C, or the half markers E or B. The quarter markers K, H, M and F are used to judge the accuracy of the circles.

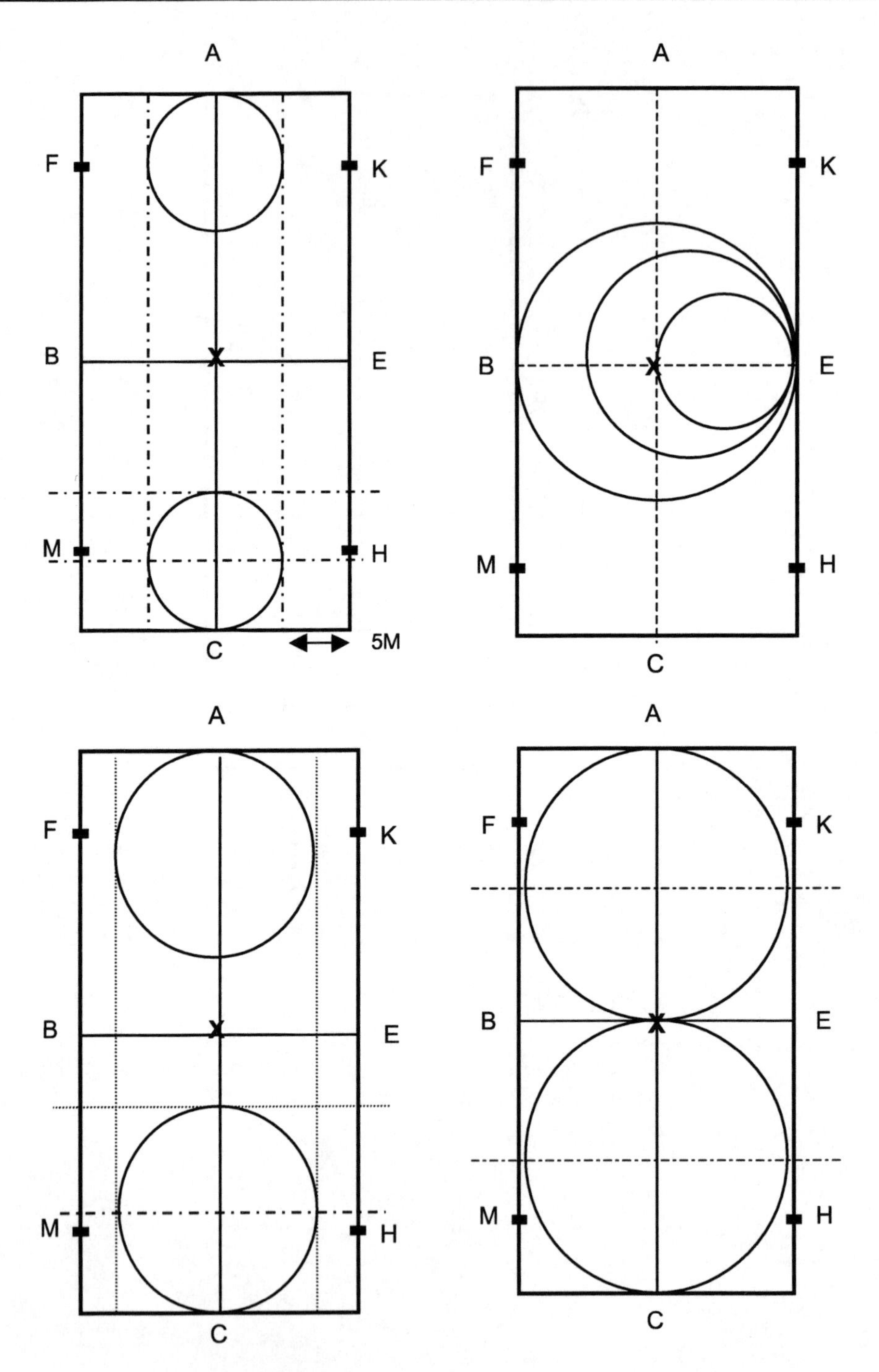

The diagrams show the dimensions and tangent points for 10m, 15m and 20m circles.

10m circles starting A and C: 5m from the side of the school, the centre line 10m from the start of the circle and 5m from side of school again. From E or B the circle will touch X at the centre line.

15m circles starting at A and C: 2.5m in from side of school, centre line 5m from X and 2.5m from side of school. From E or B: 2.5m before centre line, 5m from side of school and 2.5 m after centre line.

20m circles from A and C outer track midway between end of school and centre line, centre line at X, and outer track midway between centre line and end of school. From E or B: centre line 10m from X, outer track at E or B and centre line 10m from X.

The horse should be on the tangent points *only for a stride*. Encourage the rider to think of each circle as four quarters of a circle and to aim for each tangent point.

Half circles feature frequently in school figures. They are often used to change the rein, two half 20m circles starting at A or C or two half 10m circles starting at E or B (not shown). The half 20m circle across the school, is often used as a canter exercise.

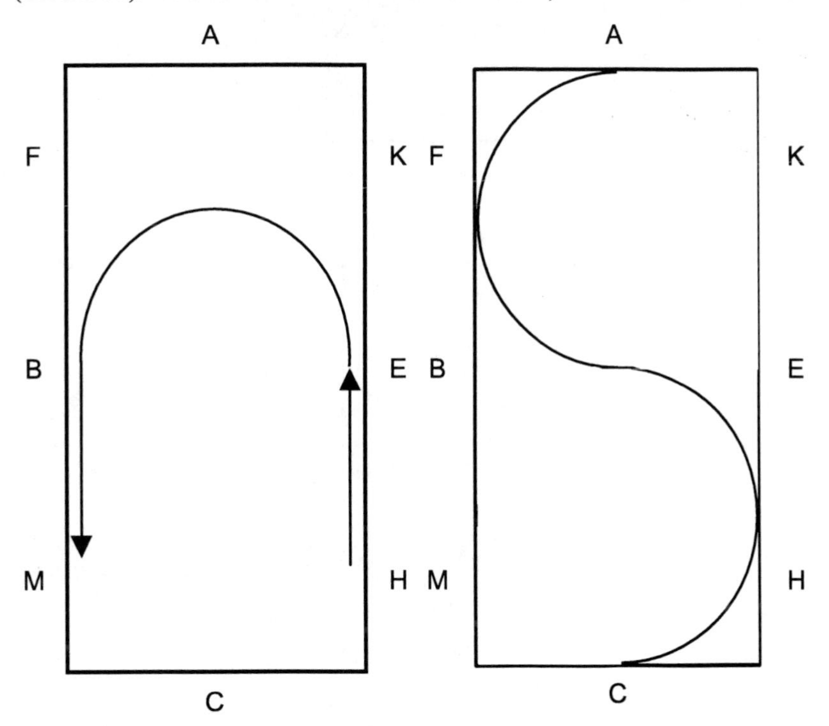

Half circles are often ridden incorrectly with riders making the shapes inaccurate, too small, unequal or too straight cutting across the school.

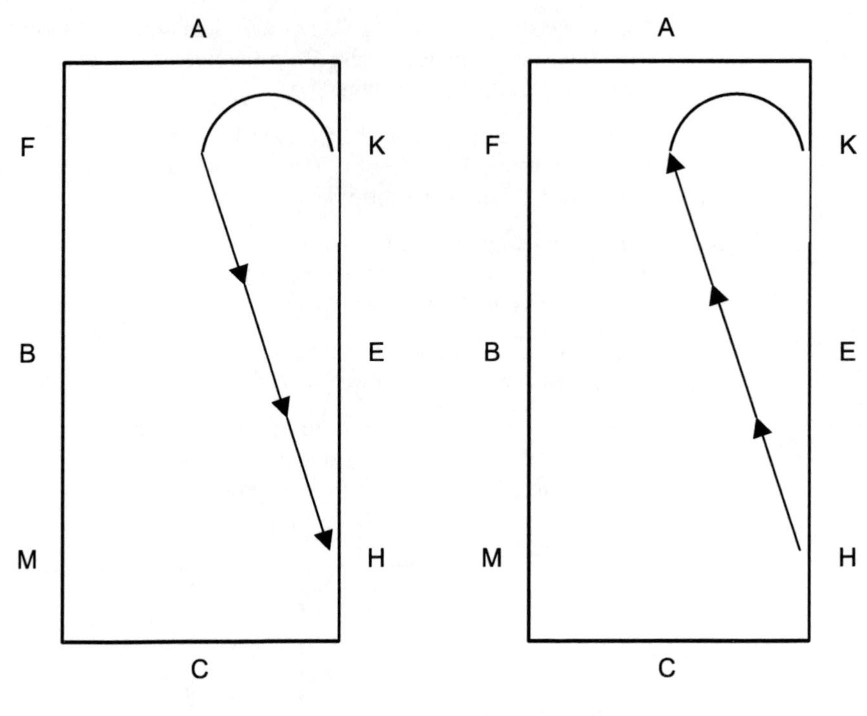

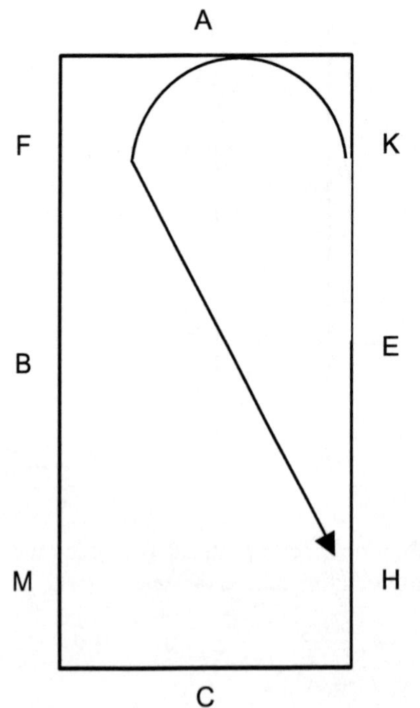

The demi-volte is a half 10m circle with an incline back to the track. The reverse demi-volte is an incline from the track into a half 10m circle back to the track.

Both these figures are used as an exercise to change the rein.

The half 15m circle and incline back to the track is also used to change the rein.

Turns

Turns include each corner of the school and turns onto other school figures, such as diagonals and the centre line. Turns need riding as accurately as circles, particularly when combined with other school figures such as straight lines.

School Figures

Other school figures are variations on the circles, turns and straight-line themes. These include serpentines and shallow loops down the sides of the school.

The three-loop serpentine is a combination of half circles and straight lines. The half circles should be the same diameter, dividing the school into three equal parts. Straight lines are ridden in between the half circles.

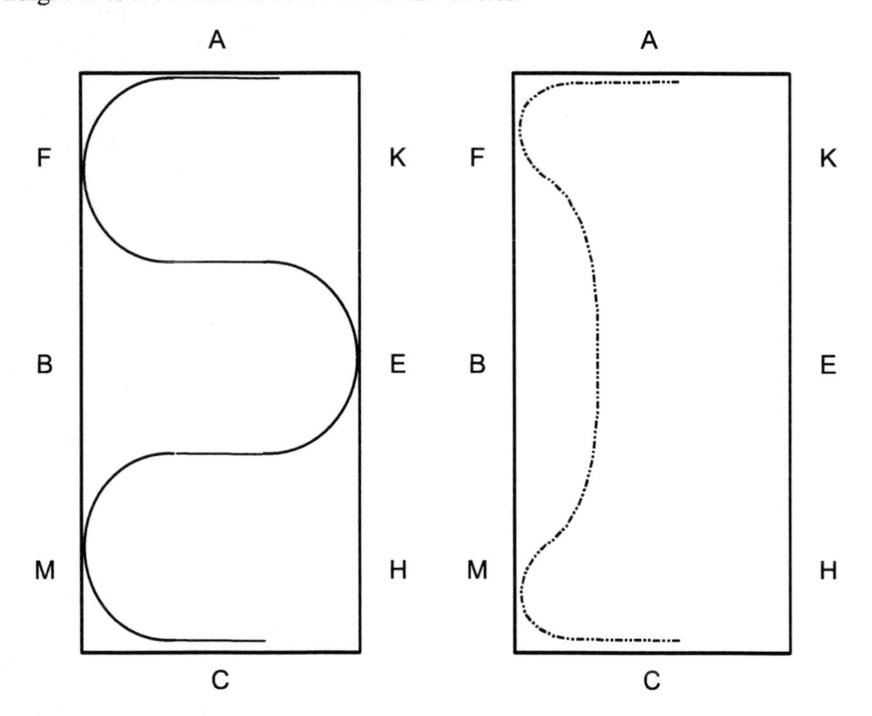

The shallow loop ridden along the long side can either be at 5m or 3m away from the school wall.

If there are no extra markers on the wall or the lesson is taking place in an outdoor arena, refer to natural markers, a spot on the school wall, the post of a fence or a particular tree.

There are other school figures such as the four loop serpentine, but those described previously are the most usual and will be taught to all riders at all levels.

Drill or Double Ride Work

To make the riders really conscious of accuracy in riding school figures, to increase their control, drill riding or double ride work can be introduced into a lesson.

This adds variety to the flatwork and it can generate a lot of fun. It makes the riders think; they have to look about them and consider another rider. It makes them look up and around which does wonders for their position.

Simple double ride work will start with two riders riding school figures around the school together.

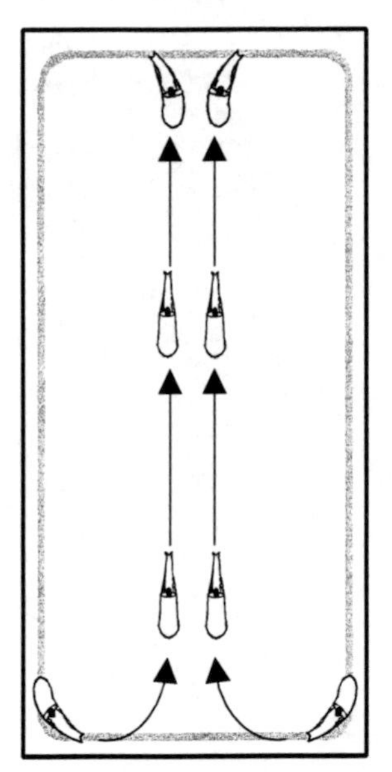

These can be straight lines, the centre line, diagonals across the school, the short line from E to B as well as down the sides of the school.

Circles can be performed with two horses together, 20m circles at A, C, E and B. The inside horse will be performing a 15m to 18m circle.

The double ride work can include two horses riding together, splitting apart then coming together again. For instance riding together down the centre line, splitting at the end of the school, one rider goes left, one goes right, going large and meeting at the centre line again, as in the diagram.

Points

Keep the plan simple at the start until the riders are more confident and familiar with the work.

- Watch that one horse does not dominate another especially when one horse is trapped on the track by the side of the school.
- Make sure that the horses are relatively similar in size, though double ride work has been performed with a horse and pony to good effect! If possible the strides should be similar.
- The riders need to be fairly competent to direct the horses, though this work is successful in improving riding techniques, teaching accuracy and control.

For many riders double ride work is a new dimension to their lessons. It teaches discipline as well as control. The rider has to keep to the same pace as his partner; he must look and judge the pace and direction. Also riders have to be firm with their horses to stop any misbehaviour when riding close.

Performing double ride work to music adds variety to the work and is another method of teaching riders about control, rhythm and pace.

Teaching Tips

Teaching riders about the seat and body aid should be done with discretion. It is only when a rider is fairly balanced and secure in the position that the seat and body aid can be used correctly and with effect. Less experienced riders can be taught to strengthen their back muscles and then release.

As they progress and improve they will begin to understand how the rider's position subtly influences the horse's movements and paces.

When teaching the school figures to a group of riders, observe the ride, the whole ride needs to ride accurately. School horses do have a tendency to cut corners, particularly if following another horse. Often, too, if the lead file rides an inaccurate line, the rest of the ride will follow the one in front. Each rider needs to be encouraged to ride individually even in a group. So if the lead file makes a mistake the second and third in line should be thinking ahead and ride an accurate line.

Riding accurate figures is good practise as a foundation for other movements, and for competitions when accuracy is essential. Also it makes riders think about where they are going, how to control the horse and how to use the aids.

When teaching circles you could mark out the dimensions in the sand with a stick, to give the riders an accurate line. With practice the riders eventually will become familiar with the circles and tangent points.

When teaching school figures and movements impress upon the rider that preparation is essential. The rider needs to think ahead, prepare well in advance. When commencing at a school marker the rider should aim to begin just before the marker. Similarly when crossing a diagonal the rider should aim to reach the track just before the marker, this will ensure that the rider actually reaches the marker instead of overshooting it.

CHAPTER 14
School Movements

School movements are exercises such as turn on the forehand and leg yield. They are used to increase the rider's effectiveness with the aids and the horse's suppleness, balance and obedience.

Turn on the Forehand

This movement is an introduction to lateral or sideways movement. It teaches the rider the independent and co-ordinated use of the aids. It increases the horse's suppleness and improves his obedience, teaching him to move away from the rider's inside leg. In practical terms it is used to open and shut gates when hacking.

The movement is performed from halt. (It can be performed from walk; the movement is then referred to as turn about the forehand.)

The turn is named for the direction in which the horse's head moves. If the head moves to the left, this is a left turn on the forehand, the hindquarters will be moving to the right. The left side would also be the inside, the side to which the horse's body is bent.

Aims

The horse steps away obediently from the inside leg aid with the hindquarters turning in an arc around the forehand.

A good halt is essential for turn on the forehand. The horse should ideally be standing square, weight equally on all four legs, waiting for the rider's aids.

The inside hind crosses in front of the outside hind. The forelegs remain more or less in the same spot, with the inside fore stepping on the spot and the outside fore stepping in a small arc around it.

Method

Instruct the rider to come in off the track to perform the turn in a safe place, away from the wall of the school.

- ❖ Prepare the horse first by asking for an active, energetic walk.
- ❖ Then prepare with a few half-halts and ride him into a square halt.
- ❖ Keep the seat level in the saddle, shoulders level and the body posture upright.
- ❖ With the inside hand ask the horse for slight bend in the direction of the turn.
- ❖ Keep the contact with outside hand to control the amount of bend.
- ❖ Use the inside leg slightly behind the girth in a series of nudges, one nudge for each step across, asking the horse to move his hindquarters.

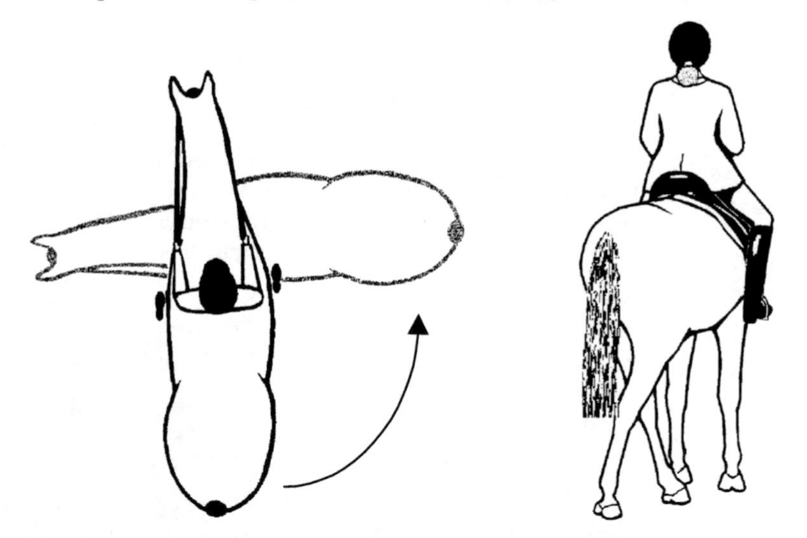

- ❖ Keep the outside leg in a passive contact near the girth. This leg controls the speed of the turn and asks for forward movement once completed.
- ❖ With both hands maintain a slight restraint (resist and release) upon the reins to prevent the horse from walking forwards.

Faults, causes and corrections

a. *The horse steps backwards.* The hands are restraining too much and the rider is not using sufficient leg aid to maintain impulsion. The walk may have been poor before the halt. Not enough preparation. The rider may be tipping forward.

Correct the rider's position, seat deeper in the saddle, the rider sitting straight and level. The rider should improve the preparation by making the horse active in the walk before the halt. The rider should lighten the hands and use firmer leg aids. Alternatively the rider could practise the turn from walk rather than halt.

b. *The horse steps forward or moves the forelegs round.* The horse may not understand or be evading the rider's aids. Not enough preparation with the half-halt. The rider may not be using the correct co-ordination of aids, legs and hands.

The rider should practise riding the horse into halt a few times first. Talk the rider slowly, one step at a time, through the turn on the forehand, explaining the aids.

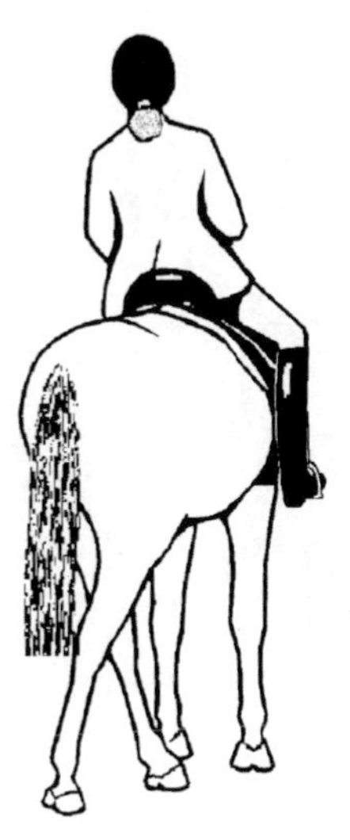

c. *The horse shuffles over but does not cross his hind legs. He may have too much neck bend.* The rider's inside leg may be clamped on in an attempt to make the horse step over, causing tension and stiffness. The rider's position may be incorrect, unlevel, the body leaning to one side.

Instruct the rider to use a firmer inside leg aid but in a series of nudges, nudge then release. Correct the position, seat and body level in the saddle. The horse may need a tap with the whip when the inside leg is used, to insist on obedience.

d. The horse spins round quickly, he may pivot on his inside foreleg. He falls out through his outside shoulder. The outside leg aid is not controlling the turn. The outside hand is not controlling the shoulder and forehand.

The rider needs to use the outside leg to control the speed of the turn. It may help if the whip is held in the outside hand. The rider could ask for two or three steps then walk the horse forward. Quality is better than quantity.

Leg yield

Leg yield is a lateral movement used to increase the horse's obedience to the rider's aids, to improve his straightness and suppleness. This movement increases the rider's 'feel' and understanding of the co-ordination of the aids.

Aims

The horse moves sideways diagonally on two tracks by crossing his inside fore in front of the outside fore and the inside hind in front of the outside hind. The horse should move forwards as well as sideways with impulsion. The horse's body is straight except for a *slight* flexion at the poll away from the direction of the movement. The horse's 'inside' is the side to which he is bent, in this case, away from the direction of travel.

Method

This movement can be performed at walk and trot. The rider can practise a couple of times in walk first. In trot the movement should ideally be in sitting trot except if the rider finds this difficult and it hinders the horse's movement.

Instruct the rider to ask for an active, forward going pace first. Explain that the horse needs to be straight in his body before starting the leg yield. This is important for a good sideways movement.

- ❖ Use half-halts to balance the horse.
- ❖ Sit straight and level in the saddle, shoulders and hands level.
- ❖ Look towards the direction of travel.
- ❖ Apply the inside leg (the leg away from the direction of travel) in the region of the girth, or just behind the girth if the horse has been taught this method.

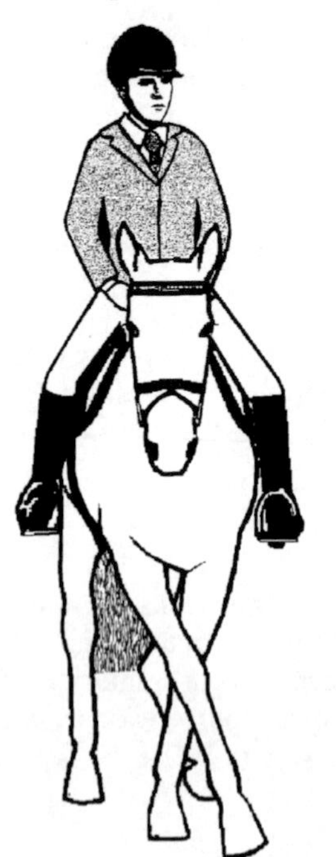

- ❖ Keep the outside leg in contact to ask for forward movement and to control the horse's hindquarters.
- ❖ With the inside rein ask for a slight flexion from the horse.
- ❖ Indicate the direction of travel with the outside hand by turning it over slightly almost as though the thumb is pointing towards the point of travel. Maintain the outside hand contact to control the flexion.

Ideally the aids should be applied independently but in co-ordination; the inside leg asks for sideways movement, then relaxes, the outside leg asks for forward movement, and relaxes. Though this may prove a little difficult for some, learning to apply an aid and then to release it, is a useful exercise.

Faults, causes and corrections

a. *The horse does not perform the leg yield but wanders across forehand first.* Poor preparation, the horse was not straight before the leg yield. Aids applied incorrectly.

Instruct the rider to prepare by riding the horse in a straight line before the movement. The rider then needs a firmer inside leg aid, perhaps slightly behind the girth to ask the horse to move his hindquarters across and a firmer outside hand to contain the shoulder. The rider should ask for two or three steps of leg yield then ride forwards. It is of more benefit if only a few steps of leg yield are performed at one time.

b. *The horse loses impulsion, shuffles across, stiffens, resists and becomes unbalanced.* Poor preparation: the horse lacks impulsion and energy. (Sometimes rising to the trot around the track and then sitting to the trot for the movement, is interpreted by the horse as a downward transition.) The rider may have tense thighs and knees; the legs may be clamped to the horse's sides restricting the horse's movement.

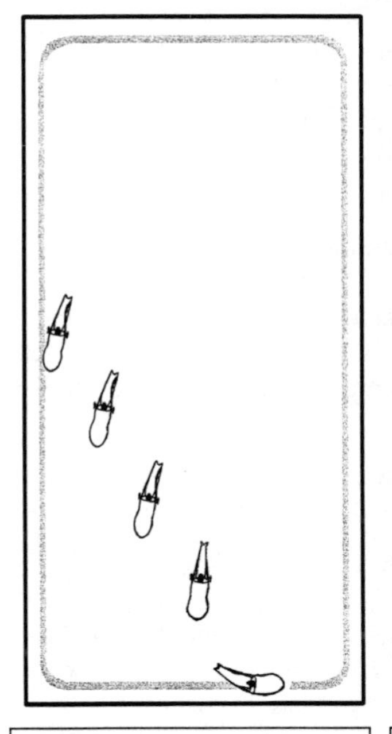

The horse is not straight, the rider may not be giving the correct aids; the horse wanders across without performing leg yield.

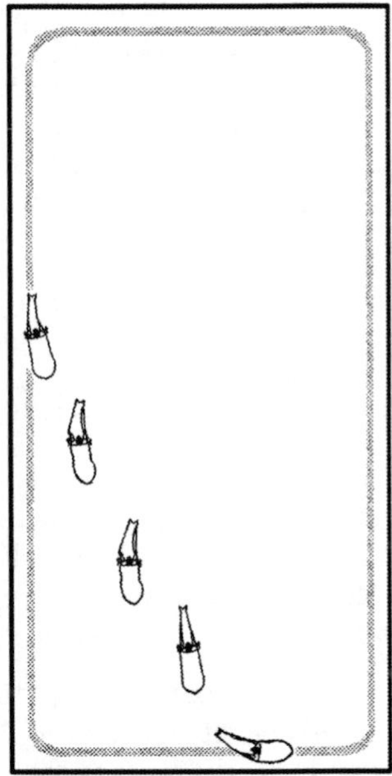

Again the horse is not straight, the rider's aids or position may be incorrect and the horse leads with his hindquarters.

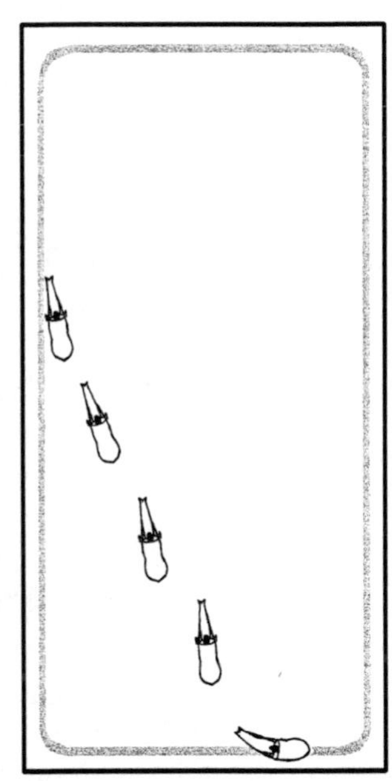

The horse is allowed to fall out through his outside shoulder. This results in making him crooked in the leg yield.

The riders are leaning first to the right to try and 'push' the horse across, then to the left to 'pull' the horse across. Both these incorrect seat positions interfere with the horse's balance and his movement.

The rider needs to create energy and activity before the turn into the straight line, then give a half-halt before the leg yield to balance the pace. The leg aids can be applied when changing to sitting trot. (The rider could rise to the trot through the movement, or take sitting trot earlier on the track.) The rider needs to relax the legs and apply the leg aids in a series of 'nudge and release'.

c. *The horse falls out through his outside shoulder or leads with the hindquarters.* The inside hand is too strong, creating too much bend. The outside hand is not controlling the shoulder. The outside leg aid is not controlling the hindquarters. The rider's body position may be unlevel and crooked either leaning away from or into the direction of travel. Leaning one way or another will unbalance the horse.

   Correct the rider's position first, seat straight and level in the saddle. Then, by using a slightly firmer outside hand, the rider can control the horse's outside shoulder. The rider may also bring his outside leg slightly forward to contain the shoulder.

Observing riders from behind whilst they are performing leg yield can show clearly if they are sitting straight and level in the saddle. From this viewpoint it will also be apparent if the horse is straight in the leg yield.

Teaching Tips

Turn on the forehand and leg yield are important movements because they introduce the rider to lateral work and to more advanced school movements. The rider learns about the effective use of the aids. The rider also begins to experience and understand how the body position really does influence the horse, his movement, balance and action.

When teaching these movements be clear and positive about teaching the aids and about the release of the aids after application. So many riders clamp the leg on, hold tightly with the reins in an attempt to perform the movements well. Release and relaxation are essential for the free movement of the horse. Take it slowly and make sure that the riders understand. It is better for riders to achieve one or two quality steps than try too hard and become tense.

Always check that the rider is sitting straight. One of the most common faults is that the rider leans to try and push or pull the horse into the movement.

Teach the aids every time you teach these movements, even if the riders state that they know how to ride turn on the forehand and leg yield. Many riders are not taught the aids through an assumption of knowledge on the instructor's part. Riders often will not admit to this lack of knowledge and struggle on, guessing and hoping for the best.

There is great achievement and reward in teaching a rider to successfully perform these lateral movements. For some riders lateral work is a mystery, try as they might, it just never quite works out. Take your time, and watch the rider's face as under your expert guidance the horse magically performs the movement.

CHAPTER 15
Equestrian Terms

Some of the concepts in equitation, whilst sounding simple, can be difficult to explain and teach, concepts such as straightness, impulsion and self-carriage. Many of the terms can also be difficult to understand through language, they need to be experienced.

This chapter describes these concepts in a practical, step by step way, to increase understanding.

The Horse

In this section the paces of the horse are described, the footfalls and how the horse should be working at a basic level in all three paces. Knowing how the horse moves, the basic principles of how he should work, the reasons for this and the influence the rider has on the horse through his own position, is the foundation of horsemanship.

The Paces

The three basic paces are the walk, the trot and the canter.

The Walk

- The walk is a four-time movement – (reading from right to left), left hind, left fore, right hand and right fore. The horse should show a clear rhythmical four-time beat.

❖ In medium walk the horse should carry himself in balance, working through from behind. He should be in front of the rider's leg accepting the rein contact, that is he should be moving actively forward, seeking the bit contact.

❖ In a free walk on a long rein, the horse moves forward with ground covering strides, over tracking. He should move through his shoulders, showing good foreleg movement. As the rider allows with the reins, the horse should stretch down to seek the contact.

The Trot

❖ The trot is a two-time movement – one diagonal pair fore and hind, and the other diagonal pair fore and hind, with a moment of suspension in between. The horse should maintain a rhythmical two-time beat.

❖ In working trot the horse pushes himself forward from the hindquarters using his hocks actively. The hindlegs should step underneath the body creating a roundness through the back and a supple swing to the steps. The shoulders should move freely, with the horse seeking and accepting the rein contact.

❖ When shortening or lengthening the stride (working towards collected and medium trot) the rhythm of the trot should remain the same. The horse when shortening will cover less ground but have more elevation (height) to the steps, when lengthening the horse covers more ground by stretching throughout his frame.

The Canter

❖ The canter is a three-time movement – outside hind, diagonal pair outside fore and inside hind and then the 'leading leg', the inside fore and a moment of suspension. The horse should maintain a consistent three time beat.

- In this pace the horse pushes himself forward from the hindquarters with the hocks coming underneath the body. The pace should be active, feel upwards and forwards, with a roundness through the horse's back. He should be accepting the rein contact.

- The canter stride can also be shortened or lengthened (working towards collected and medium canter). When shortening, the stride should show more lift and cover less ground. When lengthening, the stride covers more ground with the horse stretching through his frame.

To achieve these ideals the riders need to know the basics of straightness, balance, rhythm, suppleness and impulsion. The definitions that follow will help when teaching the rider these terms, explaining how they are achieved and how they should feel.

Straightness

Basically the straightness of a horse refers to the 'line' following his spine from poll to tail.

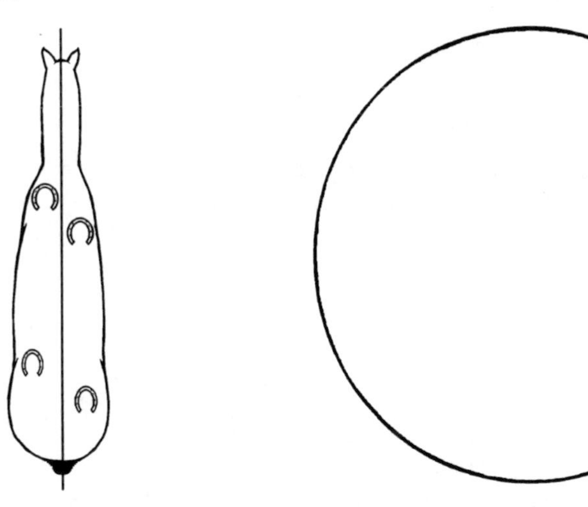

- When working on straight lines the horse's spine should be relatively straight.

- When working on curved lines the horse's spine should be uniformly bent, that is curved like the arc of a circle without any deviation at any point. The hindlegs should follow the same line as the forelegs.

Straightness is so fundamental to working the horse correctly, to achieving balance, rhythm and pace, that the rider should be taught to understand straightness first.

The rider does need the ability to judge the horse's straightness and to ask the horse to work with a regular, constant line from poll to tail.

As the horse is more flexible in the neck area and less so along his spine, he finds it easier to bend through his neck.

Here the horse is working crooked in the canter. His hindquarters are to the left. This has been exaggerated to clearly show the horse's crookedness.

If the horse is allowed to compromise his straightness, work crookedly, he will not be in balance and without balance there is no rhythm.

More importantly, over time, he will not be able to develop muscular equality; he will then find it more difficult to be 'straight'.

These diagrams show how the horse can be crooked.

The horse's hindquarters are swinging to the left.

On the circle the horse's right shoulder is falling out and there is too much neck bend.

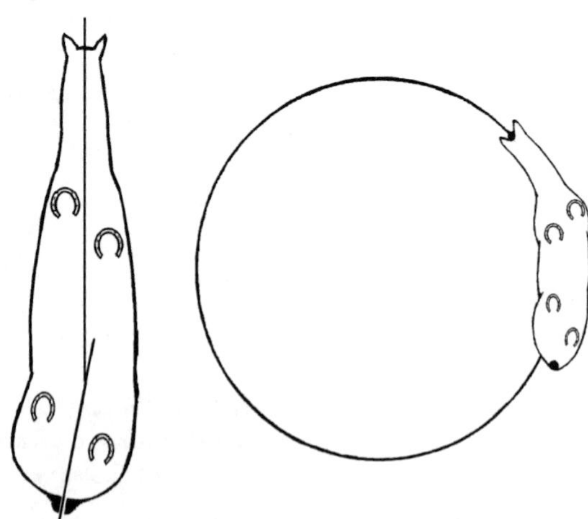

Straightness can be a difficult concept to teach and understand yet it is the key to balance, rhythm and impulsion.

Here again the horse is working crooked in the canter. The hindquarters are swinging in to the right.

Exercises for Teaching Straightness

The rider's position is important as it affects the horse's straightness. Straightness is achieved by the rider sitting level in the saddle and in balance, and through the co-ordinated use of the leg and hand aids.

When teaching straightness certain exercises are used to help the rider increase his understanding and feel, and to encourage the horse to be straight.

Leg yield - this exercise helps the rider to understand straightness, how the rider's position affects the horse and how to use the aids in co-ordination.

Straight lines - riding down the centre line, the three-quarter line, the long diagonal or on an inner track can increase the rider's awareness of the horse's straightness or crookedness and the aids required to correct the horse.

Shallow loops down long sides - changing the bend of the horse through his body, increases straightness by helping the horse to work evenly.

Teach the rider to recognise the difference between the horse's softer and stiffer sides. Begin work, if possible, on the horse's softer side so that he can warm up and loosen without tension or strain.

Balance

There are two types of balance, that of the rider and that of the horse.

❖ **The rider is in balance when he or she has sufficient suppleness to adapt to the horse's change of gravity with an independent seat.**

Through instruction and practice the rider develops the ability to maintain a balanced position whilst allowing the movement of the horse through changes of pace or direction. If the rider loses this position, needs to maintain security by holding onto the reins or by gripping tightly with the leg, then true balance has not been achieved.

- **A horse is in balance when he carries himself and his rider so that he can move with maximum ease and efficiency.**

  Young horses learn their own natural balance, then, when they are backed, they must learn to balance themselves and a rider. This is achieved through correct training and developing the right muscles.

Exercises for Teaching Balance

Transitions - all transitions should be smooth and steady. The rider needs to maintain the rhythm of the pace (using the leg aids) then balance the horse (with half-halts) before the transition. Transitions can be markedly improved by this preparation of balance. Any loss of balance will be apparent, particularly in downward transitions.

Circles - the horse needs to work without 'falling into' or 'leaning out of' the circle. The rider needs to assess his own position first, if he is leaning in or out of the circle and influencing the horse.

Rhythm

Rhythm is a regularity of beat; an evenness of footfalls. Each pace has a sequence in which the feet touch the ground; for instance, walk is a 1-2-3-4 beat. This 'beat' should be a constant and regular rhythm.

Rhythm is important within a pace. A horse should maintain his rhythm as this keeps the horse and rider in balance. An inconsistent, changing rhythm throws the rider and horse out of balance.

Exercises for Teaching Rhythm

Pole work is an excellent method of teaching the rider to feel rhythm. The horse's walk and trot are more pronounced over poles.

Counting - the rider may call out the footfalls in all three paces, checking the regularity of the beat.

Music is a great medium for checking rhythm. The rider can even discover how his own rhythm influences the horse.

Tempo and Speed

Tempo is the speed of the footfalls. The tempo of a pace should be constant, not irregular or changing. If the horse is in balance the tempo of the pace will be constant.

To distinguish between rhythm and tempo think of a piece of music; this will have a regular beat or rhythm, 1 2 3 4 or 1 2 --- 1 2. The tempo is the speed at which this rhythm is played, either slower or faster.

Speed is the rate at which the horse moves, the kilometres per hour at which the horse travels in any pace. Speed is often confused with impulsion; moving at a fast speed is often mistaken for activity.

Exercises for Teaching Tempo

Pole work - by slightly decreasing or increasing the distance between the poles the horse should maintain his rhythm but change the tempo.

Shortening and lengthening of stride - on the long sides of the school, between the quarter markers, ask the rider to count the number of steps the horse takes and then to alter this number. For instance, if the horse does ten trot steps between K and H, increase this to eleven, twelve or more for shortening; decrease to nine, eight or less for lengthening. The rider should maintain the same rhythm throughout.

Impulsion

This is 'controlled energy'; it should not be confused with speed. Speed may be energy but unless it is controlled by the rider's aids, this energy is lost.

Impulsion begins in the hindquarters with the horse using his muscles to build up the energy to push his body forwards. This energy is asked for by the rider with the legs and contained by the rider's body and seat, legs and hands. At the same time the horse (via the rider) maintains his straightness, balance and rhythm.

The horse achieving impulsion will be going forward actively and vigorously with his steps showing elasticity. He may even feel as if he is moving more 'slowly' but with extra push and elevation.

Exercises for Teaching Impulsion

Transitions - upward and downward transitions performed frequently, for instance 6 steps of walk, 6 of trot and 6 of walk again, or walk to halt to trot, encourages the horse to respond to the rider's aids, use his hindquarters. The transitions need to be ridden well with the horse going forward but the energy contained.

Shortening and lengthening of stride - these are transitions within one pace and will also develop impulsion.

Suppleness

Suppleness is the ability to flex or bend within the body. It is also the ability to move the limbs in relation to the rest of the body. The horse with a supple back will be able to move freely through his shoulders, have a lightness in the forehand and bring his hind legs underneath his body. He will have the ability to do lateral work taking his legs across, under and then away from his body.

Both the horse and the rider need suppleness or physical flexibility to work efficiently and correctly. Correct training and exercise achieve suppleness.

Though some (and not just older) riders and horses may find suppleness more difficult to achieve and maintain, this is quite possible with constant and regular exercise.

Exercises for Teaching Suppleness

Circles and turns - helps to keep the horse's back supple. Circles in alternate directions, or half circles, for instance, one circle to the left immediately followed by one to the right as in a figure of eight. Shallow loops and serpentines help to increase suppleness.

Pole work - keeps the horse's joints (hips, hocks, elbows and knees) supple.

Leg yield and turn on the forehand - increases suppleness throughout the horse's body.

Forwardness

Forwardness is a willingness and ability to move in a free forward movement covering the ground. This type of energy is essential to achieve impulsion and balance. The horse literally needs to be 'thinking' forwards, even in lateral movement.

Exercises for Teaching Forwardness

Variety in schoolwork - hacking out, jumping, lungeing, increases the horse's forward thinking and movement.

Lengthening stride - lengthened trot and canter can encourage forward movement.

Also the rider needs to be 'forward thinking'. When the rider looks up and in front of the horse, this helps the horse to be more forward.

Self-carriage

A horse is in self-carriage when he is sufficiently balanced to carry himself and the rider with ease at all paces without having to rely on support, or lean on the rider's hands. This is achieved through training, physical and mental development, discipline, considerate riding, knowledge, straightness, balance, rhythm and harmony.

Outline

The horse is in a correct outline when he moves forward freely, with the hindquarters, loins, back and shoulders free and supple. His neck arches from the withers and his face is carried just in front of the vertical. He will move with a swinging action, his limbs coming through and forward easily.

Self-carriage and outline are the results of all the other points put together; the rider's position and posture, the use of the aids, straightness, balance, rhythm and tempo, suppleness, impulsion and forward thinking (both horse and rider). Achieve these (simple!!!) and the horse should carry himself in a rounded, supple outline.

Teaching Tips

Most of the equestrian terms mentioned could be explained in much more detail, but part of the skill of teaching is to give clear and concise explanations so that the riders understand the concept first. It is through progress, when riders begin to experience for themselves and learn to 'feel', that these concepts can be understood in greater depth.

Teaching is the first step towards experience, experience creates comprehension and comprehension develops into practice and consequently improvement.

CHAPTER 16
Horses

In any Equestrian Centre or Riding School the horses are the most important part of the business. Depending on the yard's main trade, the horses will differ in standard and type. Most schools have a variety to suit different riders at various levels and to cater for the different disciplines, show jumping, eventing, dressage, students training towards their qualifications, and hacking.

Horse Management

This subject covers the organisation and care of the school horse and pony; choosing a suitable type, maintaining his care and health, and organising his workload to keep him physically and mentally fit.

Qualities

School horses need certain qualities.

- Have a good temperament; be sensible and steady.
- Have good manners in and out of the box (if the horse does have slight problems, providing he is not dangerous or aggressive, this can teach pupils and staff how to handle different horses).
- Have the tack put on and taken off without much fuss.
- Lead well out of the stable and in hand.
- Stand still whilst being mounted (or can be taught to do so).
- Sensitive and responsive to the rider's aids.
- Fairly forward going ideally, though slower horses can teach riders to use their aids more positively.
- Ideally should be capable of working in a snaffle - though having horses who are ridden in different bridles, such as a Pelham or Bitless bridle, does increase the rider's experience. If the horse can also work in a double bridle this is a bonus.
- Capable of being lunged: particularly those horses suitable for teaching adults on the lunge.

Types

The Centre should consider the type of service they wish to give. Whether they wish to concentrate on beginner riders or whether they will cater more for hacking. They may wish to offer BHS Examination courses and may be an Examination Centre. The Centre may want to cater for more advanced riders in dressage, eventing or show jumping, perhaps with the emphasis on competing. Most Centres, whilst catering for a variety of skills, will need to decide on their main priority. Only the larger establishments can successfully offer a wide scope of horses for all.

Depending on the clientele, and this may differ in various parts of the country, the type and variety of horses will need to be carefully considered.

Most Centres will be catering for adult group and private lessons, children's lessons and hacking. Certain types of horse and pony will make up the bulk of the riding stock and be suitable for most clients.

- The backbone of any riding school is the cob; they tend to be hardy, tough and steady, useful for beginners and novices up to intermediate level. Cobs can be schooled to quite a high standard for the advanced rider when they can be a joy to ride. Ranging from 14 to 15.2 hands catering for teenagers, most lady riders and lighter weight men. Types can be the Welsh Cob, Dale, Highland, Connemara, Fell.

- Part thoroughbred or Arab types. Not as hardy as cobs, but can be schooled to a high standard. Lighter in frame and normally more forward going with a more sensitive temperament, this type of horse gives the rider a different feel and variety. Can be used for intermediate riders, lessons or hacks up to advanced level for well-schooled horses. Usually 15 to 16 hands in height useful for larger teenagers, lady riders and lighter weight men. Types Anglo-Arab, Cob x TB (Thoroughbred).

- Thoroughbred x Irish Draught or Cleveland Bay. Around 16 to 17 hands catering for larger adults, these horses are usually useful for show jumping and cross-country, for novice lessons up to intermediate/advanced level for well-schooled horses and for hacking. Types: ID (Irish Draught) x TB, Cleveland Bay, Cleveland Bay x TB, Shire x TB or pure Thoroughbred.

- Ponies are created in all shapes and sizes, and in many breeds. Ponies in a Riding Centre need to be strong, sensible, fairly quiet and steady. They should be capable of being led on the lead rein and working with other ponies. Types range from the Shetland (may be head strong at times) around 11 hands, Welsh Mountain around 12 hands, Dartmoor and Exmoor around 13 hands, New Forest around 13 hands; Fell, Dale and Connemara around 14 hands and any cross-bred up to 14.2.

These will be the basis of the school horses and ponies. Depending on the focus of the Establishment other types of horses may be required. For dressage and flatwork: ex-dressage horses, medium and advanced up to ex-Grand Prix - normally Warm bloods, Dutch, Danish, British and cross Thoroughbreds. For jumping: ex-show jumpers Grade A or B or ex-eventers - normally ID x TB, British Warm bloods or pure Thoroughbreds.

Note: every Centre should always be looking to improve their standards for any discipline. This is important because the regular clientele will be improving and will eventually wish to ride horses of a higher standard. This policy will also encourage other new clients, possibly those who own their own horses, who wish to train on a schoolmaster at a higher level.

Ages

The horses and ponies can vary in age, older animals tend to be steadier, more reliable but can be stiff and take more time to work in. Younger horses can be more sensitive, lack schooling but offer a variety in the work force and give a freer, more supple feel in paces. The ages will vary from 4 or 5 years olds up to those in their late teens and twenties.

Availability of Horses

There are various ways in which the school can build up its reserve of horses and ponies.

- Young horses to be trained for the Centre or possibly sold on.
- Ex-dressage, ex-eventers, ex-racehorses and ex-show jumpers.
- Loan horses - competition horses who are older or who have a slight physical problem.
- Working liveries.
- Older horses and ponies of good quality - schoolmasters and mistresses.

Though a variety of horses are available, the Centre should be strict in its choice of type and temperament. An important part of a Centre's reputation lies in its stock of horses. No matter how good the instruction and facilities, if all the horses are old, stiff, constantly unlevel, aggressive, temperamental, difficult to ride, the clients will be deterred. Reputations are soon tarnished.

Also if the Centre constantly takes on horses who are physically unable to cope, this will result in loss of revenue with the horses off work and high Vet's fees.

Unsuitable Types

There are some horses who may not be suited to a Riding School environment either because of their temperament and conformation or because they are the wrong type of horses for the Centre's clientele.

- Any horse or pony who is dangerously aggressive, naps, has too sensitive a temperament or is unpredictable. Any horse or pony who may be considered a danger to a client. Some horses with problems can improve within a school environment providing they do not have a behavioural problem that is either dangerous or ingrained.

- No school wants to spoil their reputation or be sued, because of a horse who bucks, rears, bites, kicks, naps or bolts. There will always be a risk because horses and ponies are living creatures and behave unpredictably at times, but to put someone at risk when the horse is known to be dangerous is negligence.

Preservation of Horses

It is more economically viable to maintain the horse's health, his standard of work and his mental well being. The horses working within the Centre need to be maintained at a certain level, if possible, even improved.

1. Diet - should be suitable for the type of horse, the amount and type of work and the level of riders.
2. Should have days off, at least one a week, and an annual holiday ideally spending this time out at grass.
3. Should be schooled regularly, to preserve physical condition, muscular form, quality of paces, ability and standard.
4. Each horse should be ridden regularly by good riders.
5. Variety of work - in the school, hacking, jumping, outside in the menage, the field or cross-country, regular lungeing (without rider) keeps the horse fit and supple. Keeping the work varied prevents staleness, boredom, bad habits, bad behaviour and eventually physical illness.
6. The riders should be suitable for the horses; height and weight ratio: should match the rider to the appropriate horse. Too heavy a rider can injure a horse's back.
7. Amount and type of work should suit their breeding, temperament and ability.
8. Good stable management - proper grooming, foot care, stable and field conditions, clean bedding, careful handling, clean, properly fitting tack in good condition, clean rugs and boots.
9. Routine - though more difficult in a Centre because of client demand, the feed and hay times should be as constant as possible.
10. Health - regular inoculations, worming, worming procedures and prompt attention if injured or ill.
11. Regular visits from the blacksmith - correct shoeing.
12. Good instruction - essential for the horse's well being and preserving his standard. A good instructor will be able to maintain and even improve both riders and the horses.

Some horses suit school life and, providing their ability and health is maintained, continue to grow and thrive in this environment. Ideally though no horse should spend all his life in a Riding Centre. Some horses do not suit the life at all and these are better sold on to one owner where they will enjoy life more.

It is also advantageous to have a constant turnover of good horses, this adds variety for the clients, gives them the opportunity of experiencing different horses at different levels.

All the horses and ponies need to be monitored carefully and any attention required given promptly. The Yard Manager and instructors need to be knowledgeable about the health of the horses.

The Centre's jumping horses in particular need looking after, they generally have to take more strain and good jumping horses are often more difficult to find than flatwork horses.

As the essence of the Riding Centre, the horses and ponies need careful managing. Time spent on caring, handling and looking after them will be repaid not just in monetary gain but also in knowing that they are physically and mentally well and happy.

Horses Workload

The horses and ponies need regular work, being under-worked can be just as detrimental as being over-worked. As well as the timetable for lessons, clients and instructors, the Centre will normally have another chart showing how many hours per day each horse and pony works.

Most horses should work from one hour to a maximum of two hours in the school per day or three to four hours hacking only. This can and should be varied; for instance a horse could do one hour in the school and one hour hacking. Some horses and ponies will need slightly more work; these may work for two hours in the school and one hour hacking.

The amount of work does vary with individual horses. Some thrive on three to four hours a day, some wilt after one or two hours. Weather conditions too can effect the work periods. In hot weather horses may sweat and tire more easily.

Horses that are continuously worked too long every day though, will eventually become tired, stale or ill. It is wiser to keep the workload constant at a rate that keeps the horses and ponies well exercised but healthy.

Grading System for Horses

In most Centres the horses (and ponies) are graded by standards, levels and abilities. Grading by size of horse to weight-carrying capacity ensures correct allocation of rider to horse.

- For example - P1 smallest pony through to P5 largest pony for children and small adults, HL1 small light horse (Arab) to HL5 largest light horse (Thoroughbred) and HH1 for small heavy horses (cobs) to HH5 for largest heavy horse (Shire or Shire cross). A heavy lady or a tall, light man would then be put on HH4 or 5. In most Centres each horse and pony is known and a suitable rider will be chosen for them.

- The horses will also need grading for quality and standard. There will be the better horses capable of a standard Stage III, IV or above, ex-Grand Prix horses, Grade A and B jumpers for the better riders. The top-level horses may be used solely in private or semi-private lessons, for the students or qualified clients.

- There will be the hacking horses and the solid school horses who can be used for beginners and novices.

Any horse will benefit from being ridden by better riders for a period. The better horses should be schooled by the instructors regularly to maintain their level of work.

Work Timetable

One vital part of the organisation of the Centre is communication; *the information from the office needs to be passed efficiently onto the yard and staff.*

A list is placed in the yard so that the relevant horses are prepared in time, instructors can see what lessons they are giving and where, the yard routines can be carried out with regard to lessons and hacks taking place.

If this communication between office and yard breaks down or does not give current information, for example a late booking, the efficiency of the yard will deteriorate. Horses will not be prepared, lessons will run late and clients will be inconvenienced. A horse may even have been fed and not available for the client concerned.

The office staff, the teaching staff, the Yard Manager and the yard staff all need to work together to ensure maximum efficiency, to maintain the Centre's standards and to preserve the health and happiness of the horses and ponies in their care.

Obtaining a good stock of horses and ponies requires a large investment in finance and time. This stock is also the essence of the riding establishment. All the horses and ponies therefore need careful management to keep them healthy, happy in their work and an asset to the Centre.

Example of work timetable:

08.00	Robert	P/L 1 hour	Eeyore	Paul Turner
08.30	Jean	P/L ½ hour	Douglas	Margaret Heritage
09.00	Robert	G/L 1 hour	Oscar	Sophie Reed
			Monrush	Stephen Jones
			Murphy	Caroline Church
			Buster	Sarah Goodall
09.30	Philly	P/L ½ hour	Foley	Fiona Jones
10.00	Jean	S/M 1 hour		Rhoda Phillips
11.00	James	Staff Jump 1 hour	Sovereign	Ian Spalding
			Rufus	Alison Phillips
			Foxy Lady	Dave Thomson
			Harry	Tracey Humphries
			Bella	Diane Salt

Teaching Tips

One of the most essential duties in a riding centre is to keep the horses and ponies healthy and fit. Observe all the horses and ponies when you teach and assess their quality of work. Being able to assess when a horse is unsound, unlevel or ill is vital.

Teach to improve the horses as well as the riders. Sometimes it is difficult when riders need to learn; the horses have to cater for a variety of standards and at times endure bad riding. Having a rota, where better riders in the more advanced classes periodically work the horses and ponies, is a benefit to the yard, pupils and teaching staff.

It is the responsibility of the yard manager, staff and instructors to ensure that all the horses and ponies are kept physically and mentally in good health. Horse management is a practical subject; the horses and ponies are the essence and foundation of every Riding Centre and School.

Section Two

The Preliminary Teaching Test

CHAPTER 17
General Information

To be successful in the Preliminary Teaching Test, candidates need to show that they are capable of teaching and improving pupils in a safe and competent manner. Teaching, for some, is a natural gift and enjoyable, others find it more difficult and a little daunting. With good preparation and practice, with knowledge of the techniques, every candidate can increase their ability and enter the Preliminary Teaching Test with confidence.

Eligibility

All applicants for the Preliminary Teaching Test must

- be a member of the BHS at the time of application and taking the Test
- have passed their Stage II Riding and Horse Knowledge & Care
- be 18* years of age

* Candidates can take this Test at 17½ years if they also hold four GCSE subjects at Grade A, B, C or equivalent. One of these must be English Language or English Literature. Proof of age and academic qualifications must be sent with the application form.

The Syllabus

Each candidate will be required to **teach a group lesson**, give a short **lecture** (lecturette), show **theoretical** and **practical knowledge of equitation and of business practices** and either teach an adult on the **lunge** or a child on the **lead rein**.

Theory Candidates need a general knowledge of theoretical and practical subjects such as basic equitation, organisation of a commercial yard, safety and accident procedures for a lesson, for a hack in the country and on the Public Highway.

Lecturette Candidates should be capable of giving a short lecturette on a subject suitable for the standard of Horse Knowledge & Care Stage II, Riding Club Grade II or Pony Club Test C.

Group Lesson

Candidates should have the ability to organise a group of 3 or 4 riders showing a progressive plan throughout the lesson. They should be capable of teaching the principles of equitation up to Stage II standard working towards Stage III and improve the pupils' horsemanship on the flat and over jumps.

Lunge/Lead Rein

Candidates should have the ability to teach a suitable lunge or a lead rein lesson for a beginner/novice adult or child.

Candidates may teach in an indoor school or outside menage. Ground poles or jumps may be included in the group lesson and will be made available for use.

There is also an underlying criterion to show that candidates are able to build a rapport with pupils, deal confidently with any problems that may arise and gain their pupils' trust.

General Preparation

The important aspect of this Test is the **prior preparation and practice**. Candidates need to allow sufficient time for preparation. This should be months rather than weeks, possibly as much as six months.

Those who suddenly decide to do a 'crash course' a couple of weeks before the Test will find it difficult to be successful, or enter the Test feeling nervous through a lack of knowledge and practice.

Some candidates may have teaching experience prior to the Exam, possibly at their own establishment or at a livery yard. Whilst this type of teaching practice is useful and commendable, this should not make candidates complacent. It is a different situation teaching unknown riders on unfamiliar horses in strange surroundings with Examiners making assessments.

Candidates should receive instruction for the PTT from a qualified BHS instructor, a BHSII or BHSI if possible. The instructors should then be familiar with the current requirements, the format and standards required.

Preparing at a BHS Approved Riding Establishment will also help the candidate become familiar with the words of command and the methods of organising lessons within an educational environment. Without qualified supervision candidates may lack the knowledge to teach the correct basics of equitation or be limited in their comprehension of safety.

If candidates can study at the Centre where they plan to take the Test, this would be an added bonus. They will gain experience of the venue, the schools, the horses, ponies and lungeing equipment. If this is not feasible, candidates may find it useful to arrange at least a few practice sessions at the Test Centre.

The knowledge of the theoretical subjects comes through study, attending lectures and personal experience. The actual physical teaching and lecturing; voice control, the commands, control of a group, teaching a person on the lunge or lead rein comes from study, practice and observation; that is watching and assessing lessons.

Candidates, having mastered the basic elements of teaching, should practise whenever possible. It is essential to become familiar with the school, the letters, the best areas to perform school figures; to lunge various riders, teach children and develop the ability to organise lessons efficiently, correctly and, most importantly, with safety.

Where to Train

Preliminary Teaching courses are normally offered at establishments where the Test is held; BHS Examination Centres, Approved Riding Schools or Agricultural Colleges. Qualified BHS instructors can offer lessons or courses at other establishments, riding schools, or by freelancing at livery or competition yards.

The courses include techniques for teaching, theoretical information, the organisation of groups, the structure of lessons, teaching practice in a school for both adults and children.

Working pupils may receive tuition as part of their qualification course and should be given the opportunity to practise teaching different classes under qualified supervision; groups, adults, children, beginners, lunge and lead rein lessons.

BHS Examination Structure

The Preliminary Teaching Test can either be taken before or after the Stage III Examination. Some training establishments prefer the students to pass their Stage III before taking the Preliminary Teaching Test.

Once candidates have passed both the PTT and the Stage III Riding and Horse Knowledge & Care they will gain the Preliminary Teacher qualification, BHSPT. This qualifies them as a Trainee Teacher.

Preliminary Teachers can apply for membership of the Register of Instructors providing they have a current Health and Safety Executive First Aid at Work certificate. Membership includes freelance insurance as well as inclusion in the BHS Register of Instructors book.

To obtain the Assistant Instructor qualification, Preliminary Teachers complete a BHS Log Book to show that they have a specific number of hours of practical teaching experience. Those who teach at BHS 'Where to train' centres (listed in the 'Where to train' book) need 250 hours, those who teach at BHS Approved Riding Schools need 350 hours, whilst those teaching at other establishments need 500 hours.

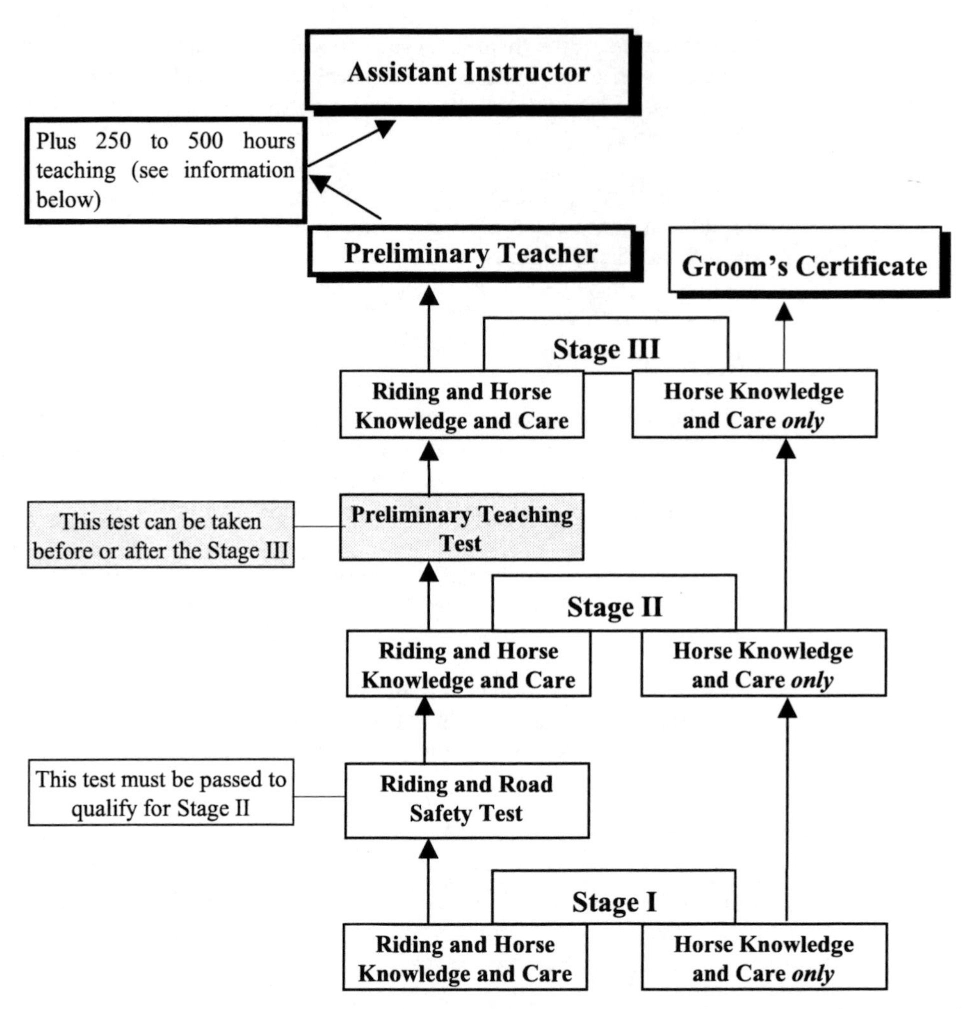

Freelance instructors, teaching at various centres, are able to count the appropriate hours when they teach at a 'Where to train' or 'Approved Riding Centre'. The teaching should include practical teaching and stable management lessons. Additionally some of the hours required can be offset by attending courses given by the British Horse Society or the 'Training the Teachers of Tomorrow'. This rule is reviewed periodically; for instance instructors over a certain age may now be exempt. Check the rules with the BHS when making the application for the AI certificate.

Some people are naturally enthusiastic, confident and competent in their teaching techniques. Others may find that teaching, lecturing a group or relating to children is unfamiliar and difficult. All candidates though, however capable, will need tuition, practice and experience to develop their skills in the variety of different types of teaching featured in the Preliminary Teaching Test.

CHAPTER 18
Theory

As well as covering subjects such as teaching and types of lessons, the Theory Section of the PTT includes general business management, dealing with clients, office duties, the management and welfare of school horses.

General Business Management

Learning about the basic organisation of an office is useful, not only on a theoretical basis, but also in practical terms. It may be necessary to run the office or reception area, even on a temporary basis. Alternatively, once qualified, the plan may include managing or running a yard.

Office management

- How to deal with clients.
- Introducing a new client to the school.
- Answering the telephone.
- Information required from a new client.
- How to keep clients.
- Client records.

The standard of an Equitation Centre depends on many aspects - the efficiency of the reception and office area, facilities for clients, quality of the staff and public relations, that is, how clients are welcomed and treated. The quality, variety and condition of the horses are important, amenities for school work, hacking and stable management, the cleanliness, atmosphere, and organisation of the yard.

New Clients

For any potential new client, first impressions are extremely important; from this they will base their assessment of the establishment.

Most new custom comes via the telephone; it is vital that clients receive a pleasant, efficient and welcoming answer. When answering the phone the receptionist should speak clearly, give the name of the establishment and possibly his or her own name.

Even existing clients can be discouraged by an unpleasant or inefficient reception on the telephone and even more so if the phone is allowed to ring continuously before being answered (or in some cases not answered at all). An answering machine is a useful item, but even this can be discouraging if used consistently.

It is important, with potential new clients, that the necessary information is given to and received from them. This is required by the instructor concerned and for those organising the horses so that the client is treated with efficiency and encouraged to return for another booking.

Information to give to a Potential Client

The conversation may proceed as follows:

'Good morning, this is X School of Equitation, Ann speaking, how may I help you?'

'I'm thinking of booking some lessons (or hacks) with you, could you please give me some information about your school?'

Information to give:

- Type of establishment and standard, a BHS approved or Examination Centre.
- Level to which pupils can be trained (BHSPT, BHSII, or BHSI - beginners to novice, intermediate or advanced).
- Qualifications of instructors.
- Types and standards of lessons or hacks.
- Times of opening during the week and weekend.
- Price range.
- Payment is required in advance (by cheque or credit card).
- Any cancellation policy, for example a 50% cancellation fee if cancelled within 24 hours.
- New clients may require an assessment lesson first.

Assessment Policy

An assessment policy is important especially for a busy yard and possibly more so when hacking is the main proportion of the service offered.

Most prospective clients accept an assessment policy especially if this is mentioned from the start. The Centre may or may not decide to charge for this. It is the policy in many Centres to book a new client into a half-hour private assessment lesson.

If a particular client refuses (and there may be one who, as an 'experienced' rider, does not believe in being assessed) the receptionist may state calmly and firmly that this is the Centre's policy. It is necessary for insurance purposes, to ensure the client's safety and welfare, and to enable the Centre to give him a suitable horse.

Alternatively the clients may be staying in a local hotel for one night and may wish simply to purchase a hack. The assessment could be organised as a quarter of an hour immediately before the hack and included in the price quoted. For a Centre that caters for hacking, even a ten minute assessment in an outdoor school is a good policy. There may be the client who needs to be led on the hack or even one who is frightened of horses.

Information from a Potential Client

To enable the client to be given a suitable horse or pony and for the client's record, the following information will be required:

- Name, address and contact telephone number during the day.
- Is the rider an adult or child? If a child or teenager ask for the age.
- Height and weight.
- Riding experience, level and any exams they may have taken.
- If they have not ridden for some time how long a gap since riding previously?
- Aims and ambitions, whether they wish to improve through lessons, take exams or simply hack out. (They may not know exactly how far they wish to progress but they may know if they want lessons to improve themselves.)
- If the client requires a lesson on their own horse, details will be required about the horse, his temperament, level of schooling, any competition experience, whether he has worked in a school previously or with other horses if this is a group lesson.
- If the rider has any medical problems such as a bad back.
- The most convenient times for them to ride (depending on availability of lessons or hacks at the Centre).
- Payment in advance - credit card details.
- Riding equipment - if they have the correct clothing.

Riding Equipment

The client themselves may ask, but certainly the Centre should request, if they have the correct riding equipment and clothing.

- Riding hat: the correct specified standard. At present this the PAS 015 or an EN 1384. The hat must have a harness and fit correctly.
- Boots - either long riding boots or jodhpur boots. Other boots are suitable providing they have a smooth sole and a heel. Boots should be high enough to protect the ankle.
- Gloves to prevent rubbing around the fingers.
- A jacket, if worn, should be capable of being fastened properly.

- Jodhpurs or loose fitting trousers, leggings or track suit bottoms. Denim trousers are normally quite tight and have a thick seam on the inside of the leg, which can cause sores. The trousers should be thick enough to prevent rubbing or chafing.
- Body protectors are an excellent idea, essential when jumping and advisable when hacking, especially for children. As most new clients or temporary riders will not have a body protector, the Centre could possibly lend these or provide them for hire.
- No jewellery apart from a wedding ring, which will normally be covered by gloves.

Ideally the client should be informed about wearing jewellery before arriving for their ride. If the client forgets or does not realise that they are wearing unsuitable jewellery such as large earrings, they should be informed politely that jewellery is unsafe and asked to remove it. They could lock it in their own car or it may be placed in the office safe until after their ride. There should be no compromise on this policy. If a client has her ear ripped or torn apart by accident they could sue the Establishment for failing to inform them of the dangers.

Hiring Equipment

Most Centres will have hats and possibly boots for hire. The Centre could have a policy whereby a voucher is given when a client hires a hat or boots. These vouchers could then be put towards buying this equipment (from the Centre shop).

When hiring out a hat or body protector this must be checked for correct fit. The hat should fit snugly. With the harness unfastened, the rider should be able to tilt his head without the hat falling off. Another check can be made by moving the hat backwards and forwards over the rider's head. The hat should move only slightly. The rider should not feel that the hat is too tight, pressing on the temples or side of the head. The harness should fit correctly and fasten easily.

Body protectors should fit correctly, snugly enough to prevent excess movement of the protector but not too tight to restrict the rider's movements.

Whatever the policy, the client should be encouraged to purchase their own equipment if they are to take up riding on a regular basis. Clients should buy a hat within six to eight weeks after starting to ride. With children, who grow out of expensive boots and hats quickly, equipment could be purchased approximately within eight to ten weeks, if they are still enthusiastic.

Further Information for the Client

Once the client has decided to book a lesson or hack they will need some further details.

- Directions to the stables; the Centre could send a leaflet or brochure that includes a small route map.

- The client should be advised to arrive at least 10 minutes before the start of the ride; this time can be used, if necessary, to hire and fit the riding equipment.
- Name of the instructor, if known.

Encouraging Regular Clientele

New clients will always be essential to any commercial Centre but it is the regular clients who are the backbone of any business. Especially if these clients can be persuaded to book two or more lessons or hacks each week and take part in other Centre activities such as competitions, special hacks or events.

The first priority is to make sure that the client is always treated with politeness and friendliness.

- The lessons should start punctually.
- The client should have the same instructor if possible. There are advantages in being taught by different instructors at times, new instructors will possibly notice different faults, they may have alternative methods of teaching that suit the rider, may teach different subjects. The client though, especially a beginner, needs to build up a rapport and feel at ease with one instructor at first.
- The horse should be ready, tacked up, with bandages or boots if necessary. At some establishments the staff bring the horse to the customer; this makes the customer feel special.
- The lesson should be the full time booked. The instructor should spend time with each client in group lessons. The client should have the standard of hack or lesson for which they are suited.
- All the staff should be polite and friendly.
- The standard of the school should be maintained in quality of teaching, atmosphere and appearance.
- Complaints should be dealt with professionally. A client should never be left to complain loudly in the yard or reception but taken into an office or quiet place away from others. Some Centres have a comment box in which clients can place a completed form.
- Regular clients should be treated just as well as new clients. These are the customers a Centre definitely wants to keep.
- Each client should have a record, kept accurately. Clients do want to feel that they are progressing in lessons. Often riders become stuck in a 'rut' on the same horse in the same standard of lesson and feel frustrated. Even if the client is not progressing sufficiently it is sometimes good policy to put them on a different standard of horse.

This can have the effect that the client tries harder and progresses well. We've all been on the 'plateau' and needed a little extra push to start advancing again. Those who hack will not want to take the same route every week.

- The client should always be encouraged to book again. Offering discounts for a number of lessons or selling discounted vouchers to be used within a specified time are excellent methods of obtaining repeat bookings as well as helping cash flow. The client can be encouraged to book next week at least. Even if they are not sure they can make a provisional booking just in case the lesson becomes full and they cannot book later. If they really are hesitant, however, trying strong persuasion can have an adverse affect and deter them.

Clients need to feel that the ambience of the Centre is an essential part of their life routine. They must feel that here they can relax either through hacking or working hard in a lesson, that they can forget their problems, at least for a time.

Promotional Advertising

As the equestrian industry is mostly a luxury service, apart from those wishing for a career with horses, extra promotional ideas can be used to encourage repeat (and hopefully more frequent) bookings by clients.

The Centre can encourage some clients to work towards the **BHS Proficiency Tests** and possibly onto their **Stage Examinations**. Working towards a Test gives the client a goal, a pride in their achievement when they are successful.

Competitions for **dressage, show jumping, cross-country** or **eventing** can also encourage clients to work towards a goal.

Special bookings such as **school parties**, **pub or picnic hacks**, **visits by celebrity riders** for **lectures, demonstrations or special lessons**, **outings to cross-country courses, gymkhana events**, **shows**, four or five day **courses for riding and stable management**.

The Centre can offer '**own a pony weeks**' or '**lease a horse**' periods. There are numerous ideas for encouraging participation by clients, inviting them to become a 'part' of the Centre.

Advertising any promotion is important. No point in having an 'own a pony week' if nobody knows about it. Posters, leaflets and booklets listing the events should be readily available and easily visible. Advertisements can be placed in the local press or tack shops.

New clients can be asked where they heard about the Centre or saw it advertised. Many new customers are advised by friends; word of mouth is powerful advertising. Some may have seen an advert in Yellow Pages or the local press. It is always useful to know what type of advertising works and is therefore economically viable.

Children's Activities

Most establishments cater for children's holidays providing special programmes aimed at the younger rider. Days at the stable, 'own a pony week', special gymkhana days, Teddy Bear's picnic hacks, fancy dress drill rides; the scope is limited only by the imagination and the Centre's facilities.

This brings in extra revenue and can be economically viable. The children may spend money purchasing goods from the shop and eating meals in the café. They may encourage new custom; advise friends or relatives to start riding at the Centre.

Safety is the most important element especially where children are concerned.

- **Constant and competent supervision**.

  The children should be supervised at all times. There should be one helper to a maximum of four children. During every activity: lunch, break time, going to the toilet, walking round the fields, the children have to be supervised. It only takes a second for an accident to happen and children can be very quick to go missing.

  They can be given a safety talk at the beginning of each day, impressing on them that they should not leave their 'team leader'. They should ask when they want to go somewhere or do something. It is particularly important that they are properly supervised when working with the ponies, grooming, tacking up and untacking.

  Ideally at least one of the supervisors should be used to children; this could be a mother. Mothers develop special instincts when it comes to children and their antics. There should definitely be a First Aider on the premises, possibly one of the leaders could be trained in basic first aid.

- **Correct clothing and equipment.**

  Correct, safe clothing should be worn by the children when handling the ponies and when riding.

- **Organisation and control.**

  The whole group should be kept away from the main yard, perhaps in the pony yard or special area. Offer variety, different activities frequently; children can become bored very quickly. Alternative activities can be planned during wet weather.

  Staff rotas will need careful organising if the children are to be supervised at all times, despite staff days off or illness.

- **Good trustworthy, sensible ponies should be provided.**

  All the tack should be safe and fit correctly.

❖ **Make all the time fun and at the same time offer training.**

Children become upset if they are trying to do a job they have been given and are not capable of doing it. Some children become frightened at tacking up the pony, not because of the pony, but in case the job is not done correctly. Children do like to do things the right way. Helpers and leaders should be friendly, understanding, constantly vigilant and, most importantly, should like children.

Organisation and Preparation

Any period whether it is a day or a week that children spend at the yard needs preparation. There should be a timetable, including mealtimes, drink breaks, scheduled activities, staff rota for those in charge, so that the office and instructors know where the children are at any time of the day. The children's activities should also be organised so that they do not clash with adult lessons in the school.

For example:

09.30 Children arrive; meet in reception. Check clothing and equipment. Take children's names and assign them to their supervisor.

Activities to include:

* mucking out
* grooming
* skipping out
* brushing the yard
* cleaning tack
* bathing a pony
* plaiting a mane
* lessons and hacks
* feeding
* mounted pony games
* filling a haynet
* walking round and inspecting the fields
* walking round a jumping course
* walking round a cross-country course
* taking ponies down to the field
* bringing them back
* tacking up, untacking
* stable management lectures

Other related activities could be:

Treasure hunts - watching videos - drawing, pony related subjects - colouring books - marking points of the horse - quizzes.

There could be a theme running through the days. In some Centres there is a gymkhana on the last day, when the children have games such as weaving round the cones; trotting races; walk, trot and canter; ducking for apples; walk and lead, and relay races.

Some have a small competition when the children do a 'dressage test' (with leaders) and a small jumping course, normally poles on the ground (again with leaders). Alternatively the children could hold a drill ride to music in front of the parents.

The children could practise this theme each day leading up to the last day bonanza. Those children who attend only one or two days and wish to participate in the last day's fun should also be included.

With safety, organisation, routine, control and a genuine desire to help, children's activity times at the yard can be real fun for everyone.

Riding Holidays

Some Centres feature specialised holidays, where older children or adults stay overnight in accommodation. Hacking, lessons, flatwork and jumping every day are offered as well as stable management lectures and practical sessions.

Other Centres will offer two or three day intensive courses with up to four hours riding each day.

For all these activities safety is the most important factor for the enjoyment of guests and staff.

Competitions and Shows

Other Centres organise competitions and shows either for their own clients or for outsiders as well. This encourages clients in their progress and brings potential new clients into the yard.

Organisation is vital for any event of any kind, keeping classes to time, sorting out judges, competitors, their numbers and times, maintaining the ground surface, roping off areas, organising fences, helpers, cashiers, stalls, lorry parking, advertising and promotion.

Helping out at these events, even as a steward or gatekeeper, increases the experience of all aspects of competition. Competing at shows or assisting a friend who is competing is an excellent method of learning about so many aspects of horsemastership.

Testing Ability

For clients who regularly have lessons every week periodic tests of their ability confirms their progress and even encourages it. It gives riders something to work towards; it inspires them to increase their knowledge.

Progressive Riding Tests

The British Horse Society offers a series of tests, **the Progressive Riding Tests**. These take the riders progressively through from beginner level, novice and intermediate level in riding and stable management.

They are excellent for those who may not work in the industry, children and teenagers, and those who have other jobs but ride fairly seriously. They encourage those who lack confidence, who want to progress onto BHS qualifications, but feel they do not have the ability to take the 'Stage Examinations'.

Riders often start taking the Progressive Riding Tests as a means of progression and find that they rise to the level where they take the BHS Stages I, II then III the PTT and beyond.

There are twelve tests, each syllabus covering riding ability and stable management from almost beginner level up to the standard of Stage III. Tests 1-9 are examined by an instructor from the Centre where they are held. Candidates taking tests 10-12 have to be assessed by an Examiner from outside the Establishment.

Successful candidates receive a card on which a special marker is placed to show that they have passed that number of tests. Passing up to Test 6 or 7 is the equivalent standard of the Stage I Riding and Stable Management Examination.

Encouraging regular clients to take these tests is a good policy, clients learn more about horses, their care and handling, it increase confidence and gives the successful candidate a sense of achievement.

This also benefits the Centre; the clientele will be rising in standard, encouraging a higher level of equitation and stable management. The Centre's reputation will increase with rising standards. The clients will need more lessons to progress through the Tests, riding lessons and stable management lectures. This results in an expansion of business for the Centre.

The Riding and Road Safety Test

This Test, run by the British Horse Society, aims to prevent accidents, reducing the amount of horse related incidents on the public highway and the suffering that these cause.

The BHS aims to increase the knowledge and awareness of riders by giving recognition to those who ride responsibly and competently on the road.

Riders are taught the rules of the Highway Code, courtesy for all road users and an awareness of the dangers of riding on the Public Highway.

It is a good policy to encourage riders to take this test, particularly for those who ride, however infrequently, on the roads and small lanes as well as main roads. This will increase the safety of horses and riders on the road.

Office Management

The office is the hub of any commercial centre. Here the bookings are taken, clients encouraged to book again, the records are kept, the horse list is often organised here, instructors informed of clients and lessons they have during the day. Often the money is kept in the office, cash taken in and bills paid.

It is essential that the office is run efficiently, if possible with the same personnel in the office as frequently as possible to keep the continuity.

The booking sheet for clients should be kept simple and efficient. Styles vary in establishments according to accounting preferences and the business emphasis.

The booking sheet should show clearly the times of lessons, clients names and any information necessary, the instructor, horses and the type of lesson or hack required.

It will need to show the price, method of payment and whether the client wishes to book again.

This should be linked to the list in the yard so that the staff know which horses to prepare and when. This is updated during the day to prevent wasted time or a disappointed client.

Office Equipment

The office should be kept tidy, clean and efficient. The office equipment may include a computer, keyboard and possibly a printer. The telephone needs to be situated in an accessible position, preferably near the booking sheets.

Cash should be kept secure in a cash box, safe or lockable drawer. Usually establishments do have facilities for credit cards.

The certificates of the instructors should be clearly visible as well as any promotional posters and timetables.

Client Records

Each client and pupil should have a record kept of their progress. This can detail their improvement, their standard, level of riding, the type of lessons they have and any problems they may be experiencing.

Keeping a record of the rider's progress ensures that tuition can be progressive even with a different instructor or when the regular instructor is away.

Example of booking in sheet

Time	Name	Comments	Instructor	Horse	Type of lesson	Amount to pay	Paid	Method of payment	Next booking
08.00	Margaret Heritage	Stage IV	Robert	Ace	P/L 1 hr.	£40.00	✔	Chq.	N/W
08.30	Tony Noble	New Client See records	Jean	Douglas	Assess ½ hour	£22.00	✔	Cash	Ring
09.00	Rob Kennedy		James	Oscar	G/L 1 hour	£23.00	✔	Chq.	N/W
	Stephen Jones			Monrush	"	£23.00	✔	Chq.	N/W
	Christine Walsh			Murphy	"	£23.00	✔	C/C BC	F/N
	Lester Moore			Pride	"	£23.00	✔	Chq.	N/W
09.30	Fiona Jones	Stage III	Philly	Foley	½ hour	£22.00	✔	C/C visa	Ring
10.00	Rhoda Phillips	Stage III	Jean		S/M 1 hour	£15.00	✔	C/C visa	Ring
11.00	Claire Turner	Staff	Robert	Eeyore	**Staff lesson 1 hour Jump**				
	Alison Phillips	Staff		Rufus					
	Lucy Parker	Staff		Foxy Lady					
	Gemma Softley	Staff		Harry					
	Diane Salt	Staff		Bella					
11.30	Amy Jones Darren Hynes		James	Douglas Ben	Semi/ P 1 hour Jump C/C	£24.00 £24.00	✔ ✔	C/C AX C/C visa	N/W N/W

The Yard

The Centre will need a sign outside the gate clearly visible for clients. The areas within the yard should also be clearly signed; reception, office, toilets, lecture room.

The yard needs to be as clean as possible, looking smart and tidy, running efficiently and with a friendly, competent atmosphere. There should be a mounting block. Other facilities may include tables and chairs, in a safe area, for clients to sit at during warmer weather, a drinks machine in a suitable place, flowers in pots.

The standard of an Equitation Centre is built up over years and this quality must be maintained if the Centre is to keep its reputation, its clientele, encourage further custom and be economically prosperous.

Test Tips

There are so many vital aspects to running a yard, often not noticed within an efficient establishment. When everything runs like clockwork, staff are efficient, friendly, polite, the horses healthy and in good condition, the lessons running on time, the work behind the scenes is not apparent.

Any Riding School, Equitation Centre, Livery and Competition Yard that caters for customers is a business. It has to make a profit to survive, and there is nothing wrong with making a profit. The higher the margin of profit the more can be spent on maintaining, improving and upgrading the Centre, expanding its facilities so that its client base becomes larger.

This includes managing the property, creating an efficient network within the office, reception and the yard, offering a good service and facilities at competitive prices and above all caring for, maintaining in good health and improving the stock of horses and ponies.

The Theory section of the PTT covers various subjects including equitation, yard and office management, and safety precautions.

During the Theory session you will be asked about teaching beginners, about what sort of lesson is suitable, when to teach sitting and rising trot, and canter. You will need to know information about the beginner's progress, when they are ready to join a group lesson.

You may also be asked how and when to introduce jumping, about the basic position, how to work over poles, what sort of fence to start with and where it should be placed in the school. You may be questioned about children's lessons and special events to cater for children.

The Theory session may also include giving information on suitable horses for different levels of riders, for lessons and for hacks.

Any practical experience you can gain will help you during the Test.

* Teaching - beginners, children, lunge lessons, flatwork and jumping or observing instructors giving these lessons.
* Check other yards, their facilities, their reception and office areas.
* Check the type of promotions they offer, competitions, special events.
* Assess the horses and ponies in your yard or centre. Observe the different types or breeds and their particular traits, characteristics and temperaments.
* Check how the yard maintains its stock of horses and ponies, how they are cared for, handled and worked. How many hours do they work each day, do they go into the field during work days and on days off? Is their work varied, in type and standard? What are they fed for the variety of work they do?

Every piece of information will be useful not only for the Preliminary Teaching Test but also for afterwards when you are teaching clients and perhaps assisting in or running a yard.

CHAPTER 19
Group Lesson: Preparation

Preparation for the group lesson consists of designing ground plans for the flatwork and jumping lessons and practising teaching these lessons. The most important factor within every lesson is safety, being able to organise and control each individual rider and horse, and the ride as a whole.

This chapter explains the preparation and planning for the group lesson. The next chapter describes the format of the actual lesson on the Test day.

Preparation of Group Lesson

Some months prior to the Test Day send for a list of the group lessons. From this list you will be able to prepare and plan for each lesson by working out the subjects, collecting the information and designing ground plans. There are 45 different lesson plans, approximately half of which are jumping lessons and the remainder flatwork. Each lesson structure can be divided into five sections.

1. Introduction and checking tack
2. Assessment and warm-up
3. First theme
4. Second theme (usually main theme)
5. Conclusion

The jumping lessons feature a flatwork section leading progressively to jumping fences. The lessons on flatwork cover school figures and movements and subjects, such as balance, suppleness or impulsion.

The preparation includes

- Designing an assessment plan.
- Collecting information on each subject contained in the lessons.
- Designing a simple ground plan for each lesson.
- Writing these out on cards ready for the Test Day.

Introduction

Once the pupils and horses are in the school, you will introduce yourself and ask the pupils for their names. The horse's tack will be checked as will the rider's clothing. After this you may assist the riders to mount onto the horses and then introduce your lesson plan. You may then proceed to organise the assessment.

Assessment Plan

The first riding section is the assessment and warm-up period. As the time allowed for the whole group lesson is 35 to 40 minutes, the assessment plan should be no longer than 5 minutes. You will need to organise the group, comprising of three or four riders, and command them through a warm-up routine.

First **design** a warm-up routine that includes work in all three paces, a change of rein and possibly a 20m circle.

For example:

- Start in walk -whole ride going large - half to three-quarter circuit of the school.
- Working trot rising going large half to three quarters way round school.
- Trot one 20m circle at A, C, E or B whichever is convenient.
- Go large after circle.
- Walk at next marker.
- With rest of the ride remaining in walk, each leading file in succession will trot, then canter at the next corner.
- Canter large around the school; trot and walk before reaching rear of ride.
- Each leading file to do this in succession.
- On conclusion of this exercise whole ride into rising trot.
- Change of rein across convenient long or short diagonal.
- Walk after change.
- Repeat canter exercise for each leading file.
- May include canter one 20m circle somewhere in school if time *(must be done away from the other riders. If rest of ride down by C, 20m circle at A.)* Watch rest of ride, judge distance.
- Trot then walk before reaching rear of ride.
- Bring ride onto centre line, check girths and stirrups, give talk on lesson theme.

This type of plan can be used for all lessons. Design a simple routine and rehearse this prior to the test. This will then be easily remembered and commanded on the day. Keeping to a familiar and well-rehearsed routine will help you relax and give you confidence. It will mean that you can concentrate on teaching the riders instead of trying to remember a complicated or unknown assessment ground plan. It will also keep this section of the lesson within the time limit.

The assessment plan detailed here includes a canter on each rein and a 20m circle in canter. This plan may need to be shortened on the day depending on

* The subject of the lesson - if this includes a lot of work. For instance if the lesson includes working on the flat progressively towards jumping three fences, as the time is relatively short, the assessment plan can be reduced.

* If the riders have already had one lesson and do not need to be warmed-up for 5 minutes.

To reduce the plan either omit the 20m circle in canter or have the riders perform canter on one rein only. During this assessment you should *teach the riders*. The teaching can be general and include making positional corrections for each rider, teaching them the aids for transitions, for the turns and circles in the school.

You will need to observe the riders and teach to help each particular rider. If a rider has a positional fault or has problems with transitions, teach them that specific point and help them to improve. You will need to be observant and discriminating in your teaching.

Some of the plans include assessing the riders with the stirrups at jumping length. Teach them about the light seat; instruct them to take the light seat on the trot circle and during the canter exercise. Some plans request you assess the rider's ability to jump a single fence. If the riders have not ridden previously they, and the horses, will still need a warm-up exercise. If they have ridden before, reduce the routine to one rein only and proceed to assess the riders over a single fence.

The assessment plan may need to be slightly modified to cover these variations or as an introduction to the lesson. For example, if the lesson is based on teaching turns and circles include turns across the school or onto the centre line. If based on straight lines or straightness of the horse, they could ride down the centre line to change the rein.

The simpler method is to keep to the routine plan but bias your teaching towards a subject. For example inform the riders about riding the turns at each corner of the school; make them aware of the aids. When they ride the 20m circle in trot, teach them the aids, how to aim for the quarter markers. If the subject is straight lines teach them to keep the horse straight when they change the rein across the long diagonal.

The important point is to **keep the plan simple**, assess the riders and the horses during this period, essential for the remainder of the lesson.

Information

The next phase is to make a list of all the different subjects contained in the lessons. Research and note down the information on these subjects. The information should cover definitions, aims, advantages, method, the aids, anything relevant that will help you to teach.

For example:

	Subject
1	Rider's position - flatwork
2	Work without stirrups
3	Transitions; upwards and downwards and to halt
4	Natural aids
5	Turn on the forehand
6	Leg yield
7	Turns, circles and half circles
8	Straight lines
9	Ground/trotting poles
10	Accuracy; school figures
11	Paces/work in trot and canter
12	Balance and rhythm
13	Balance and suppleness
14	Impulsion; forward movement
15	Position - jumping fold and light seat
16	Stirrups - to shorten and reasons
17	Single fence and with placing pole
18	Two single fences; and with change of direction
19	Three fences with change of direction
20	One non-jumping stride double
21	Two non-jumping strides double
22	Distances between fences
23	Approaches to fences importance
24	Balance for jumping
25	Stages of the jump

Researching and writing down the information about the specific topics will help you to revise and remember the points for teaching. It will help you to be clear and precise about the information you will be giving to the riders.

Collect the information in a format that suits you, for instance:

> ***Leg yield*** *- definition - practical use - aim, method and aids, faults and corrections.*

Include information that seems relevant:

Working without stirrups *- quitting and crossing stirrups, rider's position, exercises, balance and rhythm.*

* Keep the information concise, brief, to the point. Though the information you teach will need to be thorough, timing is quite important for the lesson. You will need the ability to give as much information as possible in as brief a form as possible.

For example:

Shortened stirrups:

Reasons: to reduce the angles at the hip, knee and ankles joints - supple joints allow the rider to absorb the horse's movement to remain in balance.

Increases rider's stability and security - weight pressed down into heel - thighs and knees further forward in saddle give more stability.

Allows flexibility of movement - folding from hip to alter upper body position - freedom to move arms and hands to follow horse's head

- ❖ Length shortened by at least two holes.
- ❖ To shorten the stirrups keep both feet in the stirrup irons.

For jumping, the information will include learning the distances between fences and for a placing pole, teaching the light seat, working with shortened stirrups at trot and canter.

It may also include the stages of jump, correcting the rider's position over a fence, teaching them about the approach to the fence.

This information then needs to be organised into your ground plan for each lesson.

Ground Plans

The ground plan is designed to keep the group organised so that you can teach and the riders can practise and improve.

The important points when designing the ground plans are:

- ❖ Keep the plans as simple as possible. Complicated manoeuvres are difficult to remember, to instruct and to ride.
- ❖ Often the first theme will be influenced by the second theme. Many of the lessons follow through from one subject to another.

For example:

- ❖ Work towards improving the riders' ability to make better **transitions including halt**. Improve their ability to ride **turns on the forehand**.

Working on halt transitions clearly prepares the rider for the turn on the forehand. The ground plan will contain halt transitions progressing onto turn on the forehand.

In a lesson containing jumping fences, the flatwork section will lead to the jumping. The plan for the jumping and the position of the fences will give an indication of the plan for the flatwork section.

❖ Assess the ride and work towards improving their **transitions to canter with stirrups at jumping length**. Progress on to jumping **two fences with a change of direction across the long diagonal.**

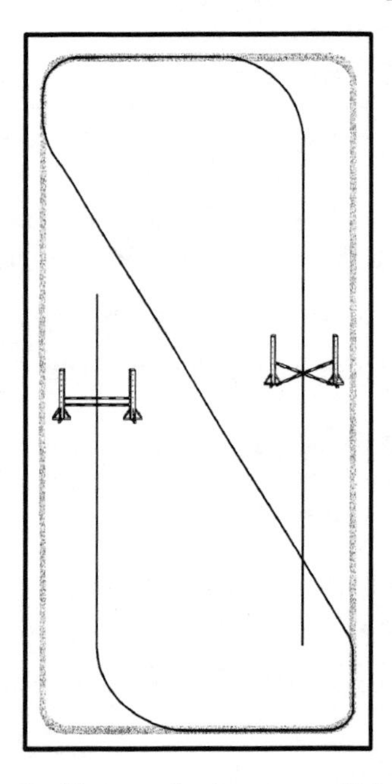

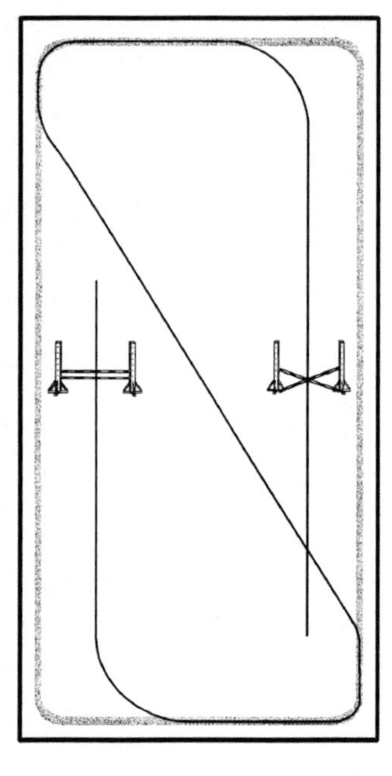

The fences can either be positioned opposite each other near E and B or slightly staggered

In this case the fences could be positioned at E and B with the rider changing the rein across the long diagonal. The flatwork section could include working the riders individually in canter, with a simple change across the diagonal.

As you work through the lessons, you will find that just a few ground plans will suit almost all the lessons. A ground plan based on school figures, transitions or the rider's position can equally be used for teaching the natural aids, balance and rhythm or suppleness.

Flatwork Plans

The flatwork lessons and the flatwork sections in the jumping lessons, cover either school figures or movements, the rider's position, the aids, transitions, balance, suppleness, working without stirrups or the horse's paces and quality of work.

Complicated manoeuvres such as figures of eight, serpentines, demi-voltes are best avoided. Though these figures can be ridden well by experienced riders, it is best not to organise these unless you are perfectly confident in the riders on the day. Also these take time to command and ride, and are rarely easy to teach.

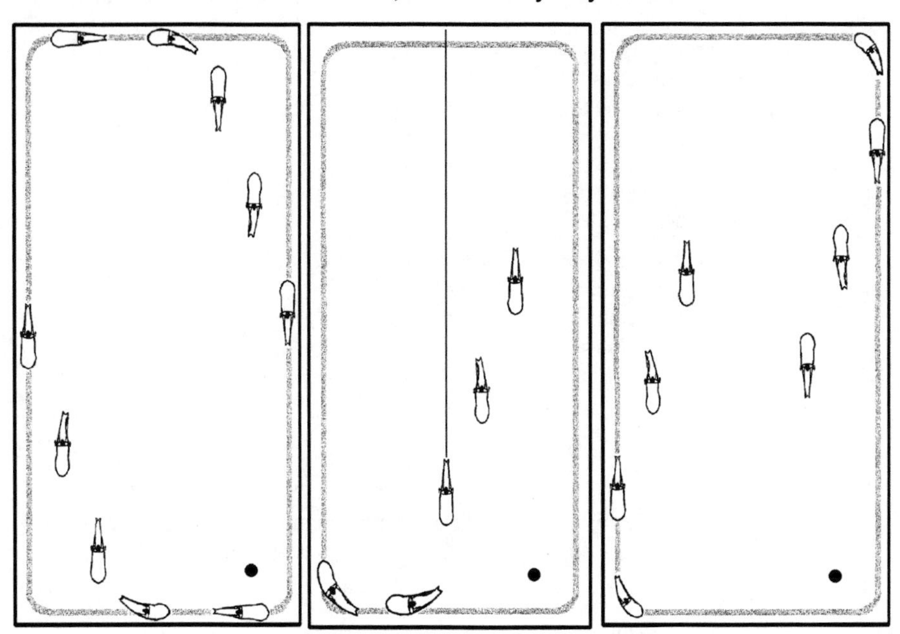

School movements such as leg yield will follow a general pattern, in walk and then trot from the three-quarter track to the wall of the school. This could progress onto riding straight down the centre line and leg yielding to the three-quarter line; or from the wall of the school to the three-quarter line.

Turn on the forehand may start with the quarter turn on the centre line either from the short end of the school or from E and B.

The riders could then progress to a half turn on an inside track around the school or on the centre line.

When teaching turn on the forehand, do not repeat the exercise too often, as turn on the forehand is not a particularly 'forward' thinking movement. It is best to intermittently do a trot or canter exercise and then repeat the turn.

The ground plans will include working the group as a ride, in open order or singly as individuals on the same rein.

The diagrams show a quarter turn on the forehand from the sides of the school on the centre line and a half turn on the three-quarter line and the centre line.

The shaded horse shapes show the movement as the horse turns.

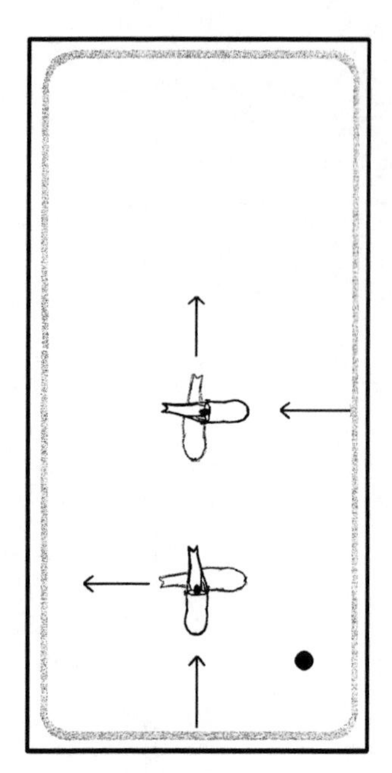

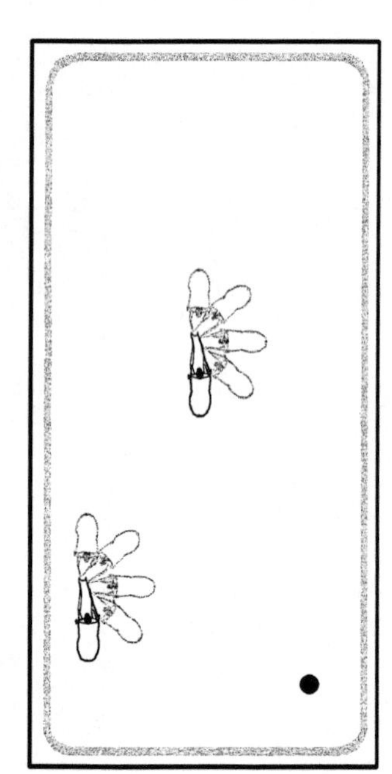

For leg yield and turn on the forehand, the ride should be organised into open order. This will also apply when working over poles.

Poles

Some of the lesson plans include working with poles for transitions to halt, to improve the horse's straightness, for turns on the forehand and as trotting poles.

Poles can be positioned so that the rider comes parallel to a pole to make a straight halt. Alternatively the rider can come to halt between two poles.

Sets of two poles placed parallel about 1m apart can encourage the rider to guide the horse in straight lines. These can be placed on the three-quarter lines down the long sides of the school.

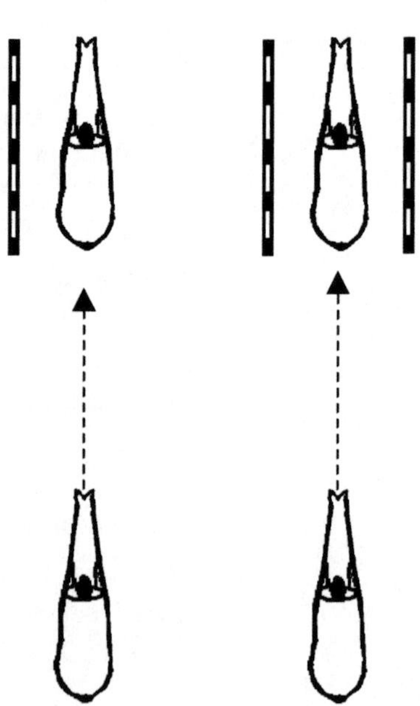

For a quarter turn on the forehand, place the poles so that the rider can walk past one pole and perform a quarter turn then walk past the other pole.

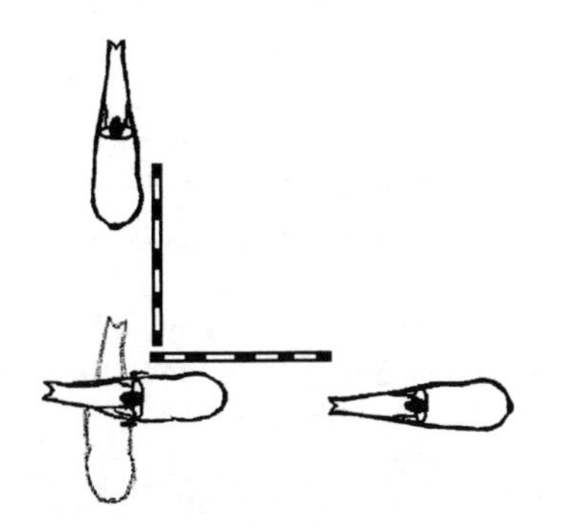

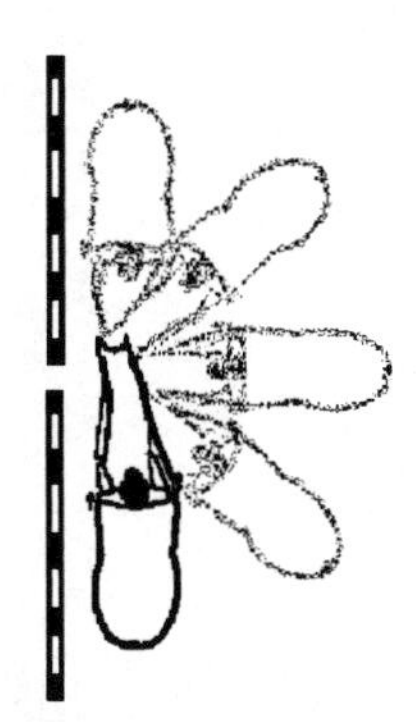

For a half turn the rider can walk parallel to one or two poles, perform a half turn and walk on.

When the poles are used for school figures and movements, make sure that the poles are used to help the rider. Instruct the rider to use the poles for accuracy. The rider should prevent the horse stepping on, stepping over or knocking the poles.

Often, too, riders are so intent on the poles that they look down and sit in an incorrect position. Encourage the rider to look up and sit straight.

When used as trotting poles, work from a basic progressive plan starting with one pole. Organise the ride into open order working in walk over a single pole first to check that the horses are quiet and accustomed to pole work.

Jumping Plans

The jumping lessons vary from working over a single fence, a fence with a placing pole, two single fences, two single fences with a change of direction in between, a one non-jumping stride double, a two non-jumping strides double, three single fences or a grid. The fences vary from a cross-pole, a vertical or a spread.

The ground plan for jumping will include:

- Position of the fences in the school; depending on the number of fences and if these are related in distance.
- Design of fences, cross-pole, small upright, placing pole, spread.
- Organisation of ride, as a ride, open order, or as individuals.
- Vantage point, where to stand.

The riders should be worked progressively towards the jumping. This means practising on the flat, with shortened stirrups, in different paces, around the track and on the approach down the three-quarter line.

Safety

For flatwork organise the plans so that riders work through school figures and movements at a safe distance from each other. This needs careful stage management.

There are times when the ride can work as a ride, at other times they will need to be in open order. When working in open order, you should remind the riders to be aware of the others and to keep their distance.

Be aware of the position of the riders around the school so that a rider working individually has space to work safely away from the others. You may need to be adaptable to cover circumstances that arise.

Plan as far as you can and then be aware of what will happen in each exercise, so that you can adapt to maintain the safety of the riders.

During jumping lessons, because the horses and riders are unfamiliar to you, it is safer to have the ride walk and then trot over poles on the ground, to test their reaction before jumping. The poles can be placed between the wings and the ride organised into open order for this exercise.

When the jumping begins, either from trot or canter, each rider needs to work as an individual. The other riders should be positioned safely in the school.

When working with a double whilst in walk and trot over poles between wings, the riders can complete this safely in open order.

Once the fences are built the riders need to jump individually with the other two riders safely situated.

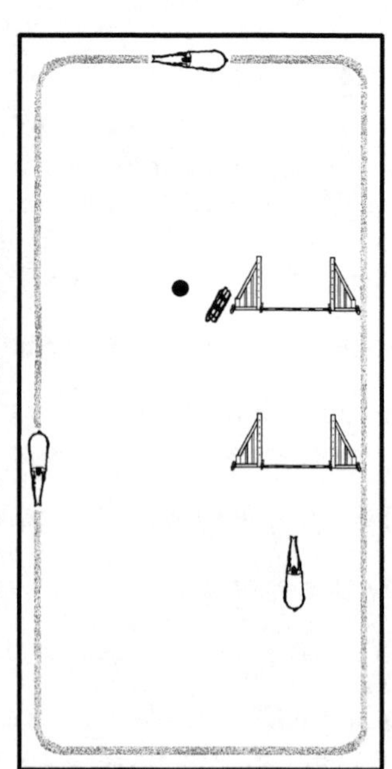

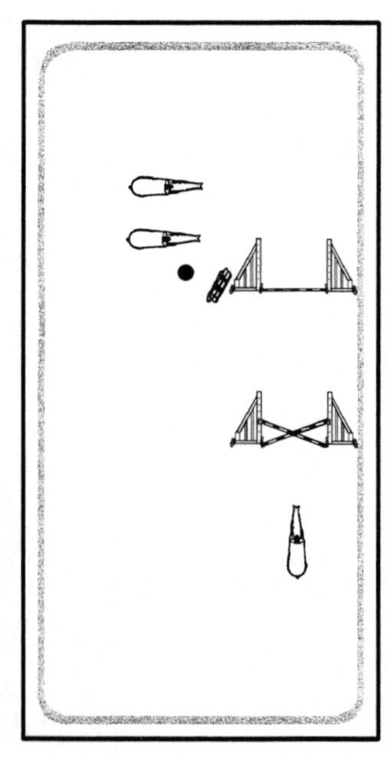

For a ride working across the diagonal when they are practising over poles at trot and canter, the other two riders need to be positioned in the corners of the school for safety.

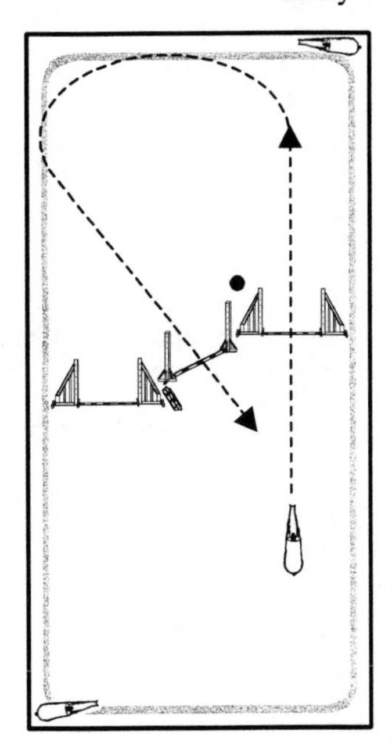

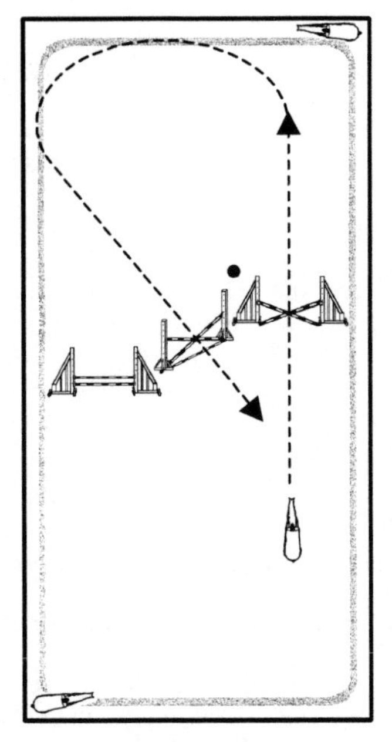

Where the lesson includes a change of rein, it would be unsafe to work as a ride across the diagonal, even in open order.

Riders need to work as individuals with the other riders safely positioned in separate corners of the school.

Here the two waiting riders and horses are situated safely in the corners of the school whilst the third rider negotiates the three fences.

Once all the subject information has been collected, the assessment routine planned, you can write out the full plan for each lesson.

Designing the Ground Plan

The ground plan can be prepared as follows:

Example:

❖ Assess the ride and **work them progressively over fences**, then teach them to ride a **one non-jumping stride double**.

Italics indicate teaching portions.

Prepared plan

Assessment plan. *Correct the riders' positions and horses' paces.*

Whole ride, prepare to turn in and halt. Check girths and put up stirrups.

Reasons for shortened stirrups. Explain the light seat. Check light seat at halt, make corrections.

In the upright position, whole ride to the track. Work as a ride.

Check light seat at walk. Then into upright position.

Canter exercise. Each leading file in succession go forwards to sitting trot, then canter. Into light seat for canter, down three-quarter line at free side of the school then large coming through to trot (in upright seat) and walk to close up to the rear file.

Watch for transition may need to teach through this.

Change rein. Repeat.

Corrections on seat position.

Bring ride into centre.

Jumping. Put wings out and second pair distance of 7.3m (24 feet, 8 of my strides). (Assess horses if smaller and shorter striding may need a shorter distance.) Poles out ready. Put ground pole between wings at first fence.

Whole ride out, open order, large around the school then come down the inner track and walk over the pole.

Corrections, straightness of horse, activity, allowing horse to stretch.

Whole ride forwards to trot and trot over the pole.

Corrections, straightness of horse, turn before fence, activity, allowing horse to stretch.

Whole ride walk, two riders turn in and halt safely in school.

Put up first jump.

Third rider go large into trot then come down the inner track and trot over the jump.

Corrections, activity, turns, straight line, position of rider, straightness after fence - all through this section.

After fence prepare to go forwards to canter come over the jump. Trot large whilst put up other fence. Forward to canter come over the two fences.

Corrections to track, approach, position.

Other two riders individually do same.

If time and all is well could put fences higher and repeat individually over double.

Watch striding of horses for second jump. May have to alter distance slightly for a smaller or larger horse.

Conclusion - cool down in walk. Finish off with any questions.

This plan now gives you a basis from which to work, including the teaching sections.

Lesson Cards

Once the plan is organised you can transfer this into personal shorthand notes to fit on a small card, postcard or filing card. These cards may be taken to the Test Centre and referred to before the group lesson when your chosen lesson is known. Writing a plan for each lesson does help to memorise the lesson plans. The plan on your card can be written in any type of shorthand, whichever suits you and your memory.

Key to abbreviations -

BICG - bring in check girths

SS - shorten stirrups

LS - light seat

FTB front to back

L - large around school

BR - both reins

OO - open order

TIOO - **two** riders **in** centre of school, **one out** on track

Example of card:

Assess. (Normal Assessment Plan)

BICG SS Explain shortened stirrups and check LS.

As RIDE Canter exercise FTB L and down ¾ line - BR

Walk large - put out wings 7.3 metres

OO Walk over pole then trot over pole.

TIOO

Trot over one jump; canter over one jump, then two, individually.

TIOO - repeat for other riders. If time repeat.

Conclusion - cool down. Questions and advice for future.

General Practice

It will probably be difficult to practise every lesson before the Test day, but you will need to practise at least three or four. This is important for several reasons:

Timing

The lessons do need to be timed. Some of the plans are relatively uncomplicated, some are more difficult to fit into 35 minutes and for these, each section will need to be completed fairly quickly.

Each stage in the lesson needs to be carefully timed; the assessment, putting out the fences, the content and the length of time it takes the group to perform a school movement or jump two or three fences.

Positioning of poles, wings and jumps

For one or even two single fences the positioning is clear, for a double or three single fences the positioning needs careful planning. The distances need to be correct.

The placing of the ground poles in the school and, for jumping, the wings before the fences are built needs to coincide with your plan for the riders. If the riders are to do a large circle at A, the poles or wings need to be positioned at a distance from A so that the riders are not obstructed by them.

Voice and stance

Voice projection and tone will need developing through practice, particularly in an outdoor menage when the acoustics will be poor. The vantage points, the position to stand so that you will be able to see the riders for the maximum amount of time, will need checking.

Teaching

Being able to assess pupils, observe their problems and give relevant corrections needs practice, particularly with different riders on unfamiliar horses. **The Examiners want to see you teach the pupils not just to command them around the school.** They need to see that you can improve the pupils and build a rapport with them.

The commands for control of the riders will need learning and practising.

Systematically planning the lesson, the ground plans for school movements, figures and exercises will help the lesson run smoothly and show your efficiency and competency. Thorough organisation of the lesson will give you the freedom to really teach, demonstrating your knowledge and ability.

Test Tips

This may seem a lot of preparation for the group lesson but as you work through the lesson plans you will find that many of these are similar. You will eventually use three or four different plans for all of the lessons.

If you are experienced at teaching and teach regularly you will already have some plans that you use for groups. You will have experience of positioning jumps and riders and be aware of the dangers involved when the positioning is incorrect. It is still advisable to plan and practise as much as possible.

Most candidates though have little experience of teaching groups. Good preparation and thorough planning will give you a solid foundation from which to work. This will build your confidence and you will look efficient, professional and able to cope with any problems should these arise.

Planning lessons on a school or menage diagram is useful for positioning of jumps and riders. Working out the route for each exercise will help to prevent mistakes and will give you an idea of how the riders should be organised.

You may have your own method of planning and preparing group lessons. Whichever way works for you is the best method to chose for the PTT.

Time spent in preparation and studying will be well spent. The teaching cards may be used again for your own group lessons when you have qualified.

CHAPTER 20

Group Lesson: Practical

The group lesson for the PTT is based on teaching a small group, normally three or four riders in a school or menage. The standard of the riders will be from novice up to Stage II working towards Stage III.

This chapter describes the format of the group lesson, the introduction, the content and how to command and organise the riders during their lesson.

Test Format

At the beginning of the Test, between 08.30 and 09.00 a.m., you will be asked to choose a slip detailing the group lesson subject. Alternatively the Examiners themselves may give you a lesson plan.

Occasionally the Examiners do not give a lesson plan but ask the candidates to plan their own lesson. They will specify that this should either be a flatwork or jumping lesson.

Lesson Brief

1. Assess the ride.
2. Teach to improve *the riders in front of you.*
3. Use ground poles and jumps progressively to ensure safety.

After the lesson, you will have a short discussion with your Examiner.

A short time, about ten minutes, is allowed to prepare for the lesson after which the first group giving the lesson will be requested to go to the school. The first candidate will begin the lesson.

The other two candidates will normally watch and at some time during the lesson may be requested to help put out poles, wings and jumps.

The two important points are to keep to the lesson plan you are given and to keep the teaching appropriate to the riders.

Introduction

From the moment the lesson begins you are in charge and should control the riders and horses to give them confidence.

The riders are normally dismounted and should be stood by their horses lined up on the centre or three-quarter line of the school. They may already be mounted, possibly having just completed a previous lesson. Introduce yourself clearly.

'Good morning my name is...... I will now come round to each of you individually, learn your names and check your tack.'

Ideally the group of riders should be positioned so that you can stand in front of the ride, adjacent to the Examiners where they can see and hear you.

The previous lesson will probably finish in this position. Or, if you enter the school before the group, arrange the ride so that they are lined up correctly for you.

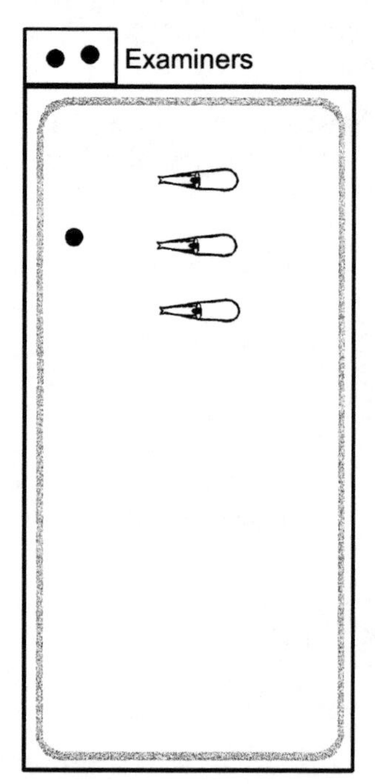

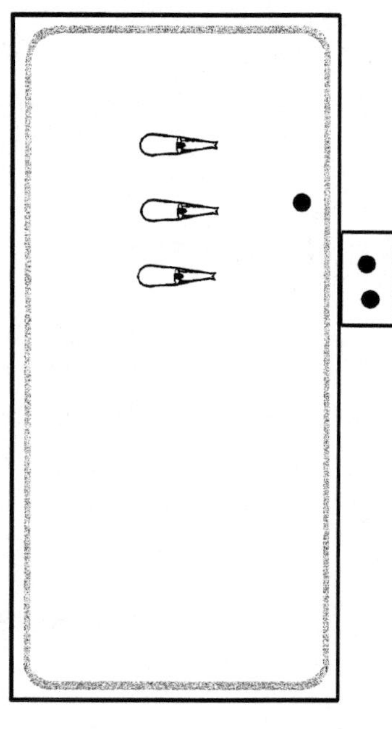

Checking the Tack

This is VITAL. Always, always check the horse's tack and the rider's clothing. For a jumping lesson check that the saddle is a GP or jumping saddle. If the horse is wearing a dressage saddle and the lesson includes jumping mentioned this to the Examiners. Request that this is changed.

Check that the girth is the correct length. If the girth is too long, or too short, (on the last hole of the girth straps) mention this to the Examiners. This will be changed as well.

Briefly check the bridle for fitting and condition, and any boots or bandages to make sure they are fastened properly.

Check the rider's clothing. The hat has to be of an approved standard. Some hats look correct but are not the compulsory specification. If in doubt ask, *'Is your hat a PAS 015?'* (or the alternative EN 1384). Riding Schools could have problems with insurance and legal claims if a rider is injured and the hat is below the approved standard.

The rider should also be wearing gloves, suitable boots, jodhpurs or suitable trousers, a fastened jacket if the weather is cold, or a long sleeved shirt.

Check the whip. For flatwork only, a long whip is acceptable, but for jumping the rider has to have a short whip. You should mention this if the lesson is to include jumping and one rider has a long whip only. This could be an important point; a long whip could be dangerous when a rider is jumping.

Rider Information

Whilst checking the tack, ask the rider's name, the level of riding, any qualifications, if the rider has ridden or jumped this horse before, any problems, such as a bad back. Ask also about the horse, his or her name, abilities, problems, such as, is he a good lead horse or is he a kicker?

When asking the rider's name have eye contact. This begins the rapport between teacher and rider.

'Your name is .... and the horse is ....

Have you ridden this horse before? Can you tell me anything about the horse, is he forward going, sluggish or does he have any problems? Have you jumped him before?'

Mounting

The riders may need help to mount. This may mean a leg up or requesting a mounting block. Never be afraid to do this, it is more important for a rider to mount safely than struggle from the ground.

When the rider is mounting, watch where the rider holds the whip. If mounting from a leg up the whip should be held over the neck of the horse on the offside. If someone holds the offside stirrup, the rider holds the whip on the near side. Assistants are often caught in the face by a whip if held on the wrong side.

If the riders are already mounted ask them if their stirrups are comfortable. Check that the stirrups are of equal length.

Points

Though the introduction involves a number of essential actions, such as checking tack, clothing, helping riders mount and so on, this part of the lesson needs to be completed fairly speedily, within five minutes.

If the riders are in the school already mounted, the tack and clothing should still be checked, this is so important. There may be something that was overlooked previously.

If the riders have just completed a previous lesson their stirrups may still be at jumping length. These may need lengthening for flatwork.

Assessment

After completing these introductions with all the riders, return to the front of the ride and prepare them for the assessment phase.

The theme of the lesson today will be …………………

First to work the horses in and to allow me to make an assessment, you will begin with a warm-up exercise.'

Instruct the riders to form a ride with one horse as leading file (normally the larger horse), one second and one as rear file (the smaller horse).

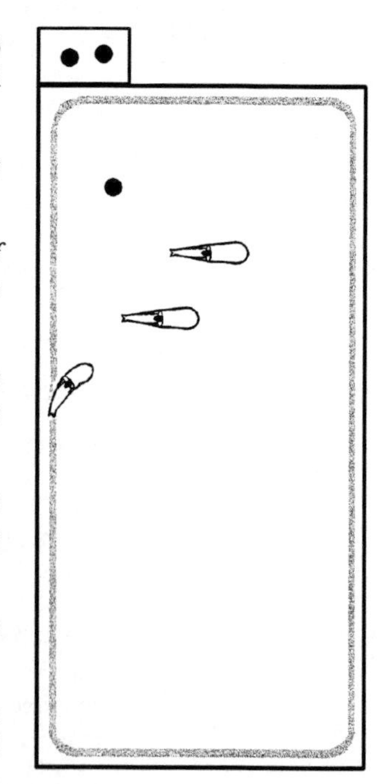

'Form a ride in the following order, Margaret as leading file, followed by Anne and then Christine.'

'Margaret, as leading file, keep an eye on the rest of ride, regulate the pace so that is not too fast or too slow.

The rest of the ride must remember ***to keep a safe distance of one horse's length between your horse and the horse in front.***

If you find yourself getting left behind, turn before a corner to close up. If you are becoming too close, ride further into the corners'.

'Whole ride preparing to walk. On my command you will walk straight to the track and track left.'

It does help for the ride to know in advance in which direction they will be riding; the riders can then hold their whips in the correct hand.

'Whole ride walk-march straight to the track and track left.'

If you choose an order of ride where lead file horse is in a different position, for instance in the middle, you can call out the rider's name first.

'Whole ride prepare to walk straight to the track on my command, Anne walk-march straight to the track and track left, followed now by Christine and now by Margaret.'

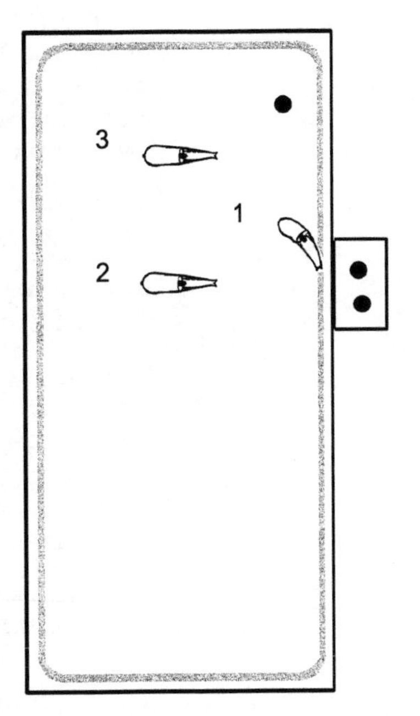

Take up your vantage point, where you will stand for most of the lesson. This is normally in one corner of the school near to the Examiners.

Observe each rider, assessing their ability so that you are able to teach them by making corrections and improvements during the lesson.

'To warm the horse up properly, encourage the horse to walk actively from the start. Allow the forward movement by following the horse's head smoothly with the hands.

You need to encourage the horse to walk with a longer stride, so that he uses his shoulders and stretches his frame.

You can also ask the horse to bend a little deeper into the corners. Think of each corner of the school as a quarter of a circle. Keeping the seat level in the saddle use your inside leg by nudging him in the region of the girth. With the inside hand ask him to bend in the direction of the corner. Allow this bend whilst maintaining the contact with the outside hand. Encourage the horse to bend through his body by applying the inside leg aid.'

Comment on each rider's position, one good point and one correction.

'Margaret, your body posture is good, you are sitting up tall and straight, now just raise the hands slightly and bend the elbows. Good.'

The riders and horses will need to do at least half a circuit of the school in walk to allow them time to relax before beginning the trot work.

Normally PTT guinea pigs are fairly competent and will be able to trot as a ride. **Emphasise the point about safe distances.** If the ride does trot and one rider is obviously having trouble keeping the horse at a safe distance, calmly bring the ride forward to walk and either alter the order of the ride so that the faster horse is in front or do the trot exercise as individuals.

'Whole ride, prepare to go forwards to rising trot, remember to keep your distance from the horse in front. And whole ride trot on.'

Preparing the Riders

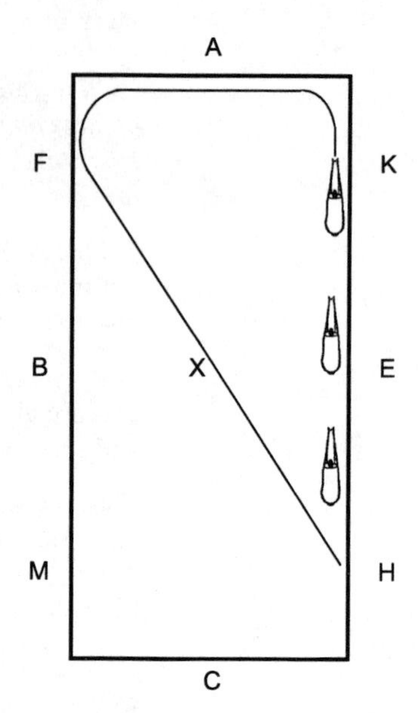

Before asking the riders to do anything, a transition, a change of rein, a school figure, always give them preparation time; always give them a few seconds to prepare themselves and the horse.

'Whole ride prepare to go forwards to working trot rising, ...and whole ride trot on.'

'Whole ride prepare to go forwards to walk, sitting up tall, keep the legs on and whole ride walk.'

For a change of rein, or a school figure such as a 20m circle, the ride needs preparing **before** the marker at which they will commence the manoeuvre. The amount of preparation time depends on the pace; the faster the pace the more time required to prepare.

At walk allow at least a quarter way round the school for the riders to prepare.

To make a change of rein from F to H through X the ride in walk will need to be prepared at K.

To make a change of rein from F to H through X, the ride in trot will need to be prepared at E.

'Whole ride, prepare to make a change of rein from F to H. Look up and ahead, ride an accurate turn before the diagonal and aim for the track just before the H marker. Keep the horse straight and ride him forwards.'

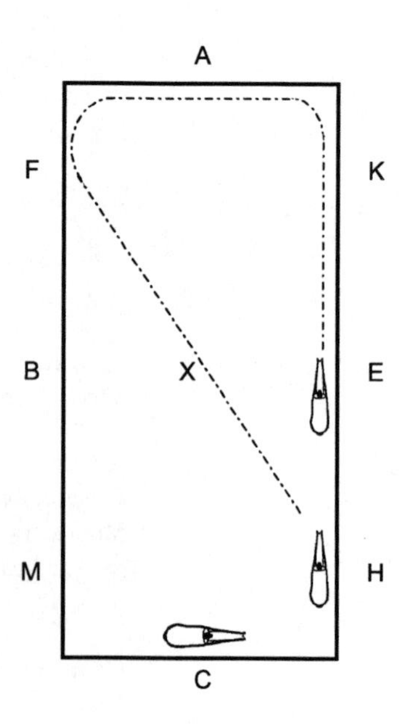

Points

If the riders are told abruptly and given no preparation time to make a transition or a change of rein this will cause confusion.

The ride will either make a hurried, poor transition, or completely miss the change of rein.

Alternatively giving too much time can frustrate riders and horses and cause the horses to anticipate.

Trot Work

Whilst the ride is trotting, keep teaching them by giving general reminders or corrections to position.

For example:

'Whole ride in rising trot, at E commence riding a 20m circle. To ride an accurate 20m circle, look for the quarter markers.

Keep the seat level in the saddle, upper body straight and relaxed. Apply the inside leg aid to encourage the horse to bend around the circle, keep the outside leg in contact slightly behind the girth to control the hindquarters. Guide the horse with the inside hand, but keep the contact with the outside hand to control the bend in the horse's neck.

Or you could make corrections:

'Margaret turn your shoulder more, bring your inside shoulder slightly further back. Good. Anne raise your hands do not let the inside hand fall, keep it level with the outside hand. Good. Christine you need firmer inside leg aids, give a firm nudge then relax, nudge then relax. Good.'

'Whole ride, after the circle, go large at E.'

The ride should normally go large after one circuit unless you specify that they should continue circling. On the warm-up phase though, because time is short, the ride should only circle once, and it does no harm to specify that the group should go large after the circle; this removes any doubt from the mind of the leading file.

Points

When preparing riders for the warm-up session, do emphasise the point about the safe distances, one horse's length from the horse in front. Keep observing the ride; if at any time the distance varies, correct it.

If one rider continues to ride too close, reorganise the ride. For the rider who cannot keep up, instruct them to turn before a corner to close up. Avoid commanding a rider to 'cut a corner' or to 'catch up'.

Keep comments and corrections brief and to the point when the riders are on the move.

Watch carefully for incorrect diagonals in rising trot and ask the rider to change.

'Anne, can you feel that you are on the wrong diagonal? Change it as usual by sitting to two beats and rising again.'

Canter Work

The canter work will be performed as individuals. Bring the ride forward to walk. Instruct the rider that they will now do a canter exercise.

'On my command each leading file will go forward to working trot rising, take sitting trot and in the next corner ask for a canter transition. You will remain in canter large around the school coming forwards to trot and walk before the rear of the ride.

Leading file prepare to trot and with remainder of ride in walk, trot on.

At the next corner, go forward to canter. Prepare now by sitting to the trot, half-halt to prepare the horse. Apply the inside leg aid and stroke the outside leg slightly back behind the girth. Good.'

Command the downward transition, so that this is performed in time before reaching the rear file. *'Prepare to come forwards to trot, half-halt, sit up, leg on and trot. Prepare to come forwards to walk, half-halt and walk.'*

Points

If a rider performs a bad transition into canter, ask the rider to return to trot, and repeat the preparation and transition. Talk through the transition to prevent the same problem.

If the horse is sluggish the rider may need to use the whip behind the inside leg.

If the horse is rushing off, perhaps running in the trot first and then launching into canter, the rider can bring the horse forward to walk. From walk the rider asks for a couple of strides of sitting trot, just before a corner, then canter.

Always watch for the downward transition. Downward transitions are often ridden poorly. Talk the rider through.

If, because of a bad transition, one rider receives only a short canter, you could include a 20m circle in the school away from the rest of the ride. Alternatively include a half a 20m circle across the school, rider go large and make the downward transitions before the rear of the ride. You may have to adapt and improvise to handle situations.

Watch for a wrong lead in canter. Ask the rider to bring the horse to trot and repeat. Explain the aids for canter, so that the rider does know that it is the *inside leg aid* that is important to ask the horse for forward movement. The outside leg should not be brought too far back or used too strongly as this will encourage the horse to swing his hindquarters inwards.

After the warm-up, instruct the ride to walk and to turn into the centre of the school near the Examiners, to halt on the centre line, quarter line or three-quarter line.

'Whole ride, prepare to turn in together and halt on the centre line. Whole ride, turn in now.'

Always **check the girths and stirrups again** now, or instruct the riders to shorten their stirrups if starting their jump practice.

Lesson Content

After allowing the riders a few seconds to check girths and alter stirrups, you can expand on the lesson theme. For instance if the subject is about transitions, you could explain briefly what transitions are, how to prepare for transitions, the importance of the half-halt, direct and progressive transitions, balance and rhythm in transitions.

If the lesson is progressive, leading from one subject to another, you can explain this.

'*In the first part of the lesson, I will be teaching you about transitions to halt, this will prepare you for the second part of the lesson when I will be teaching you about turn on the forehand. The transition to halt is an important part of this school movement.*'

Or '*the simple change of lead practised in this part of the lesson will be preparation for jumping the fences in the second part of the lesson which will include a change of direction.*'

Give as much information as possible, but as briefly as possible. The ride does need to be resumed without wasting time.

If poles, wings or jumpkins are needed these can be brought out at this point and placed in position or in a safe place in the school. You may ask for help or the Examiners will request that the other candidates assist.

The ride is sent out onto the track, either as a ride or in open order. You will by now have assessed the riders and know if they are sufficiently competent to work in open order. Repeat the information about safe distances, even in open order the riders need to know that they should keep their distance.

Keep this part of the lesson on a continual ground plan, keep the ride moving, doing different school figures, transitions, trot or canter work whatever is relevant to the theme. Vary the movements and change the rein occasionally. Avoid the group continually riding large around the track.

If the lesson theme is to ride school figures in relation to jumping fences afterwards, the ride could practise the school figures once or twice through the wings (in open order) at walk and trot.

Points

The ride can work in open order at walk and trot. For canter organise the group as individuals for a canter from the front to the back of the ride or with a single rider cantering in the school and the other two positioned in safe areas.

Whenever the poles or wings are brought into the school the ride should either be at halt or in walk. Poles and wings should not be carried into the school with the ride in trot or canter. This is dangerous.

When jumping from canter the rider should ask for canter before the long side prior to the fence. The rider will then have the opportunity to establish the canter, to create activity and balance before the fence.

If horse is rushing, the rider could approach the fence at trot or ride a circle before the fence, balance the horse and then ask for canter. If the lesson specifies that the fence is to be approached at canter but the horse is too hot or the rider cannot cope, then the rider should trot in and canter afterwards. This is safer. You are in control.

Conclusion

Towards the end of the lesson if you have finished your brief, you may ask the riders to walk their horses around the track on a loose rein.

If you find that your lesson is not completed but the Examiners tell you there is just five minutes remaining, continue for another two or three minutes then finish.

Bring the ride in to halt on the centre line and give your assessments on how each rider worked and improved. Give good points and corrections, and advice about future progress.

'Margaret, your position is good, you have a secure seat. You do tend to look down and this causes stiffness in the neck. You did improve this during the lesson, could you feel how much better your position was when you looked up? You also need to bend your elbows a little more and raise your hands slightly. Your jumping seat was good, well done.

Christine, you worked the horse well, but you seem a little stiff in your back. Perhaps a few lunge lessons, and exercises may help to loosen that area. Well done.

Ann, your jumping was good, you have a secure lower leg. You need to create more impulsion in the horse, establish a forward going canter before the fence. Then the last strides before the fence will be more balanced and the horse will make a better jump. When you achieved this, your last jump was much better. Well done.

Thank you, I really enjoyed teaching you all.'

If the ride has to dismount you may need to check that this is done safely before you leave the school.

Points

If you go to talk to each rider individually about their progress, you will need to talk more loudly so that the Examiners can hear your assessments.

Test Tips

The most important aspect in these lessons is safety. Any candidate who includes in their lesson anything which is considered unsafe, even something as simple as having horses come too close to each other, will not be successful. Remember always check the tack and clothing, remind the riders of their distances. Keep the exercises, school figures and movements simple and safe. Observe the riders, keep your control over the group. If any problem occurs deal with it quietly, calmly and efficiently.

Make sure that all wings, poles, cups and pegs are positioned safely in the school, depending on your ground plan for the lesson.

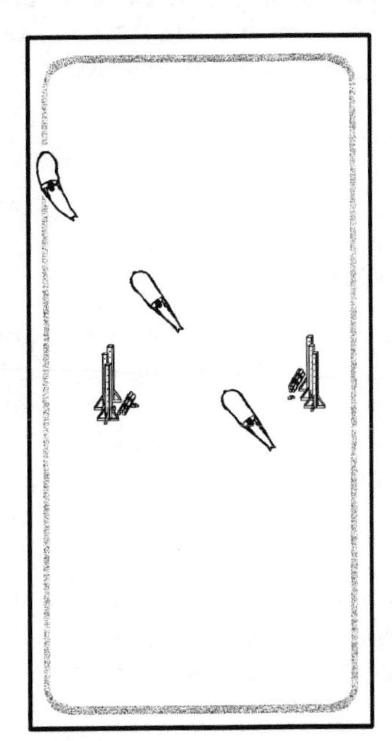

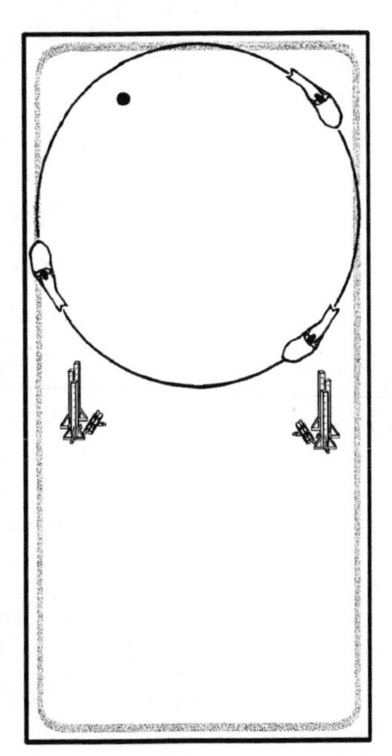

You may be a little nervous during the introduction; it is often difficult to concentrate on checking tack and clothing whilst suffering a state of nerves. This part is vital though. Forgetting to check the tack, in most cases, will be detrimental to your success. Take a deep breath, take a few deep breaths, and concentrate on this phase.

Design your own warm-up assessment plan, together with 'lines' to learn throughout the routine. During the warm-up do observe the riders and give relevant corrections. The first few minutes are important as this gives the Examiners their first impressions of you.

You need to show your control and organisation of the group whilst observing and teaching the riders in front of you.

Remember your vantage point, stand where the Examiners can hear you. Avoid standing in the centre of the school or moving about constantly.

Do not worry if at some time you have a panic attack. '*Oh no what do I do now? What was I supposed to be doing next? I have forgotten my plan. She's done that wrong what should I do? That was a bad transition should I stop her and do it again?*' Many candidates have at least one panic attack during the lesson, just take your time, breath, think. If the transition was bad but it is too late to change it, mention it and request that, next time the transition can be ridden more correctly. '*The transition to canter was a little hurried. When you next ask for canter, take your time, sit for a few strides of trot first and then slowly ask for canter.*'

If an incident occurs that could be potentially dangerous, coolly take control. For instance, one rider is doing the canter exercise around the school, whilst the rest of the ride is in walk. Rider cannot stop horse cantering. 'I can't stop the horse,' cries the rider.

Firmly state, '*Come onto a circle now. Rest of the ride, prepare to halt and halt.*'

Now with the rider on a circle, '*Sit up Carol, take a firmer contact with the reins, now sit up again and bring the horse to trot. Good. Now to walk.*' Mentally make a note this horse has the control.

Keep the lesson safe. If the plan is to improve the canter but one rider is obviously having trouble and becoming anxious, keep this rider in trot most of the time. If the rider is supposed to jump from canter but the horse rushes off leaving the rider behind, bring them through in trot. When or if, you consider it safe, then ask them to canter for a short space, but only if you think it is safe. If the Examiners question you afterwards, as long as you can give practical reasons for your actions, this will be acceptable.

Use cones, poles, the school letters or markers on the walls; use the arena to your advantage. Though there are many variations and positions to place the poles, when giving lessons in the Preliminary Teaching Test, you need to keep the lesson safe, simple and quick.

Most of all believe in yourself and what you are saying. It really does show if you have faith in what you are teaching.

CHAPTER 21

The Lecturette

The lecturette is chosen from a list of subjects covering stable management, horse care and handling. Though comparatively short compared to the other sections of the PTT syllabus, the lecturette is important. The Examiner will be assessing preparation, presentation and practical experience.

Test Format

At the beginning of the day each candidate will be given a slip describing the subject for the lecturette. The group giving the lecturette first will have a few minutes to prepare. The other groups are normally given some preparation time at the beginning of the day or between their group lesson and theory session.

Lesson Brief

Give an oral lecturette of up to 5 minutes suitable for BHS Stage II, Riding Club Grade II or Pony Club C students.

General Preparation

Study the list of subjects and organise a lecture plan for each one. Though most seem quite simple, when studied in detail some are more complicated than on first appearance. Other subjects cover such vast areas that deciding on the key points and making these as brief as possible is a test of organisation and planning.

The preparation includes

- Collecting information on each subject.
- Organising this into a logical sequence, listing the key points.
- Reducing the information into a brief form.
- Arranging the information onto a lecture card.

Information

The information for each of the subjects is collected from books, from stable management lectures and from personal experience.

Though this information is not needed in great depth (there is not sufficient time to deal with any subject in detail within five minutes) you will need to study the subject matter well. You need to keep the information relevant, follow a logical sequence and insert any important details, in as brief and clear a manner as possible.

The list of lecturette subjects covers a wide selection of topics relating to horses, their care, handling, stable and grassland management. The subjects are described below to give you an idea of the range covered. The actual list of subjects is occasionally updated so you will need to obtain a current list prior to your Test.

The subjects include

Saddlery	Stripping, cleaning and reassembling a bridle Fitting a snaffle bridle Checking a saddle for safety Fitting a GP saddle Types of martingales, functions and fitting Organising the Tack Room Storage of tack
Clothing	New Zealand rug, functions and fitting Cleaning and storing rugs and blankets Rugs: types, functions and fitting Brushing boots, types, functions and fitting
Safety	Fire precautions and fire drill Safety precautions in and around the yard Safety precautions when handling horses
Public relations	Receiving and looking after clients and visitors
Yard Management	Maintaining an indoor school Maintaining an outdoor school
Bedding	Mucking out/Skipping out Types of bedding, advantages and disadvantages
Routines	Daily routine, reasons for Importance of the routine
Feed	Rules of watering and feeding Organisation of the feed room Feeding school horses Preparing feedstuffs Bran, advantages and disadvantages Cooked foods, function and preparation

Horse Care	Keeping school horses fit and well Preventing staleness, sourness and other problems in school horses School horses, possible problems and prevention The horse's foot: care of, signs for shoeing Signs of good and bad shoeing Roughing off, procedures Grooming; types of, reasons, procedures Turning horses out into the field; method and safety Catching horses in the field, safety aspects
Conformation	Good and bad points of conformation How conformation affects action
Grassland Management	Checking the fields before turning the horse out
Clipping	Types of clip, reasons for Preparation of horse for clipping including clippers Role of assistant when clipping Safety rules when clipping
Equine First Aid	Signs of good and ill health How to treat minor wounds Taking temperature, pulse and respiration Sick nursing and isolation procedures Worms and worming procedures, worm control

Organising the Lecturette

After collecting the relevant information, organise this into a logical pattern, highlighting the key points.

For example - **Bedding types: advantages and disadvantages.**

Reasons for bedding

1. To prevent the **jarring** effect on the feet and legs of a horse standing for hours on a hard surface.
2. To provide **insulation, warmth** and **protection** from draughts.
3. To encourage the horse to **stale**.
4. To allow the horse to **roll and rest** in comfort.
5. To prevent the horse from **slipping and falling**.

Types - The main types are Straw, Woodshavings or Woodchip (often called shavings), Peat moss, Shredded paper and Rubber matting.

Straw

Traditional type of bedding.

There are three types of straw

1. **Oat**; palatable, likely to be eaten by the horse. Porous, tends to become saturated and heavy.
2. **Barley;** palatable and, though modern farming methods are making this less likely, may contain sharp ears or awns irritating to the horse's skin.
3. **Wheat**; best type, one most commonly in use, less edible, contains no awns.

Straw, advantages and disadvantages:

Advantages	Disadvantages
✓ Easy to obtain ✓ Economical to buy ✓ Bales are convenient to store ✓ Permits free drainage, as long as the stable floor has drainage outlets ✓ Bright, comfortable, warm bed	✗ Labour intensive, must be mucked out thoroughly each day ✗ Straw may be eaten by the horse ✗ Can be dusty or contain fungal spores causing respiratory problems ✗ May be difficult to obtain good straw constantly, no guarantee of good quality so buyer must always be observant to avoid bad straw

Woodshavings or Wood chip

Shavings of wood packed into plastic bags called bales. Several varieties to choose from: large wood chip or softer, finer shavings.

Bales available in different sizes, from the smaller bale of 20 to 25 kgs, to the larger bales of 30 to 35 kgs.

Advantages	Disadvantages
✓ Economical ✓ Easy to obtain ✓ Bright, comfortable bed ✓ Labour and time saving if kept clean and droppings removed frequently ✓ Will not be eaten by the horse ✓ Good for horses with respiratory problems	✗ A bed of shavings needs to be kept clean, as it is quite porous, becomes soggy and dark in colour. Droppings and soiled patches need to be removed frequently ✗ Cannot be disposed of easily ✗ Not quite as comfortable as straw unless a very thick bed is laid ✗ Not as warm as straw because there is no trapped air ✗ It is more expensive than straw

Rubber matting

Rubber matting is being used more often as a stable bedding. It can either be used on its own or with other bedding material on top.

Advantages	Disadvantages
✓ When used on its own it is dust free ✓ Easy to muck out as the dung is removed and urine cleaned by hose pipe or a proprietary cleaner ✓ After the initial outlay there is no other bedding to buy, so upkeep can be cheap ✓ If used alone reduced risk of infection for a horse with an injured lower leg, no shavings or straw to irritate wound	✗ It may not allow the horse to lie or roll in comfort, if at all ✗ It can appear revolting when not cleaned properly and the dung is trampled around by the horse ✗ There is often a smell from the ammonia fumes ✗ Urine often streams out into the yard ✗ The stable needs good drainage to allow the urine to drain away ✗ May not offer warmth ✗ There are no banks for insulation, to protect from draughts or to prevent the horse from becoming cast

There are now different types of rubber matting on the market that is more comfortable and provides efficient drainage. Rubber matting works well combined with some shavings or straw.

Shredded Paper

This bedding consists of paper pieces.

Advantages	Disadvantages
✓ Dust free, good for horses affected by stable dust ✓ Inexpensive to buy ✓ Benefit to horses who may suffer from allergies	✗ Being absorbent, paper becomes heavy when saturated which makes it difficult to muck out ✗ When dry the paper can blow about the yard in windy conditions ✗ Shredded paper is often made from old printed newspaper that can leave stains on the horse, particularly a grey ✗ Needs skipping out frequently

Peat moss

This can provide a comfortable bed but needs cleaning frequently.

✓ Not palatable ✓ No dust or spores ✓ It does not catch fire easily so particularly useful where there is a risk of fire	✗ Expensive to buy ✗ Becomes very soggy and heavy ✗ Tends to be dark in appearance ✗ Difficult to purchase ✗ Can be difficult to dispose of even though it is an excellent garden manure when rotted

These are the main types of bedding used. There are also various new beddings on the market such as shredded cardboard, specially treated hemp bedding, and dust extracted chopped straw.

Lecturette Cards

When the information has been collected, condense it into note form and write this onto a filing card.

The information can be written out in long hand or short hand. Short notes are quite sufficient as the base of a lecturette.

The information for each subject is then placed into a logical order.

- ❖ Introduction
- ❖ Key points with relevant information
- ❖ Conclusion

You may refer to the card during the lecturette, though often having collected the details and written the cards out, you will remember the information and may only need to refer to the card either prior to the lecturette or once during the lecturette.

Example of lecturette card

Introduction	**Lecturette on types of bedding: their advantages and disadvantages**
Reasons for use	prevent jarring, provide insulation and warmth, stale, roll and rest, prevent slipping and injury
Types of bedding	**Straw** - 3 types, **Oat**: palatable/porous, **Barley**: palatable and contains awns **Wheat**: best and most popular
Advan	Good availability, economical, easy to store, drains well, bright comfortable bed
Disadvan	Labour intensive, eaten, dusty, fungal respiratory problems, difficult to recognise good quality
	Wood shavings, bales in plastic bag
Advan	Economical, easy to obtain, labour saving, not eaten, less dusty, bright bed
Disadvan	Porous, dark and soggy, difficult disposal, not as comfortable, not as warm
	Peat Moss
Advan	Not eaten, dust free, fire proof
Disadvan	Expensive, soggy and heavy, availability difficult
	Shredded Paper, newspaper, magazines
Advan	Dust free, fairly inexpensive
Disadvan	Porous, heavy when wet, blow about, fire hazard, stains from print (grey horses)
	Rubber Matting
Advan	Dust free, once installed inexpensive, reduced risk of infection
Disadvan	Uncomfortable, cannot roll, cold, ammonia fumes, bad drainage, no banks
Conclusion	Straw traditional and most widely used. Good for most horses. Shavings little more expensive; beneficial for horses who eat straw or for respiratory problems. New types of bedding always being introduced - include shredded cardboard, specially prepared hemp, dust free straw cuttings and various types of rubber matting more comfortable, good to use with straw or shavings. More expensive though and difficult to obtain, straw and shavings remain the most popular.
Notes	**Could use black or white board to write down types. May obtain samples if poss.**

Each subject can be planned and prepared in this way. It may take a little time, but you will sound so much more efficient, be more confident and give a more professional lecturette on the day through proper planning.

Once the lecturette is organised, you should practise in front of a mirror and then with a few friends or colleagues to improve your presentation. You will need to practise from your notes on the card, checking timing, voice projection and tone, body posture, eye contact, use of props and blackboard.

Timing

During practice, you will need to time the lecturettes by reading them out loud. At first you may find that the time is too long; especially when there is a lot of information contained in one subject.

Reduce the information to the most important details. If the time is too short add in more details. Aim at the five minute mark or just over.

Timing is important because you want to show that you know the subject by being able to give all your information. If the lecturette is too long the Examiner will probably stop you in mid flow. If too short, it may appear that you do not know the subject or have not prepared the information sufficiently.

Even in five minutes it is clear whether a candidate knows the subject or not. In an unprepared lecturette there will be lots of repetition, hesitation and information irrelevant to the subject matter.

Timing the lecturette is part of the planning for the PTT and will show that you are willing to work at preparation.

Voice Control and Projection

Practice helps with voice control and projection. Speak *slightly* more slowly, sound waves need time to reach the audience. Speaking at a normal speed often sounds rushed, garbled and inaudible. A slower speed allows each word to be spoken clearly, the meaning as well as the sound of the word needs to be understood. This also allows you to take more breath, which in turn increases the voice projection.

Voice projection is the ability to increase the distance and audibility of sound without shouting. Think about speaking directly to a person (or an imaginary person) at the back of the room. Automatically the voice will be louder than talking to someone on the front row.

Breathing is also important, words are sounds formed by air being pushed through the vocal chords, speaking takes breath. Breathing a little more deeply and a little more frequently increases the voice production.

Another important aspect of public speaking is mannerisms, those little automatic, habitual phrases that creep in unnoticed by the speaker but which are a constant annoyance to the audience.

'Erm....' 'You know what I mean?' 'Right'.

Notice them, then try to eliminate them.

Presentation of the Lecturette

On the Test Day your group of four or five candidates will be taken to a lecture room and each of you will be requested to give the five minutes lecturette on the chosen subject. You will stand in front of the audience, which will include the other candidates and an Examiner. Occasionally all the candidates are gathered together to give their lecturettes but this is unusual.

Take a deep breath and introduce your subject.

'Good morning everyone, my name is……… I shall be giving you a lecturette on types of bedding, their advantages and disadvantages.

When in his stable the horse needs some type of bedding on the floor. The reasons for this are to protect his feet and prevent jarring, to provide insulation and warmth, to encourage the horse to stale, so that he can roll and rest and to prevent him slipping and injuring himself.

The traditional bedding is straw of which there are three types, oat, barley and wheat. Oat straw is palatable and is likely to be eaten by the horse, barley has awns which can prick the horse when he lies down. The best type of straw is wheat.

The advantages of a straw bed are…..'

As you are giving this lecturette the main points may be written on the board.

Types: Straw - oat, barley, wheat

Shavings

Peat Moss

Shredded paper

Rubber matting

Having given all the information on the card you will then conclude:

'Straw is the traditional and most widely used bedding, good for most horses. Shavings are a more expensive; but are beneficial for horses who eat straw or for those who have respiratory problems.

New types of bedding are always being introduced on the market; these include shredded cardboard, specially prepared hemp, dust free straw cuttings. These new types of bedding though are normally more expensive and difficult to obtain. Straw and shavings remain the most popular bedding for horses'

You can look at your audience and ask,

'Are there any questions on the information I have given?'

The Examiner may then ask a question such as:

'Which is easier to stack straw bales or shaving bales?'

Answer - *'Straw bales. Most commercial shaving bales are wrapped in plastic that slips; also the sides curve outwards so they are not level when stacked on top of each other.'*

Practical information gained from experience is essential. Though no candidate will be expected to know everything about every topic, information gained from practical experience is as valuable as that gained from study.

Through the lecturette, keep your voice natural, as if talking to a friend or colleague; this will give your voice rhythm, cadence. Often when speaking in public, through nervousness, the voice becomes dull, monotonous, one toned. This is boring, uninteresting, unenthusiastic, lacks energy and power.

Stance and Posture

Stance and posture are essential to voice projection, standing upright, chest expanded with relaxed shoulders and neck will increase the volume.

Posture is important for appearance, authority and relaxation. The way a speaker stands and carries the body is a visible sign of confidence, ability and competence, which in turn indicates authority. This helps the audience to relax, increases their listening and awareness; they become involved in and part of the communication process.

A poor stance, shoulders bent, hunched back, gives the appearance of tension and nervousness, incompetence, reduces the voice projection, the audibility and makes the audience feel uncomfortable.

Frequent movements of the hands, or even the head can distract an audience's listening. In a short lecturette this may not be a vital point but it is worth noticing for future reference.

Eye contact

The speaker needs to involve the audience; there is no surer way of doing this than to make eye contact. This is an important point.

Look at each person eye to eye for a few seconds at a time. Occasionally, when thinking, your eyes will stray to the back of room, but then look and make eye contact with each person again.

A speaker who constantly looks at the back wall and never makes eye contact with the audience appears nervous, unclear, uncommunicative and is uninteresting.

Make eye contact with each separate person in the room, not one individual constantly. This will make them feel embarrassed.

A smiling, relaxed face, looking at each listener, speaking with enthusiasm, energy and vitality in a clear, concise way will create a captive audience.

Props

Many of the lecturette subjects are made more interesting by the use of props; tack (saddle, bridle or martingale), feed, grooming kit, medical kit, rugs, boots or bandages, anything that may be borrowed from the Test Centre. The yard manager will normally make equipment available on the Test Day. You will need to request props during your Lecturette preparation time. This is another reason why the preparation of lecture cards is useful; you will have more time to collect any props you require.

The blackboard (or whiteboard) is a useful aid; you can write down the key points included in the subject.

Preparation for the PTT lecturette, will not only help you succeed in the Test, it also acts as a preparation for your career afterwards. Organising stable management lectures and designing teaching cards can be useful for teaching in the future.

Test Tips

To keep up to date on current information, new technologies and inventions on the market, read the advertisements in the equine magazines. These are full of information on new products, foodstuffs, prices, equipment and types of Wormers available, all of which will add to your practical experience.

Practising in front of people is **vital**, friends, relatives, co-workers, even if you have to bribe them with a cup of tea and a slice of chocolate cake. Those in the audience with equine knowledge will be useful to comment on any points that are either incorrect or not clear. Those without equestrian knowledge can indicate if the information is understandable.

At first you may be self-conscious but this type of practice will help. You will become clearer, more confident, able to arrange and relate the facts in a logical manner. Your voice will become steadier, louder, more audible and the subjects will become much clearer in your head.

Ask your audience for feedback, are the words too short, too long, too simple, too complicated. Did you understand all that I was saying, the points I was making? Can you hear me? Do I come over as being confident? Any comments or criticism you receive will help to improve your style.

Do not worry about criticism, you can choose whether to accept it or not. Some criticism is valid and increases your understanding and competence; some criticism is personal opinion and may or may not be relevant. Taking criticism and using it to positive advantage is one of the skills of life.

Preparation, practice and organisation for the lecturette will be amply rewarded. This type of education will increase and develop your skills far beyond the Preliminary Teaching Test. It will be a solid foundation for all future lectures, lessons, conferences and any further public speaking throughout your career.

CHAPTER 22
The Lunge Lesson

For the lunge lesson in the PTT you need to be competent at lungeing a horse, being in control. You will then need to practise lungeing the horse whilst teaching a rider at the same time. You will also need to be knowledgeable about correcting faults and giving exercises to improve the pupil.

Test Format

During the Test Day the lungeing is normally held in the afternoon, though occasionally it is scheduled for the morning. The time allowed is 15 minutes approximately, in which you are requested to lunge the horse, then to teach the rider.

The lunge and lead rein lessons normally take place at the same time, being organised so that some candidates give a lunge lesson, some a lead rein. This is normally half of the whole group, chosen at random.

Lesson Brief

These are the aims for the lunge lesson.

- Assess the horse on the lunge.
- Use the equipment safely with confidence and competence.
- Teach the rider in front of you giving appropriate exercises.
- Teach so that the lesson is progressive, the rider should improve.

The rider will be an adult up to novice level. The work will begin with stirrups and reins and then, at your discretion, the rider can be lunged without stirrups and reins.

The Examiners may give you one of the following subjects, which should be included in your lesson.

- Improve the rider through relevant exercises
- Work on transitions between walk and trot
- Improve the use of the weight and leg aids
- Rising and sitting trot
- Sequence of footfalls at walk and trot
- Riding without stirrups
- Increase the suppleness in the rider

General Preparation

The first part of the preparation is to practise lungeing the horse only, until you can use the equipment with confidence, controlling the horse's paces with the aid of the lunge line, whip and voice. Practise using different horses in various situations, indoor schools, outdoor arenas, until you are confident.

Practise assessing his obedience and response, upward and downward transitions, reactions to the lunge line and whip. Experiment by varying the feel on the lunge line, by changing your body stance slightly. Observe the horse; watch his gaits, his changes of pace when you change your body stance. This will help you become 'attuned' to the horse's own body language and will provide a good foundation for teaching riders on the lunge.

The next part of the preparation is to practise teaching a rider on the lunge. Though lungeing itself is learnt and practised for the Stages II and III, it is quite different lungeing and, at the same time, teaching a rider. You need full control so that the rider can concentrate on the teaching and riding without worrying about the horse.

This practice, particularly at the start, should be under the instruction and supervision of a qualified, competent instructor. At the beginning the rider may be competent, may even be able to help and give some useful information. As you progress, teaching novice riders will expand your knowledge and experience.

You will need to develop observation, to be able to distinguish the relevant points to improve the rider. Though there are standard exercises that improve most riders, the skill of the good lunge instructor is having the ability to observe and give relevant corrections for each individual rider.

Some time prior to the Test prepare a list of lunge exercises. These can be divided into exercises that improve the general position and exercises relating to specific problems, for instance, stiff, tense hips.

As time for the lunge lesson is short you need the ability to make a quick assessment of the rider, to observe and recognise problem areas, and to give appropriate exercises for improvement. After the lunge lesson, the Examiner may question you about the rider's problems and the relevance of the exercises.

Practice should also include mounting and dismounting the rider. Safety is just as important at these points.

Lunge Lesson Structure

You should be wearing a riding hat with the harness fastened, jodhpurs, boots, gloves, shirt and tie or stock, and jacket properly fastened.

On the Test Day the horse will be tacked up for lungeing when handed to you. Organise the lunge line and then proceed to check the tack. Check that the stirrups are secured for lungeing with the leathers looped through the stirrup irons.

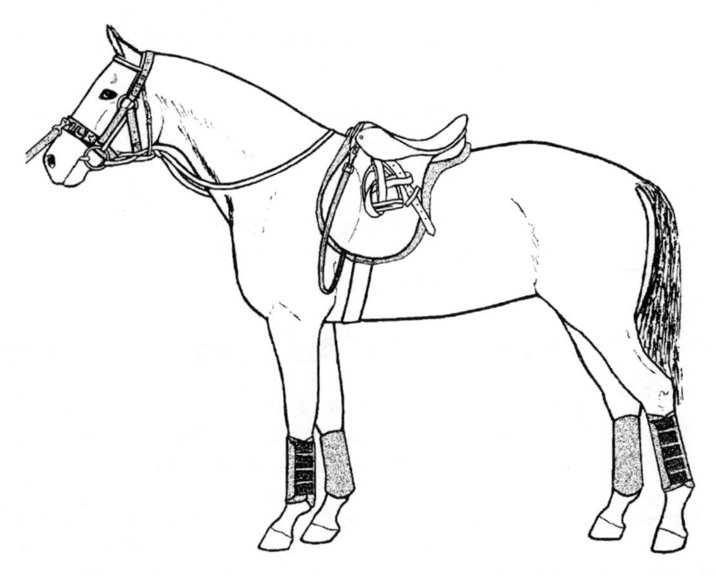

The reins should be looped through the throatlash and the side reins safely fastened to the 'D' rings of the saddle.

Assess the fit, condition and suitability of the lungeing equipment. You may be asked to give your opinions, for instance, whether you prefer leather side reins to synthetic ones. Make these checks efficiently to avoid wasting time.

The lunge lesson will be structured as follows:

- Introduction
- Warm-up and assessment (horse)
- Mounting the rider
- Warm-up and assessment (rider)
- Content
- Conclusion
- Dismounting the rider

Introduction

The lesson begins with introductions between you and the rider. You should observe the rider's clothing, hat, gloves, boots; a whip will not be required. If anything is incorrect mention this either to the candidate or the Examiners, for example if the rider is not wearing gloves request that some gloves are made available now.

'Good afternoon, my name is .... I shall be giving you a lunge lesson today. Your name is?'

You can be speaking to the rider whilst checking the tack, but remember, you should also make some eye contact with the rider to start the rapport.

You will normally be expected to warm the horse up briefly before asking the rider to mount. Explain this to the rider.

'Before your lesson I will warm the horse up by lungeing him for a couple of minutes and check his responsiveness to my voice. Please stand over there and I'll call you when I am ready.'

If the horse has already been used for a previous lunge session, you may warm him up again briefly to check his obedience. Alternatively you may be asked to continue with the lesson immediately.

Warm-up and Assessment (Horse)

During the test (and whenever a rider is taught on the lunge) the horse is lunged first before the rider mounts. This is the time to make your assessment of the horse and to develop his obedience to your commands.

The horse is lunged at this point without the side reins (loose lunged). This should be brief because the time is limited. Walk the horse for one circuit then two in trot. Halt the horse and fit the side reins.

Fit and fasten the outside side rein first as this saves time. Stay on the same rein; this also saves time and the lunge line does not need to be swapped around. Continue for two or three circuits; change the rein, repeat for two circuits.

When changing the rein, the horse may be turned in a large arc without having to unfasten the side reins.

When fitting the side reins keep the whip safely out of the way. Collect the lash and hold it with the whip handle so that it does not drag on the floor where you or the horse may step on it.

The warm-up session should take no more than four to five minutes. If the horse is obedient on the lunge, is working well and going forward actively, you can reduce the warm up period slightly, allowing yourself more time to teach. You may wish to explain this to the Examiners afterwards *'As the horse was going well in the warm-up I decided to continue with the lesson.'*

Mounting

Once the warm-up and assessment is completed the rider is called over to mount. The rider may check the length of the stirrup leathers and alter them if required.

Undo the side-reins and unfasten the bridle reins before the rider mounts.

Check the girth again and tighten if necessary. The rider mounts as normal either from the ground, by a leg up or from a mounting block. The girth and stirrups can be checked again. The side reins are fitted now at the start of the lesson.

Whilst the rider is preparing to mount, you may use this time to ask for some background information such as the rider's standard, or any problems.

'How long have you been riding? Have you had a lunge lesson before? Have you any problems you would particularly like to work on?'

This stage should be completed efficiently, safely and fairly quickly so that time is not lost before the lesson begins.

Warm-up and Assessment (Rider)

You will need to assess the rider's position first with stirrups and reins, in walk and rising trot.

'First to allow you time to warm-up and so that I can assess your position you will ride a couple of circuits in walk and trot, with reins and stirrups.'

Keep the horse working into the contact from the whip to the lunge line, and maintain the 'triangle - pizza wedge' shape between the lunge line, the horse and the whip.

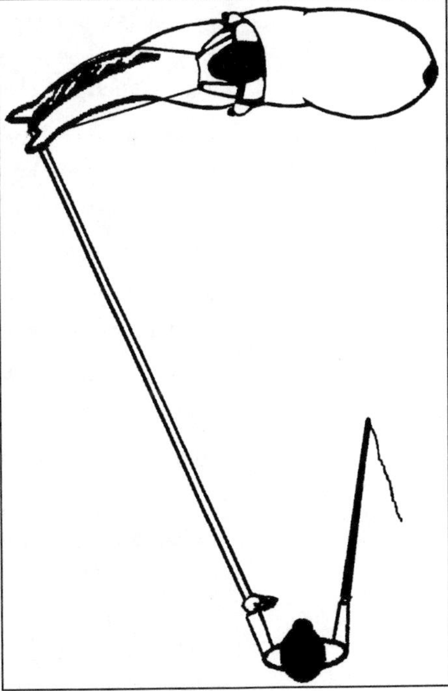

After a few circuits, change the rein and assess the rider's other side.

'I am now going to change the rein so that I can assess you in the other direction.'

Whilst the rider is warming up you can give corrections and helpful advice. The corrections will obviously be different for different riders.

'Good, now relax, lower the shoulders. Allow a little more weight to drop into the heel by gently stretching the back of the calf muscles and relaxing the ankle joint. Good.'

'You appear a little more stiff on this rein, bring the inside shoulder back slightly and the outside shoulder forwards so that you are sitting more correctly. Now lift the inside hand, so that it is level with the outside hand. That's good, can you feel the difference?'

The warm-up phase should last approximately three to four minutes.

Content

This section will consist mostly of working the rider without stirrups, at walk and trot, and of doing exercises to loosen muscles and joints, and to correct faults.

The horse is brought forward to walk and halt. The rider can be requested to quit and cross the stirrups. Check that the rider **takes both feet out of the stirrups.**

'You are now going to work without stirrups to improve your position. This will help you to loosen and stretch the hips and thighs, opening the angle of the hip and allowing the legs to stretch and lengthen.'

The bridle reins may be knotted into a loop; the rider can then hold this and the pommel of the saddle at the same time with both hands.

'Hold onto the saddle with both hands to begin with; this will help you to flow with the horse instead of stiffening against him.'

When ready the horse can be commanded to go forward into walk. After a few steps in walk the rider can learn to feel the horse's movement.

'Relax your hips so that you can feel the horse's movement through your seat. Can you feel the footfalls?

You may make corrections to the rider's position.

'Carry your upper body upright, head looking around the curve. Now relax your neck and shoulder muscles. Good. Stretch your legs down, dropping the weight into the heel, slightly raise the toe, but do not force it. The legs need to be supple and relaxed.'

After a few circuits at walk you can introduce some trot work. The rider should continue to hold onto the pommel.

'I am now going to command the horse to go into trot, so sit, relax, breathe and go with him through the transition.'

The rider can again be instructed to feel the rhythm of the trot pace through the seat. This does help to relax the pelvis area.

Make the transition from walk to trot as smooth as possible. The rider needs to maintain the balance without being suddenly thrown backwards by a sharp forward change, or be sat waiting for a sluggish, reluctant transition.

You will need to observe the rider in trot. By this time you will have assessed the rider's standard. If there is any stiffness or tension, you may need to keep the trot short to begin with and return to walk. The amount of trot work does depend on the fitness and suppleness of the rider. The rider may be good but begin rather stiff, in which case keeping the trot for longer helps to supple and loosen the body. You will need to make your own judgement.

You can bring the horse forward to walk and proceed to give the rider a couple of relevant exercises to improve position, balance or suppleness.

If the rider has worked well at walk and trot, you may progress by asking for two or three transitions between walk and trot. The rider needs to feel balanced through the transitions, avoiding stiffness in the hip area. You need to use your judgement on how much you can improve the rider through transitions.

The content plan does depend on the subject you have been given for the lesson.

After a few circuits, you can bring the horse to halt and change the rein. Repeat the exercises and transitions on the new rein.

Conclusion

After approximately five to seven minutes, you will need to bring the lesson to a conclusion.

With the horse at halt the rider takes back the reins and the stirrups, which may need lengthening. Assess the rider's position in sitting and rising trot on one rein to see the improvement.

Bring the horse to halt and give a brief précis of the lesson including the improvements.

'Well done, your back began to soften and relax, and your hips were flowing with the movement. Were you able to feel that? You need to concentrate on looking up and keeping the weight into the heel. You showed good improvement during that lesson. Thank you.'

You can explain what the rider needs in the future for further progression.

Presentation

This is as important in the lunge lesson as in every other type of lesson. You will need to be polite and professional to the rider so that you gain the rider's trust and confidence. At the same time you will need to build a rapport, be pleasant, smile and be welcoming, eager to teach the rider.

Timing, voice projection, body posture, stance and eye contact are important to the presentation of the lunge lesson.

Timing

For the PTT the time for the lunge lesson is so brief. By the time you have checked the tack, introduced yourself to the rider, warmed the horse up, prepared the rider, checked stirrups and girth, assessed the rider on the horse, there is not much time left for teaching.

You will really need to practise the timing before the Test day so that you know how efficiently to organise this lunge session.

If anything is incorrect, such as the stirrups not secured properly, this all takes more time. Fifteen minutes is not long, you will need to crack on with each section.

Voice Control and Projection

Voice projection is vital, particularly in the Test. You will need to sound louder than will normally be necessary when teaching a rider on the lunge. Your voice needs to be heard by the Examiners.

If you start to talk personally and quietly to the rider, the Examiners may call out that they cannot hear you. A quiet voice also sounds nervous and unsure, unprofessional and inefficient. Even when asking the rider's name and details, make sure the Examiners can hear you.

Even the most obvious of instructions or explanations need to be in a good loud voice so that the Examiner will hear what you are doing. For instance:

'I am first going to assess your position in walk and trot rising. Take up a contact with the reins and prepare to walk, and walk on.'

Stance and Posture

When lungeing your stance will need to be relaxed, confident and in control. Keeping the chest expanded, ribcage raised and the head up, will help with voice projection. Remember to breathe.

Do not move about unnecessarily, you should be able to keep to one spot when lungeing, just moving at the centre of the circle.

Keep the lunge line taut and in contact with the horse, straight without twists. Keep the whip pointing to the horse's hocks. When moving into and around the horse keep the whip out of the way so that you do not accidentally hit the horse or the rider.

Eye Contact

The rider will often turn around to look at you when you make a correction or comment. Though you will need to observe the horse to give commands and watch the rider's position, you will need to look directly at the rider at certain times.

Test Tips

Teaching equitation through lungeing, if done correctly, is a superb method of improving riders. You will need to learn this skill from an instructor who has the ability of teaching on the lunge. Watching qualified instructors giving lunge lessons is a useful method of expanding your experience and knowledge.

There are some important points to remember for the lunge lesson. As soon as you enter the school you are in charge of the horse and rider, not the Examiner. You will need to assess the tack, the equipment and the rider's clothing, pointing out anything that may be incorrect. You will need to have a confident attitude showing both the rider and the Examiner that you are in charge.

You will need to control the horse's paces, keeping the walk and trot active. The rider will achieve little if the horse is sluggish and reluctant to move forwards. When warming the horse up before the rider mounts, assess the horse. If he is sluggish, now is the time to make him more obedient. Send him forwards so that he realises you mean business, this should make him more obedient with the rider on board. If the horse is still sluggish during the lesson, you may need to take up some lunge line and step in towards him to make him move or even touch him with the whip just above the hocks.

Avoid sending the horse off sharply with the rider on board; this may cause the rider to lose balance. This does need careful and capable control.

Do not ask the horse for canter on the lunge.

Keep the exercises appropriate to the rider so that these will help towards improvement. When giving corrections say something complimentary first, then something constructive. If the rider is fairly competent at one exercise, move on to something else. Do not continue teaching something if the rider does not need it. Progress on to another exercise or make the exercise more difficult. Always remember safety though, do not give any exercise that may make the rider unsteady or cause pain.

If there is a problem deal with it swiftly but calmly. For instance if the horse is a little fresh, take immediate control, bring him to walk and halt, ask the rider to take back the stirrups and proceed at a quiet pace. You may even shorten the side reins slightly for more control. If the horse is obviously unsuitable you may even need to stop the lesson and request another horse. This is your lesson, your responsibility, use your judgement.

If you have prepared for this section of the Test, you will feel confident and be able to build a rapport with the rider, showing that you can give a good lesson on the lunge.

CHAPTER 23
The Lead Rein Lesson

This chapter explains the lead rein lesson and the preparation required. The structure of this lesson is described in detail with examples of the language required when teaching children.

Test Format

The lead rein lesson lasts for 15 minutes, and takes place in an indoor or outdoor school during the afternoon. The arena may be divided into two or three smaller areas with two or three candidates teaching children at the same time.

Lesson Brief

The aims for the lead rein lesson are:

1. Assess the child; this includes assessing if the child is capable to be let off the lead rein.
2. Teach the child an appropriate lesson for improvement.

The lesson should be relevant for the child you are teaching. The Examiners, however, may set a specific subject, which should be included in the lesson.

- ❖ Mounting and dismounting.
- ❖ Checking and altering girths and stirrups.
- ❖ Basic riding position.
- ❖ How to hold and shorten the reins.
- ❖ The natural aids.
- ❖ Transitions, between walk and halt.
- ❖ How to hold, use and change the whip.
- ❖ How to ride turns, circles and changes of rein.
- ❖ Trot work at sitting trot.

General Preparation

Teaching children is different in many ways to teaching adults. Whether or not you are used to children, you will need to practise teaching children and supervising them around ponies. As preparation for the Test, practise giving at least one child a couple of lead rein lessons. If possible give two or three different children lessons to increase your experience.

Design a short lead rein lesson for a child. Work out every detail from the time the child is introduced. Even the simplest of actions may need to be explained, for instance the child may not be able to mount, not understand about walking too close to the pony's hindquarters, may not know how to hold the reins, tighten the girth or alter the stirrups.

Plan the explanations you will use for mounting, holding the reins, asking the pony to walk forward, to halt, to turn a corner. The technical aspects need to be correct but the language needs to be that of the child.

Lead Rein Lesson Structure

If you are chosen to give a lead rein lesson, you will be allocated a pony and introduced to the child. From that point you are responsible for the child and the lesson.

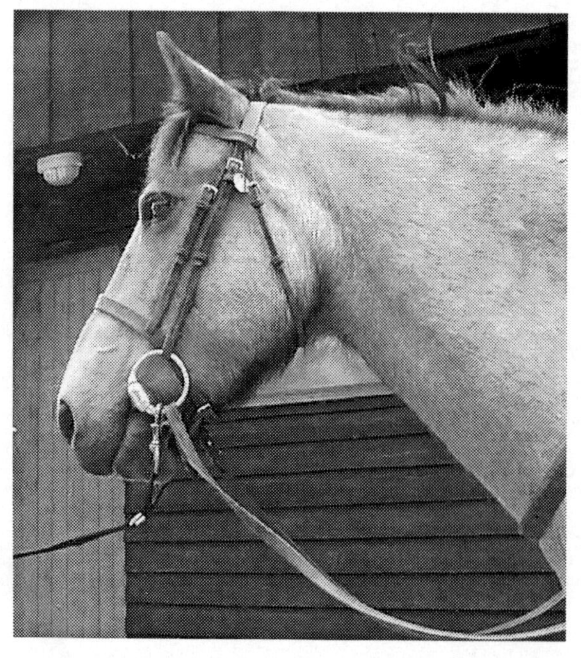

- Check the pony's tack, saddle, girth, stirrups, bridle, lead rein, neck strap.
- The stirrups should be the correct size for a child, ideally safety stirrups. The child's foot can easily slip through a large adult stirrup and become caught.
- The bridle reins should be the correct size; too long a rein can become looped around the child's foot.
- The lead rein should be attached using a link or coupling of leather or chain from the bit. There are special lead reins with this coupling attached. Alternatively the pony may wear a headcollar under the bridle or the lead rein can be fastened to a cavesson noseband.
- The pony should be wearing a neckstrap or breastplate.

If anything is incorrectly fitted, worn or missing, mention this to the Examiners at the start.

You should check the child's clothing. This is important. The child should definitely have the correct hat, gloves and suitable boots.

You may wish to test the hat for fit by gently pulling it backwards and forwards on the child's head.

The boots should have a heel and a smooth sole. Many small children wear wellingtons with a flat or ridged sole; if this is the case, this should be mentioned to the Examiners.

Even if the child has just had a lesson check the pony, tack and child's clothing again. The child is now your responsibility.

You will need to wear a riding hat with harness fastened, boots, gloves and carry a short riding whip.

Introduction

The lead rein lesson is of a short duration so the introduction and mounting should be performed efficiently. The introductions are made first.

'Hello I'm Gemma. And your name is ……? I'm going to give you a short lesson on this pony today.'

As you prepare for the lesson remember to keep the child in your sight. If you have to walk the pony and child into the school, make sure the child stays by your side. You could ask questions to maintain her attention and keep mentioning her name now and again; this also creates the rapport.

'How old are you Helena? Have you ridden before? Do you have lessons? Have you ridden this pony before? Do you know her name? What colour is she?'

Keep speaking to the child, to give her confidence, to build up a rapport and to encourage her to enjoy the lesson. Keep the child near you, do not let her wander off on her own or walk around the back of the pony.

'Do you know how to approach a pony? That's right from the side towards her shoulder. You can say Hello Apple Pie so that she knows you are there. You can pat her on her neck and shoulder.'

You may show how to check and tighten the girth; remember to check both sides, and explain why this is important to hold the saddle level.

'What's the first thing you should do before mounting the pony? What should you check on the saddle first?' Pause to see if the child can answer.

'Do you know how to check if the girth is tight enough? I'll show you how to tighten a girth. You should check both sides, do you know why?'

'When you walk around the pony to the other side, should you walk around the front or the back of the pony? Why?'

Encourage the child to chat and give answers. Keep smiling; facial expression is important to a child, you can show delight, amazement, they love it.

Mounting

To prepare for mounting, explain how to pull down the stirrups.

'First take the leather from under the iron. Now pull the iron down the leather gently. If you pull it down quickly it will make a loud noise which could frighten the pony. Also this will rub the leather and ruin it. Now walk with me around the front of the pony and show me how to pull the stirrup down on the other side.'

To save time, the stirrups can be pulled down at the same time as checking the girth on both sides. If the child is tall enough you could demonstrate how to measure the length of leather against the child's arm.

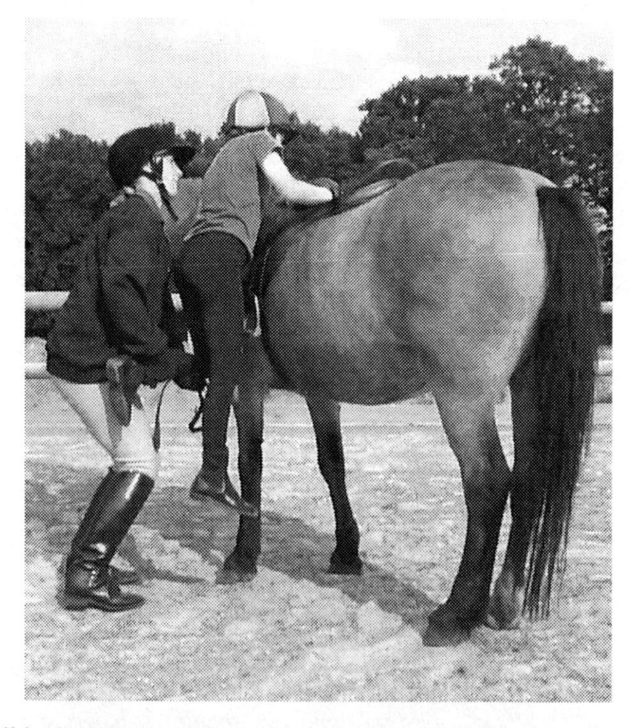

Show the child where to stand for mounting, how to hold the reins and some mane. Explain about putting the right hand over the saddle, not to hold onto the cantle. The child may not be tall enough to mount on her own. Some children are quite able but a smaller child will need to be given a leg up or physically lifted onto the saddle.

Make sure your riding whip is kept safely tucked under your arm or out of the way as you lift the child into the saddle.

Check the stirrups; often children need shorter stirrups until they have developed strength in their legs. Check that the child's foot is in the correct position in the stirrups; that is with the widest part of the foot on the stirrup iron. Check the girth again.

Ask if the child knows how to hold the reins and if not show and explain. Instruct the child to shorten the reins until they can feel pony's mouth. If the child is small and likely to be unsteady, the reins can be held with both hands whilst the child holds onto the pommel of the saddle or neckstrap for stability.

This section of the lesson needs to be completed fairly quickly, within five minutes.

Content

You can begin by explaining the rider's position, in simple language. Though the child may not be able to manage the whole position, this will help her in the future.

'Sit up tall, head looking forwards so you can see where you are going, shoulders relaxed, elbows bent, legs a little further back and the heels down.'

With the pony at halt, **you may now check the child's position from the rear** either by holding the end of the lead rope, or if the rope is not sufficiently long, by asking an assistant to hold the rope. An assistant will give you the freedom to check safely and more accurately from the rear and to make adjustments to the child's position if necessary.

The child's body should be straight, shoulders level, feet level in the stirrups. The child's spine should be in line with the pony's spine. (The pony needs to be standing level on all four feet, not resting a leg.)

Once completed you can begin to explain the natural aids for walk and halt.

❖ **Always warn and prepare the child before doing anything. Always give her the time to prepare and adjust for a change of pace or direction.**

'Now you are going to ask the pony to walk on. I want you to nudge her on her sides with both your legs.'

Though it is difficult for some children to use the leg aids effectively and it is very tempting to tell them to kick, teaching them to nudge with the inside of the leg will eventually develop the correct muscles. If the pony does not respond instruct the child to give a really firm nudge whilst commanding the pony to walk on.

'Good, now we're going to ask the pony to stop and halt. Sit up straight, keep the legs by the pony's sides, squeeze on the reins and at the same time ask her to whoa.'

The transitions to walk and halt can be repeated a couple of times.

The child can then be taught how to turn the pony around corners and to ride straight lines.

'You are going to ask the pony to turn to the left. Ask with the left rein and nudge with the legs. Look where you are going.'

Make any corrections when necessary so that the child understands and improves.

'Now ask her to turn to the right. You will need to shorten the reins so that the pony can feel it when you ask her to turn.'

'You are now going to change the rein. Do you know what that means Helena? Which rein are you on now? Which rein are we going on?'

If the child is older you may explain about the inside and outside of the pony.

Trot Work

The child may then try some short distance at trot starting with a few slow steps.

'Have you trotted on a pony before? Do you know how to rise to the trot?'

If the child is small and unsteady she should hold onto the neckstrap. You may need to hold onto the child's clothes at the back for security. For a small child the trot will be sitting, for a more capable child the trot can be rising, though some practise in sitting can be included in the lesson.

For a larger child, if you assess that she is confident and secure at trot, she may be able to hold onto the reins only.

'You are going to ask the pony to trot. Shorten the reins (children tend to have the reins too long). Now remember sit up and look ahead. Use the leg aids with nudges and say trot on.'

Keep the trot on straight lines. Avoid trotting around curves until you have assessed if the child is capable of doing this. Small children tend to lose their balance on corners and may slip out to the side. Make this first trot fairly brief to allow you to assess the child without problems or running out of breath.

Exercises

At halt, and then at walk, a few simple exercises can be introduced to help balance and confidence. Arm circling, 'the windmill', 'aeroplane' with arms in the air at shoulder level turning slowly from side to side, touching toes; left toe with the left hand and right toe with the right hand.

You can make the lesson more interesting by asking simple questions about the tack and the pony.

'What colour is the pony? How tall do you think she is? How many legs has she? What does she have on her feet? Can you think of anything on this pony which begins with B, S? What is the metal thing she has in her mouth? What is the hair on the top of her neck called? Do you know where her shoulder is?'

You can make the questions simple for a small child, a little harder for older children, then pretend to be amazed when the child answers correctly. *'Gosh you are clever Helena. How did you know that? Let me think of a harder one.'* They will love it.

For older or more experienced children who can ride corners and change of rein, progress onto more difficult exercises such as riding a large circle, figures of eight or weaving in and out of cones.

'You are going to ask the pony to go onto a circle. So take up your reins and ask the pony to walk on. You know that now, good.' (Encouragement, lots of it, praise.)

'Use both legs and ask with the inside rein. Do you know which is the inside rein?'

Even if the child does not fully understand the information, if said simply without fuss they will eventually learn the correct method.

For a more capable child it may be possible to do some trot around a large circle, perhaps varying this with transitions from trot to walk and then halt. If cones are available make use of these, mark out corners for turning, a square, a circle or a line of cones for the weaving exercise.

Conclusion

At the end of the lesson instruct the child to bring the pony to halt. Ask if there are any questions about the lesson, if there is anything they did not understand. The child can pat the pony as a thank you and prepare to dismount.

Dismounting

Before the child does dismount, briefly explain about this. How to take both feet out of the stirrups, hold onto the pommel of the saddle or some mane, swing the right leg over the back of the pony without hitting her and slowly slide down to the floor.

'What do you do to dismount? From which side do you dismount? Remember not to kick the pony on her back with your leg, she won't like it. Now put the stirrups up, remember to walk around the pony's front.' Children do often forget (as do adults).

Small children will need lifting off. With older children, stand by the side of the pony so that if the child does need help, if they slip backwards, they can be caught and held safely.

'Pat the pony and tell her thank you. Well done, you rode very well. I'd like you to have another lesson with me, would you like that? Good. See you next time.'

Points

With older children you will need to vary your explanations and corrections accordingly. Older children do not like being talked down to; you may treat them almost as adults.

Always explain and talk through everything. This is important not just for the child but to allow the Examiners to assess you.

Do not make abrupt turns and halts. Always warn and prepare the child.

Be aware of the child and pony. Be observant, keep an eye on the child, particularly in trot, to make sure the child is steady.

Frequently turning round to make eye contact will also build up the rapport between you and your pupil.

Keep the lesson flowing, do not spend a lot of time talking or lecturing. A child's attention span is short and they will become bored. Talk a bit then continue, talk a little more, then proceed.

Never let the lead rein become lose or fall on the floor.

Use your whip with discretion on the pony's hindquarters if the pony is sluggish. Sometimes ponies only need the threat of the whip, bringing it closer to their hindquarters, to encourage them.

Make explanations simple, to the point. Have loads of imagination. Use the props in the school such as the cones, the letters on the wall or fence.

Progression

After about five minutes of the lesson you should be able to assess if the child is capable of controlling the pony herself. If so, you may let the lead rope out and hold it near the end so that the child independently rides the pony, under your guidance.

After another few minutes if the child, in your judgement, is wholly capable of controlling the pony and the pony is quiet and reliable, the child can be let off the lead rein. This will show that you are able to assess when a child is ready to progress.

You do need to use your own judgement. If you are in **any doubt** as to the child's ability or the pony's reliability, **keep the lead rein fastened**.

As you may be unfamiliar with the pony, you may ask the Test Centre's instructor if the pony is suitable to be let off the lead rein. This could be done at the beginning of the class lesson, if the child looks as though she would be safe off the lead rein.

If questioned afterwards about your decision honestly express your opinion:

'I felt the child was progressing well but she was still a little unsteady and I did not want to let her off the lead rein within this short time. I let the lead rein out so that she could control the pony by herself. However she did cope well and the next time I would definitely let her ride on her own during the later part of the lesson.'

If the lead rein is removed, stay by the pony's side prepared to give help if necessary. You do not want to be stood in the centre of a circle, whilst the pony decides to go 'walk about'.

If the pony is off the lead rein and something occurs, such as a tractor starting up in the next field and the pony looks startled or the child looks anxious, put the lead rein back on. Explain the reasons to the Examiners afterwards should they ask.

In all circumstances, the lead rein lesson should always be **safe**; it will then be enjoyable and informative.

Test Tips

If you are not used to being with children, or even if you are, it has to be stressed that it is advisable to practise giving a child a lead rein lesson before the Test day. Some candidates have done well in all the other sections only to be let down by the lead rein lesson.

The introduction and mounting should be completed fairly quickly, time is short and the Examiners want to assess your teaching. Do not rush the child though, explanations will still need to be thorough and certainly audible by the Examiners.

Stay with the child at all times. Never leave a small child mounted on a pony unattended. For instance if using cones either place these out around the school before the lesson, or lead the pony and child around with you to position the cones.

Avoid doing physical games such as 'round the world' in the Test. These are not safe; a child could easily slip off the pony. That is the last thing you need in the Test.

Part of the assessment is about how you interact with children, how you gain their attention and obedience. This is a whole new subject for many who take the PTT. Children have a different perspective on life; they are eager to learn but have a short concentration span. Building a rapport with children is important; you need to be friendly and encouraging but also firm and in control.

You will also need to speak louder than normal so that the Examiners can hear and assess your teaching.

Often the 'child' is a staff member or a teenager. You will still need to treat the rider as a child, using the language and actions appropriately.

Occasionally the rider is a beginner adult on the lead rein, you should alter your teaching appropriately.

CHAPTER 24
Safety

All through the training scheme the British Horse Society emphasises the importance of safety when working with, caring for and handling horses. There will always be an element of danger because horses are living creatures with minds of their own. They react to situations through instinct and, even when highly trained, their instinctive behaviour can still be a source of injury.

The objective of the BHS training scheme is to minimise accidents by increasing the awareness of danger and by developing knowledge so that accidents can be prevented. The BHS also aims to teach the correct, safe method of dealing with accidents and incidents whenever they occur.

Prevention of Accidents

Preventing an accident is better than having to deal with injury, pain and trauma. All trainers and instructors of whatever level need to be aware of situations that may result in accidents. This awareness can be developed from personal experience, by learning through the experience of others and through study.

Knowing what type of situation leads to accidents is a major part of preventing such injuries from happening. This is the importance of creating safety within the yard, stable and school. The instructor, yard manager or the person in charge needs to control, as far as is humanly possible, the students, clients, pupils and horses.

Educating and informing staff and pupils is part of that control, creating awareness for all types of hazardous situations and how to prevent them.

The candidate of the PTT needs to be particularly conscious of safety and accident prevention when teaching various types of lessons.

Lessons

In any type of lesson the instructor needs to keep as much control as possible over the riders, their horses and the environment.

All the riders should be taught and made aware of the school rules.

All tack and clothing should be checked for fit and condition before mounting. This is the ultimate responsibility of the instructor.

All riders should be taught the correct basics from the start; this is **vital** for their safety. Often teaching these fundamental basics is overlooked through the assumption of knowledge. Often too riders forget or become apathetic to the danger.

All riders should be taught how to:

- check the tack, bridle, saddle, breastplates or martingales, brushing boots or bandages
- to tighten the girth smoothly and safely to avoid causing the horse pain
- to pull down and alter the stirrups
- to mount correctly from the ground, a leg up and from a mounting block
- to be aware of how and where to hold the whip when mounting
- to alter the girth and stirrups correctly when mounted
- to dismount correctly and safely
- to wear the correct safety clothing
- to lead the horse safely and correctly

In a lesson it is the instructor's responsibility to enforce these rules and safety methods for the protection of all the riders and horses.

Safety in children's lessons is essential. There are children who genuinely do not know or understand about horses and ponies. It is easy, having worked around horses for years, to forget that even the simple rules have to be taught and then repeated, until firmly imprinted into the child's mind.

Leaders should be taught how to lead, given instruction at the beginning of the lesson and be competent to deal with children.

All types of lessons should be situated in a safe environment. If, for some reason, there is an unusual disturbance near or in the school, the instructor should either stop the disturbance or take the class somewhere else for safety. Often it is the riders who are unsettled by something unusual; this passes quickly to the horses.

Horses do have their moments deciding that the lady with the umbrella will change any moment into something particular distasteful and nasty. Unless the rider is competent, knows the horse and can genuinely deal with this type of situation, the instructor needs to anticipate and prevent an incident.

Any disturbance, children running in the yard, a noisy audience, people clambering up nearby straw bales or chairs should be asked politely but firmly to stop.

Riders do have to learn to deal with awkward situations, but there is a time and place for this and putting the whole group or other riders at risk is irresponsible.

Stable management lectures should include the subject of safety, on the yard, in the box, in the field, working and handling horses.

Most safety precautions are common sense and for anyone working around horses these become second nature. Occasionally accidents do happen and, for those involved, knowing what action to take will greatly reduce the risk of further injuries or damage.

Rider Fitness

Another area where problems occur is rider fitness, or rather unfitness. Riding takes physical fitness, suppleness and, to some extent, strength. It also takes balance and this needs developing as much as muscle tone, supple tendons and ligaments.

Adult beginner riders, who have never ridden previously, do find riding physically demanding. It is better that the first lessons are short, no longer than 30 minutes, once or twice a week until the physical ability has increased to allow for an hour's riding.

Progress too needs to be steady, at a rate to suit each individual. Some beginners will be able to advance more quickly than others. Some will need time to adjust to the movements of the horse, to walk, then sitting trot, rising trot and canter.

Accidents occur when beginners are pushed too quickly. To ask a rider who is not balanced, fairly secure in the saddle or physically able, to canter large around the school could result in a fall and possible injury. Always assess the riders on their own merits and keep the pace within their ability.

Progressing too quickly may result in straining muscles, tendons, ligaments, may cause stress to the joints.

Children, though their young bones and muscles are more flexible, tire easily. They become physically and mentally tired. Again shorter lessons are more beneficial until they have grown older and developed physical strength.

You will need to be aware of rider tiredness and stress. Adult riders often will not admit to being tired, working around the school in sitting trot, in pain. You will need to read body language and facial expression. It is also simpler to instruct the rider at the beginning of the lesson that they do tell you when they are tired. Tiredness, stress to the physical frame, will only result in tension, pain, exhaustion and gripping.

As well as regular riding lessons, riders can improve their fitness by exercising at home, visiting a gym, or taking up another complimentary sport such as swimming.

Fire Precautions

Fire in a yard is always a potential threat because of the materials used for stabling, barns, and storage. Even though this is a life threatening danger, many yards seem unaware and completely unworried about fire hazards.

Regular fire drills are essential; to prevent panic and to save lives.

Fire prevention action such as proper storage for hay and straw, no smoking, regular checks of electric cables, should be a routine matter in any establishment.

Knowing what action to take in the event of fire, where everyone should go, how the horses should be dealt with, how to use the fire extinguishers, can save so much pain and agony. The local Fire Officer could be invited to the yard to give a lecture on the regulations and actions to take in case of a fire.

Training Staff

All staff should be taught about safety. This can be a vital part of the Preliminary Teacher or Assistant Instructor's responsibilities.

New staff can be given a safety lesson and lecture before they begin work. They can be taught the basic safety procedures for working in the yard, with stable equipment, how to carry tack, handle horses correctly, how to lead a horse, how to bring a horse in and out of the box.

There could be regular safety lectures weekly or monthly, with staff being encouraged to contribute with anything they think may be unsafe or inefficient.

There should certainly be regular fire practices, with staff practising the fire drill, directing clients and students to the meeting areas.

The yard could introduce regular first aid courses. These can vary from half a day to four-day courses during the year. Alternatively it could be part of the staff's training schedule to take and complete a first aid course outside the establishment.

It is recommended that no person under 16 years of age should be left solely in charge of an establishment, be allowed to instruct or be in charge of a lesson or ride.

Accident Procedures

Being safety conscious and taking a responsible attitude to training will prevent accidents and injuries. However even in the most efficient and safe establishment accidents can occur; it is part of being around horses. All staff should be taught and know the procedures in case of an accident.

Assess the situation

Prevent further accidents

Assess the **casualty**

Send for **help**

Remember the mnemonic - APACHe

Assessment - **P**revention - **A**ssess **C**asualty - **He**lp

Assess the situation

Use the first few seconds to assess the situation, vital if further accidents are to be prevented. Take a deep breath, keep calm and reassure those around you. Observe the situation and obtain information about the incident by asking what occurred, if this is not clear.

In all situations KEEP CALM. Taking control and remaining calm will prevent panic.

Prevent further accidents

This is essential if there are to be no further casualties or injured horses. The first rule is never put yourself at risk or into danger.

Make the area safe first to keep the others out of danger. Take charge, stop the ride if necessary, and ask someone to catch a loose horse if this is going to cause problems for the other riders or the casualty.

Control the traffic if this is a road accident.

If the horse is loose in the countryside, wood or forest, deal with the other riders and the casualty first. The horse will stop in time and may even return to the others.

Assess the casualty

When the area is safe assess the casualty.

In most cases the casualty will be able to stand and move within a few seconds after the accident. Always, though, advise the casualty to visit a doctor as soon as possible. The casualty may be suffering from an injury that is not apparent at the time, for example internal bleeding or delayed shock.

In the case of injury, broken bones, sickness, vomiting, head pains, back pains or any injury that is causing discomfort, keep the casualty quiet, relaxed, calm and send for professional help.

Unconscious Casualty

If the casualty is quiet, not moving possibly unconscious;

Remember the mnemonic - DR. ABC (Doctor ABC)

Danger, Response, Airway, Breathing and Circulation

First check if the casualty is in **danger** and make him safe. For example if he is lying in a ditch with his head in the water, the casualty will need to be moved to prevent fatality.

Check the casualty's **response**. Call his name, gently take hold of his shoulders. Observe his appearance and check responses if any: such as, eyes opening, trying to speak, movement.

Open and **clear the airway**. With one hand on the forehead and the other hand under the chin, gently tilt the head backwards so that the airway is open.

When a person is unconscious the tongue can slip backwards and block the trachea. Check the mouth for obstacles.

Check breathing by placing your ear near to the casualty's mouth, looking towards their ribcage. Listen for 10 seconds for sounds of breathing, to feel any air on your cheek and watch the casualty's ribcage for movement.

Check the circulation by pressing two fingers gently on the casualty's neck by the side of the windpipe and feeling for the pulse in the carotid artery. Continue to check for at least 10 seconds.

Send for help immediately

Recovery Position

If an unconscious casualty has to be left unattended, for example so that help can be summoned, the casualty has to be placed in the recovery position. Even if you are remaining, it is still vital that the casualty is put in the recovery position. This prevents the tongue falling to the back of the throat, or vomit shutting off the airway, both of which cause suffocation.

- Remove any glasses and bulky objects from pockets. Clear and open the airway first.
- Take hold of the casualty's nearest arm and place it on the ground, palm uppermost. The arm should be almost straight out from the shoulder with the elbow bent at right angles to the body.
- Bring the other arm over the casualty's chest and lay the back of the hand against the casualty's nearest cheek.
- Take hold of the leg on the far side and bend it gently at the knee.
- Holding onto the casualty's bent leg and the hand lying against the cheek, gently and slowly roll the casualty over towards you onto one side.
- Cover the casualty with a coat or blanket.

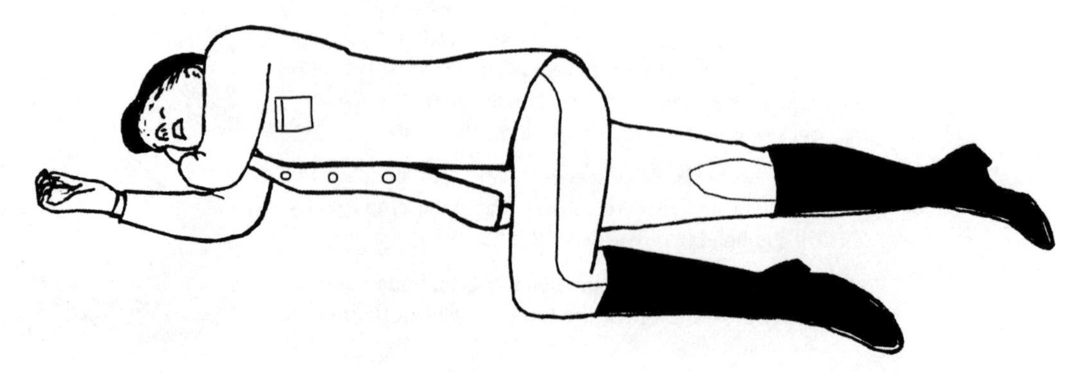

Conscious Casualty

Never try to deal with a situation on your own.

- **If in any doubt always send for help**

First aid may be given until help arrives for a life threatening injury or wound. In cases where there are several casualties, always attend to those that are quiet first. Someone who is groaning, moaning or screaming is obviously able to breathe. It is the casualty who is quiet who may be in the greatest danger.

When the casualty suffers an injury **do not allow the casualty to eat, drink or smoke**. Do not move the casualty unless absolutely necessary, give emergency treatment in the position found.

Remember the three B's, Breathing, Bleeding, Bones

Breathing: deal with any breathing problems first, if the casualty is not breathing every other injury is less important.

Bleeding: stem any serious, arterial or venal bleeding by ***direct pressure*** and by elevating the limb if possible, raising it above the level of the heart to slow down the rate of blood loss. Serious bleeding leads to shock and is fatal within minutes.

Bones: keep the casualty still, do not move them unless in a life threatening situation. Support the area of the injury with a sling for an arm, broken ribs and shoulder injuries. For leg injuries, place padding between the legs and tie the legs together above and below the injury.

Revision

Stage III. Broken bones, slings. Assessing a casualty, body check. Applying first aid practically.

Shock

This is serious and in accidents, whether or not the casualty is injured, most will suffer shock. It is also possible for those around to suffer shock, other riders, bystanders, those that come to help. Watch for the symptoms: a pale, sweaty, cold, clammy skin; shallow rapid breathing, yawning, gasping for air, dizziness, feeling sick; aggressiveness or anxiety.

To treat shock, first treat any injury; then lay the casualty down on a coat or blanket to prevent cold. Raise the casualty's legs above the level of the head; loosen tight clothing, a tie, shirt, belt. Cover and keep the casualty warm. Send for medical help.

Accident Report Book

After every accident the facts should be reported in the accident report book or form. This will include the date, time of the incident, name of casualty, horse, instructor and the basic facts describing the events. Also included should be any follow up information such as a stay in hospital or medical care. In the case of an accident on the public highway, an accident report form should be filled in as well as the book.

It is important to complete an accident report. If anyone needs to refer to the incident at a later date the facts are available as they were written down at the time. For insurance purposes or in the case of a lawsuit, this is vital.

Reports also help in the prevention of further incidents. If particular accidents keep occurring this would indicate there is a problem that needs solving or altering. Also reports give an indication of the type of accidents that occur so that all staff are made aware of dangers or hazards and can take appropriate action.

Administering Medicines

The rule is that no medicines should be given except by professional medical personnel or by the casualty himself. For instance, in the case of breathing difficulties where the casualty may be an asthmatic and need their inhaler, *the casualty must administer their own inhaler. A dose should never be given by anyone else or from someone else's inhaler, because of the possibility of giving an incorrect drug or cross-infection.*

First Aid at Work

Every yard should be equipped with a first aid kit, consisting of basic supplies, such as bandages, sterile pads, wound dressings, disposable gloves, eye pads, waterproof plasters, safety pins and scissors. There should also be a leaflet giving instructions for basic first aid.

The telephone numbers of the local doctor, hospital and veterinary surgeon should be available either in the first aid box or somewhere equally accessible.

Provision should also be made to have a qualified First Aider on the premises, possibly two or three so there will always be at least one on site. The equestrian industry is a high-risk category and having properly trained personnel on hand could, and often does, save lives.

Accident Procedures

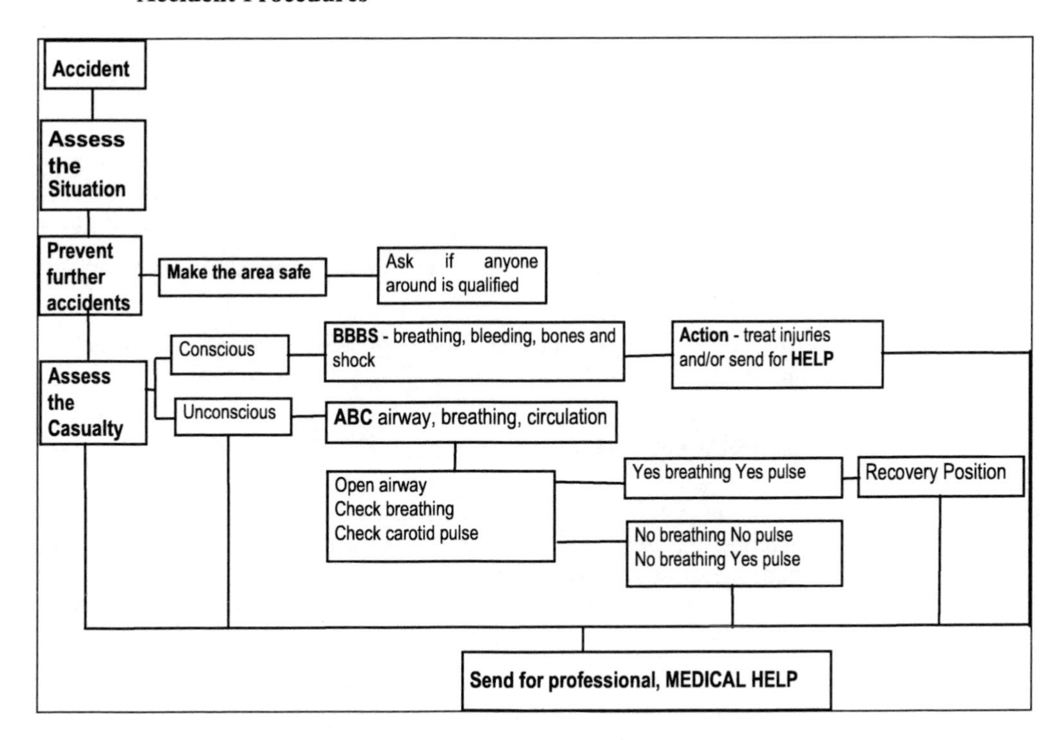

Personal Safety

When dealing with casualties and treating injuries, you will need to be aware of hygiene, of protection against diseases and infections. Infections, diseases and viruses are transferred through contact with bodily fluids absorbed through the mucus membranes, or through broken skin, that is via cuts, grazes, skin diseases.

When you need to treat open wounds or situations where bodily fluids are present, wear protective clothing, such as plastic gloves. Keep cuts and wounds covered with a waterproof dressing until properly healed. Always wash your hands before and after treating a casualty.

Proper protection may not always be possible particularly in situations occurring away from the yard or home, but being aware of the possibilities of transference of diseases and infections will create more care when treating casualties. A casualty who is bleeding can often apply direct pressure to the wound himself and stop or reduce the blood loss. If not, using a plastic bag to cover your hand, several layers of dressings or clean clothing will minimise the risk.

Another point is contact with casualties, how you touch a casualty and treat them. When treating a casualty always explain what you are doing and only touch them when and where necessary. Even if you are just remaining with a casualty until help arrives and giving them assurance by holding their shoulders, explain fully what you are doing and why.

Touching casualties needs care and thought, especially in the case where they are unconscious or half-conscious. The person who regains consciousness just as you are trying to loosen their clothing may not realise at first that you are trying to help.

Always talk to the casualty; tell them what you are doing even if they appear fully unconscious.

Always be aware of touching a casualty, keeping away from sensitive areas unless absolutely necessary.

Safety with riders

It is a sad fact that many today are frightened of being accused of sexual harassment, improper touching. In most cases this is clearly not so, especially when trying to help someone who has had an accident. However in many incidents instructors or assistants will not touch or be in contact with someone who has fallen off, through fear of being accused.

Even when teaching riders in normal circumstances avoid touching anyone around the legs, the thighs, the abdomen, the lower back and for ladies around the chest area. Avoid touching altogether if possible, but if necessary, perhaps to 'mould' into a basic riding position for instance, keep the contact to an absolute minimum.

This is also true with children. Touch only when necessary and never become over familiar or too tactile.

In most situations when dealing with people there are no problems. But instructors do need to be aware of their actions and behaviour so as not to put themselves at risk.

Test Tips

Safety precautions and accident procedures will be covered during the Theory section of the PTT. The Examiner may describe a hypothetical event about which you will be questioned, testing your ability to cope with problems, incidents and injuries. Not only will you be tested on your knowledge of accident procedures, but the way in which you answer, confidently and calmly will show how you react in situations.

For example you are teaching a group of students in the indoor school. The ride is in trot whilst the lead file is taking up canter and cantering large, coming back to trot before the rear of the ride. Halfway around the school the horse spooks and the rider falls off. The rider lies on the ground quietly whilst the horse speeds off around the school. What would you do? What would be your first action? How would you deal with the loose horse? What would you do with the casualty?

The first thing is to remember APACHE. Assess the situation quickly; prevent further accidents by dealing with the rest of the ride, bringing them to walk and then halt. Quietly catch the loose horse, or send someone else to do so, in case he causes more panic or tramples the casualty. Assess the casualty. If conscious keep him still and quiet, check responses. If unconscious do ABC, airway, breathing and circulation. Send for help. Your answers need to be calm, in a logical order, and sound confident and competent. This is how you will react in a situation.

It is strongly recommended that you revise the Safety sections in the Stages I, II and III books which cover First Aid, recovery position, bleeding, wounds, broken bones and shock.

If possible take a first aid course; whilst this will help you in your Test it is also a tremendous bonus to your life in general, at work, at home and even just out on the streets. Accidents happen anywhere, anytime and having the confidence to deal with these is tremendous. You may even save a life.

CHAPTER 25
Test Information

The Preliminary Teaching Test is the first actual teaching examination in the British Horse Society training scheme. For most candidates this will be their first experience of a teaching test and for some this may be a daunting prospect. Training and preparation is essential to achieve the confidence necessary to teach and lecture in front of Examiners.

Training Preparation

Candidates need to learn about the different aspects of horsemanship then practise to put this knowledge into terms that can be communicated to others. Candidates need to be capable of planning, preparing, designing and organising lessons to run progressively and in safety.

To achieve this does require time and work, practising as often as possible, teaching various lessons, increasing experience and competence. Consequently candidates will gain confidence in their teaching ability.

Assessment

For those being taught at a BHS Examination Centre, the instructor in charge will make continuous assessments. For those studying on a freelance basis or in a riding establishment that is not a Test Centre, an assessment from a qualified instructor is advisable. Ideally this should be done at a Test Centre where the instructors know the requirements and standards necessary for the Test.

Even for those teaching on a permanent and continuous basis, an assessment is still useful. They may need to learn the appropriate technical terms, how to control a small group of unfamiliar riders and horses in an indoor school or outdoor menage. Some aspects of teaching in a Riding School are different from the requirements of the Preliminary Teaching Test; candidates need to know the format and structure of the Test to be fully prepared.

Applying for the Test

The British Horse Society will supply information on request about the Test, together with the application form, addresses of Exam centres with dates and the current fees. All candidates will need to be members of the BHS when they apply for and take the PTT.

The address is:

British Horse Society,
British Equestrian Centre,
Training and Education Dept.,
Stoneleigh Deer Park,
Kenilworth,
Warwickshire CV8 2XZ

Telephone 01926 707700

Prospective candidates can telephone the BHS before applying for their chosen Test Centre, to check that the venue and the date required are available.

On acceptance of the application the BHS will send a confirmation letter with accompanying notes. These should be read carefully.

During the winter months many Test Centres do not offer the Preliminary Teaching Test. If candidates wish to take their Test during these months they are advised to apply for dates to the BHS in plenty of time to avoid disappointment and delay.

Test Preparation

When the Exam Centre and date have been confirmed, check the location and the route to the Centre if this is unfamiliar. If possible travel to the Centre at least once before the Test, this will alleviate the anxiety of trying to find the venue on the day. Make allowance for rush hour traffic, this can increase travel time considerably.

Clothing

Check that all your clothing and equipment is correct. An approved standard riding hat, PAS 015 or an EN 1384, (check for current standards) with a properly fitting harness, hacking jacket, gloves, jodhpurs or breeches preferably beige, long boots, a shirt and tie or stock. A long sleeved shirt should be worn; occasionally in hot weather the candidates are allowed to remove their jackets. A short whip should be taken, and possibly a long whip.

Candidates should also take a waterproof jacket or a long riding waterproof coat; even in the pouring rain, candidates may have to teach outside.

Long hair should be tied back or placed tidily in a hair net and no jewellery should be worn apart from a wedding ring. Earrings and studs should be removed for the Test.

Books

There will be time during the Test for candidates to do a little research for the lessons, lecturette and theory. Often the candidates are given 15 to 30 minutes, after the introduction by the Examiners, to go back to their cars, collect any equipment and read up any notes available. There is occasionally time between the scheduled sessions to prepare for the next part of the Test.

It is a good idea to take books so that any information can be looked up or confirmed. The Stage I and Stage II Riding & Stable Management books are useful. These books have been designed so that information is easy to find and refer to at the level required; this is particularly useful for the group lesson and the lecturette. The Stage III book describes the flatwork, jumping and stable management in more depth.

Any books that are clear, concise, easy to refer to and at the level required will be a help even to confirm the information already learnt and prepared beforehand. A pen and paper are useful to make any further notes.

The Test Day

Candidates need to arrive at the Centre at least 30 minutes before the Test. They will then be able to check their times and lesson slots before the Test starts. They may also be able to check which riders and horses they will be teaching, discover where the wings and poles are kept, or whether there are any 'props' available for the lecturette.

If it is possible, check the school and the menage to assess the space available and where to position the riders for safety during the jumping.

Any information that can be collected is useful preparation and may help the candidate during their Test Day.

Format

Normally the Test starts either at 08.30 or 09.00 a.m. and candidates should book in at Reception or the Office at the latest fifteen minutes before. The Examiners will introduce themselves and all the candidates will be given name tags and numbers to wear for identification.

Candidates will be organised into groups and their schedule for the day explained. Each group will be informed as to where they are first, the school, lecture room, or a separate room for the Theory.

The Test is divided into sections. The theory, lecturette and group lesson will normally be completed in the morning with the lunge and lead rein lessons being taken after lunch. The lunch break is normally scheduled at 1.00 p.m. for 45 minutes.

A timetable will show the times and sessions for each group. The whole Examination finishes about 4 - 5.00 p.m. This timetable can and does vary from Test to Test depending on the venue, timings and the discretion of the Examiners.

Example of a Preliminary Teaching Test Timetable.

PTT Examination - 3rd July					
08.30 - Briefing - then candidates prepare for lessons and lecturettes					
Class Lesson	**Indoor Arena**	**Outdoor Arena**			
Time	Can No.	Can No.	Time	Can No.	
09.00 - 09.40	**1**	**2**			
			09.15 - 10.45	**7 - 12**	**Theory then lecture**
09.40 - 10.20	**3**	**4**			
10.20 - 11.00	**5**	**6**			
11.00 - 11.40	**7**	**8**			
			11.15 - 12.45	**1 - 6**	**Theory then lecture**
11.40 - 12.20	**9**	**10**			
12.20 - 1.00	**11**	**12**			
1.00 - 1.40	**LUNCH**				
2.00 - LUNGE NOVICE ADULT, LEAD REIN BEGINNERS					
2.00 - 3.30	**Lunge**	**Lead Rein**			
3.30 Examiners' Discussion - Results					

The Test finishes after the last candidate has completed the lead rein or lunge lesson. The Examiners confer and the results will be given as soon as possible, 30 minutes to one hour later. Candidates may then ask for information and advice from the Examiners about aspects of their Test.

Test Tips

Naturally there is so much more to being a good instructor and teacher besides improving pupils. This is especially so when the instructor works in a large yard. Being an instructor is primarily about relating to other people: staff, co-workers, students, clients, management, office personnel, employers, other instructors and part time freelance teachers.

It is about being able to communicate with others, having the ability to discuss and, more importantly, to listen to other people. It is about creating an atmosphere of harmony, encouragement and enjoyment.

The Preliminary Teaching Test is also about communication, how you communicate your ideas to the pupils, and then your knowledge and teaching ability to the Examiners. Communication is not just based on words but also on posture, body language, eye contact and your ability to show confidence and competence.

In the Test these qualities will be evident by the way you create a rapport with your pupils and also with your fellow candidates. You need to be confident without being over-confident or egotistical. You will need to show authority without being bossy. You should be pleasant without being too familiar. You may need to take control of situations in a quiet, professional manner and through this you will achieve trust and respect.

If you study and practise sufficiently, learn the subjects so that you also understand them, the methods and the reasons for these, you will gain the ability to teach.

Then, believe in yourself, this will create enthusiasm and enjoyment in your teaching.

Good Luck

APPENDIX A

Recommended Lectures and Practical Sessions

This is a plan for a series of study sessions to help candidates work towards their Preliminary Teaching Test. It describes the theory and practice sessions recommended to cover all the sections in the Test.

1 Theory 1

- Discuss types of lessons, their advantages and disadvantages for various riders.
- Discuss the structure of lessons, planning and presentation.
- Discuss format of lessons for beginners and novices.

2 Theory 2

- Discuss jumping lessons, pole work, distances for ground poles and jumps.
- Discuss the types of horses suitable for schoolwork and their management.
- Discuss safety and accident procedures.

3 Theory 3

- Discuss and study the Office routine, management, dealing with clients, booking clients in and pricing policies.
- Discuss office equipment and communication between the reception/office staff, the instructors and the yard staff.

➢ Look at some different types of reception/office areas, booking systems and work sheets. Assess the advantages and disadvantages of these systems.

4 Group Lesson

- Discuss the preparation for a group lesson.
- Look through and briefly discuss the list of possible lessons.
- Choose a topic and make a plan for one of the lessons.

5 Group lesson Practical 1

- ➢ Use a plan already prepared and run through a group lesson.
- ➢ Use poles and jumps and position these in the school for the lesson.
- ➢ Using the knowledge gained from the practical session work through more of the lesson plans.

6 Group lesson Practical 2

- ➢ Give another group lesson with the emphasis on controlling the group around the school.
- ➢ Work through more of the lesson plans checking the timing for bringing out jumps, wings, poles, shortening stirrups, checking girths etc.

7 Group lesson Practical 3

- ➢ Work through other group lessons so that they include the introduction, the warm up phase, the content and the conclusion in the time allowed 35 minutes.

The practice for the group lesson may take several sessions until you feel confident and are achieving the timing. It is an advantage if you can practise further by giving lessons at the School or by organising a group of your own.

At home you need to work through all the BHS group lesson plans writing the finished plans down on cards in a shorthand version.

8 Lecturette

- ❖ Work through and briefly discuss the lecturettes in the BHS list.
- ❖ Work through the lecturette plans writing these down on cards in a brief version. Work on keeping the lecturettes very brief. Mark out the key points.

9 Lecturette Practical

- ➢ Using the prepared plans give a number of short lecturettes to check timing.
- ➢ Work in front of a group to check posture, voice projection and timing.

10 Lunge Lesson

- ❖ Discuss lunge lessons, their function, aims, advantages and disadvantages.
- ❖ Discuss the types of exercises that the rider can do whilst being lunged and their objectives.
- ❖ Discuss points of safety whilst lungeing.
- ❖ Plan and prepare some lunge lessons.

11 Lunge Lesson Practical

- Check the lungeing equipment and lunge a horse for 3-5 minutes.
- Give a lunge lesson for 10 minutes. This may be done at least twice in a one hourly session.
- Observe and assess various lunge lessons.
- Practise giving lunge lessons in the time as often as possible.

12 Lead Rein

- Discuss teaching children and how to communicate with them.
- Discuss safety procedures for dealing with children.
- Discuss the plan for a lead rein lesson.
- Prepare plans for some short lead rein lessons.

13 Lead Rein Practical

- Give a lead rein lesson to a child; be aware of the time factor.
- May do this two or three times in a session.
- Observe some lead rein lessons and assess.
- Practise giving lead rein lessons as often as possible.

14 The Test

Do a Mock Test.

Discuss the Test Format.

Revise any sections necessary.

15 The Timetable

Plan a timetable that includes all the study sessions mentioned. One method of preparing a timetable is to work backwards from the date of the Test. Mark the Test date on a calendar and allow yourself a number of days or weeks to study each section. Allow some days or a week for unforeseen circumstances, holidays, illness, workload, and some time for revising the various subjects.

Prepare this timetable to suit you, your commitments and the availability of lessons at your study centre. The timetable should be fairly adaptable but also followed as far as possible to plan so that all the subjects are covered and in sufficient depth.

Index

H

I

J

L